ALSO BY SCOTT RUSSELL

The Rink: Stories from Hockey's Home Towns
(co-author Chris Cuthbert)
Ice Time: A Canadian Hockey Journey

SCOTT RUSSELL

OPEN HOUSE

Canada and the Magic of Curling

{ DOUBLEDAY CANADA }

Doubleday Canada and colophon are trademarks.

NATIONAL LIBRARY OF CANADA CATALOGUING IN PUBLICATION

Russell, Scott, 1958–
Open house : Canada and the magic of curling / Scott Russell.

ISBN 0-385-65922-9

1. Curling—Canada. I. Title.

GV845.5.C3R88 2003   796.964'0971   C2003-902419-9

JACKET IMAGES:
(*Montreal C.C.*) National Archives of Canada (PA-029045)
(*Scoreboard*) Corbis/Magma
JACKET AND TEXT DESIGN: CS Richardson

Printed and bound in Canada

Published in Canada by Doubleday Canada,
a division of Random House of Canada Limited

Visit Random House of Canada Limited's website: www.randomhouse.ca

FRI   10   9   8   7   6   5   4   3   2   1

For Joan Mead and "The Chief,"
teachers and storytellers.

CONTENTS

The gathering of the clan

I CAN SEE THEM AS PLAIN AS IF IT WERE YESTERDAY.
My mother and father standing in the family room of our
house in suburban Don Mills, just to the north of downtown Toronto. They had donned matching ivory, heavy
wool sweaters that dropped to mid-thigh on both of them.
They wore turtlenecks underneath—the sweaters zipped up
to their high collars. More intriguing were the crossed
kitchen brooms hovering over smooth, circular stones with
odd-looking handles all knitted lovingly into the sweaters'
fronts by my grandmother. My parents wore tams on their
heads like some Scottish people I had seen—although the
accompanying kilts were thankfully absent on my folks.

"We're on our way to Avonlea," my father advised.
"Should be back by eleven." Thoughts of Anne of Green
Gables ran through my head, but it turned out their mission
would be executed at an ice rink much closer to home.

Having informed me of their whereabouts for the next
few hours, the two of them padded to the front door in their

sock feet and proceeded to put on their boots. My father's were brown, lined with white fur, and came up just past his ankle—he carefully arranged the bottoms of his grey flannel slacks over the tops of them. My mother's footwear was much more festive. Shiny black leather—almost patent, as I recall—the top cuff a bright red tartan.

"Don't forget the beaver tails, dear," my mother reminded Dad on the way out. He reached into the closet and pulled out two brooms with long white necks and business ends made of straw. "I'll need this tonight," he chuckled. "Alex never comes out of the hack straight and has trouble with the in-turn. But if we get on it right away, most of the time we can swing it right onto the button." It was all a foreign language to me. With murmurs only they could understand they saluted me with their weapons and were off into the frost-filled night. They were going curling.

The game of curling merits a single observance in John Robert Colombo's book of Canadian quotations. It comes from the late actor Raymond Burr of New Westminster, British Columbia, the man who for years portrayed the lawyer Perry Mason and then a private investigator by the handle of "Ironside" on American television. "Sure I curl," he told an interviewer from the *Toronto Star* in 1972. "We all curl in Canada!" A startling declaration that is surely untrue but still, it has a certain ring to it. When I reflected on Burr's words it struck me that most, if not all, of us know what curling is and probably a large majority of people who grew up in this country have, at the very least, some sort of distant connection to the sport.

"There is something very, very unique to the game," Vic Rauter told me once. Rauter is the voice of curling on TSN and has described the action at the highest levels of competition for seventeen years. "I don't think there's another game that actually represents the country as a whole like this one," he continued.

Rauter was speaking from the broadcast booth at the Pengrowth Saddledome in Calgary, the site of the 2002 Canadian men's curling championships, the Brier. This event brings together the best men's curling teams from each of the ten provinces as well as northern Ontario, which warrants a separate entry. There is

Vic Rauter: Curling's familiar voice

also in the field a combined squad from the Yukon and Northwest Territories. It was a Thursday night and the final games in the preliminary round-robin competition were about to take place. There were 15,000 boisterous fans from all over Canada in the nearly full hockey arena to observe matches that were, on the surface, of little consequence. The playoff positions had long since been decided, with the traditional powers of Ontario, Alberta, and Saskatchewan advancing.

Rauter peered down from his perch at one end of the dome alongside his analysts, Ray Turnbull and Linda Moore, both former Canadian champions. The play-by-play man smiled knowingly and gestured out to the sounds of the arena. Cowbells clattered, air horns were honking amid the shouts and shrill whistles of partisan groups

3

representing far-flung reaches of the nation. Fans had their faces painted in the green and gold of Saskatchewan, and some from Nova Scotia had their hair dyed an electric blue.

"You could be a Newfoundlander living in B.C. and for two weeks a year at the Brier, you're a Newf again," Rauter claimed with delight. He went on to voice a much more ambitious sentiment about the game that has so obviously enraptured him. "I love the people who play it. I love the people who watch it," Rauter said. "They are honest-to-goodness down-to-earth folks. They are folks who are hard-working and salt-of-the-earth kind of people. It covers all the demographics and I love that about the sport."

I looked at the program in my hands and flipped to the biographies of the four-man teams that had each won provincial playdowns and ventured to Calgary for a chance at the coveted crown. Most who follow curling would argue that the Brier is the most difficult title to win given the depth of talent there is across all regions of this country. Yet there were no professionals in the field—none of the players listed made his living by playing this game.

Quebec's top man Francois Roberge worked as the supervisor of shipping and receiving for Sears Canada in Quebec City. He was taking on Russ Howard, a professional golfer now living in Moncton and representing New Brunswick. Over on ice sheet C, Saskatchewan's chiropractor skip Scott Bitz of Regina faced twenty-three-year-old John Morris of Ottawa. Morris was taking time away from his kinesiology studies at Wilfrid Laurier University in Waterloo to throw rocks for Ontario. Shawn Adams, Nova Scotia's hope and an employee of Coca-Cola, was going head-to-head with the City of Winnipeg transit manager, Mark Lukowich.

"God yeah, I've got another life outside of this," the defending Brier champion Randy Ferbey of Alberta confirmed. "For a week here we get to live the life of hockey players and superstars but on Monday morning at eight o'clock it's back on the desk." Ferbey operates the Tartan Rental Outlet in Edmonton and doubles as one of the best curlers on the face of the earth. His challenge was similar to one faced by each of the forty-eight sportsmen present that night in the championship field—the elite players of men's curling.

As I watched them curl, it became clear to me that, despite their amateur status, they were indeed athletes. Athletes who were easily identifiable by their ability to glide effortlessly over the ice, throwing surgically precise strikes at their opponent's stones. Recognizable by the strength and balance so obviously required to manipulate their brooms with a subtle, almost invisible effect on granite rocks. The players also demonstrated uncanny consistency. Presented with a different set of circumstances upon each delivery, they were, as a group, nearly flawless over the course of matches that lasted close to two hours each. It was like witnessing an episode of hand-to-hand combat with action on four fronts—the crowd roaring and swaying as hits, misses, and brilliantly engineered surprise attacks, once figured to be impossible, came to amazing completion.

What was even more surprising to me that night was the absence of a figure who could be considered heroic. Things seemed much more understated in this arena than in the countless others I had found myself in. There was no valiant quarterback throwing the ball into the outstretched arms of the speedy receiver dashing to the end zone, an eternity away. No heavily armoured goaltender standing fearlessly in the way of driving black bullets and calmly snatching them out of midair. The athletes in front of me appeared all too human—in fact, I might as well have been out there myself.

There is no padding in curling—nothing to guard against the body contact that never comes. The participants do not wear masks or helmets; you can see every expression on their faces as the competition progresses. They wince and smile, some yell loudly, urging their sweepers to "*Hurry hard!*" as soon as the rocks are released. Curlers talk to themselves, to the other members of their team, to the crowd, and even to their opponents throughout the most critical of matches. Curlers, it appears, have nothing to hide from anybody.

"It would be like hearing a hockey coach talk to his guys on the bench or the pitching coach going to the mound," one-time Brier finalist Guy Hemmings of Quebec figured. "It would be amazing to hear the participants discussing things and to understand what is really going on."

Hemmings is arguably the most popular figure in the sport, not because of his ability to win championships or to make the most difficult shots but because he cultivates a devoted following wherever he plays. Teams from Quebec have rarely won the Brier. Jim Ursel, a native of Manitoba, was the only man to turn the trick while representing his adopted province at the 1977 championship in Montreal. Hemmings came close a couple of times in the late nineties but it was his fraternizing with the western Canadian crowds in a humorous hybrid of both official languages that won him hearts. He still believes that the connection to the field of play is one of the game's great attractions for observers.

"You can get it if you are watching closely," he said. "Curling creates a special bond between the athletes and the fans."

The importance of the social side of curling should never be overlooked. Curling provides a sense of community in this nation, one common to young and old, wealthy and not so wealthy, on both coasts and in spots in between. It is a sport that goes far beyond the boundaries of the sheet of ice 148 feet long by 14 feet wide. It extends to the clubhouse and the lounge and into everyday life as an example of something that, while not peculiar to the Canadian experience, reflects many of the country's characteristics.

"It was something like hockey in that you may have been weaned on it," said my old curling pal Bruce MacInnis. "It was a very social thing. The rink was a place to go to have fun and it became a venue for flirting with girls. Only in Canada could you possibly say that."

There are more than a million registered curlers in Canada who, for invariably reasonable fees, frequent thousands of clubs in cities and towns of every size. Each club I have visited over the course of this journey has been welcoming and familiar. Curling clubs are uncomplicated places and combine the frigidness of ice surface with the coziness of a basement recreation room that your father might have finished himself. There's a certain eclectic, unassuming quality about these clubs. The bar in the lounge might have fixed swivel stools reminiscent of an old-fashioned diner. There's likely to be a dartboard, a few ancient and yellowed photos, and a stove on which you can warm up some hot chocolate. Maybe there's a roaring fireplace to one side, and there are certainly people hanging around slumped on comfy-looking chairs with nothing on their feet but wool socks—their shoes cast hastily to the broadloom. On the bulletin board of every curling club are notices about skill clinics and league schedules. There are also announcements of births, deaths, and upcoming weddings.

In the case of the Mayflower Curling Club in Halifax, Nova Scotia, the senior women who curl in the house league over the noon hour may find a woman who, more than once, has been a world and Canadian champion throwing rocks by herself on the sheet of ice right next door. She is likely to interrupt her practice session and stop for a chat with a neighbour or to comment on someone's improving delivery.

"They don't care, which is really nice." Colleen Jones laughed off my inquiry at her lack of celebrity status. "I never feel like a high-performance athlete. I just know I love to play. What I get tired of is the pressure of playing. If I could just go and throw rocks at the Mayflower—that's enough to keep me happy."

Jones is a mother of two, works full-time, and has been at the top of her game for decades. The same is true of other champion curlers—their resemblance to everyday Canadians is remarkable and endearing. The late Sandra Schmirler, the only Canadian skip to win the Olympic gold medal, had two small children, hailed from the tiny town of Biggar, Saskatchewan, and waged a much-publicized battle with cancer, a battle she ultimately lost late in the winter of 2000. Her death caused an outpouring of grief in Canada, and her memorial service was broadcast live on network television— a rarity in this country and something reserved for its most cherished citizens.

In her moment of victory at the Nagano Games of 1998, however, Schmirler was the nation's darling, and along with her team of Marcia Gudereit, Joan McCusker, and Jan

Betker, she surely captured the imaginations and hearts of Canadians. There was an immediate bond forged between these four women and millions of people at home who could see themselves in the champions' faces.

Holding their flowers on the podium with gold medals around their necks, Schmirler's team sang the national anthem and shed tears of joy. Schmirler wore spectacles and her Roots Team Canada chapeau was not tipped forward in a suggestion of cockiness but instead rested on the back of her head so as to reveal her brilliant smile. She looked, for the world to see, like somebody's mum. And, in an instant, Canadians could understand the special nature of her victory.

"Women out there love us because they believe we are just like them," Joan McCusker said. The second on

Canada's golden girls: The Schmirler rink in Nagano

Schmirler's curling team has enjoyed considerable visibility in the wake of the Olympic victory. She is now a popular television sports commentator and is in constant demand to appear at curling events across Canada. McCusker understands that the glory of Japan solidified an unspoken respect she and her partners garnered from a vast number of onlookers. "The people saw that it could be them," she concluded. "Ordinary people doing extraordinary things is the attraction to the everyday person."

Perhaps it is this, their apparent ordinariness, that has kept curlers at the edges of my imagination until now. I have always subscribed to the notion that the stars of sport should be capable of things beyond the reach of mere mortals. Unlike spectators, they deliver superhuman feats that inspire awe.

The most vivid recollection I have of watching curling on television goes back to 1974. It was a broadcast of the Brier from London, Ontario, and the man who would eventually win was a bruiser named Hector Gervais. He hailed from St. Albert, Alberta, and underneath his blue cardigan Gervais attempted to disguise a stomach the size of a medicine ball. He was an enormous man who looked like a transport truck driver sporting an Elvis-like coiffure, complete with slick, jet-black hair and oversized muttonchop sideburns.

As I watched I marvelled at how this guy could be considered the best in the world. I could picture Gervais sneaking a drag on a foot-long cigar while downing a bottle of ale as each end of the climactic last match was completed. But world champion, surely not. The whole scenario seemed to lack glamour. Nothing like the escapades of the gods and

Hec Gervais: The giant with the gentle touch

goddesses I had seen during the Olympics or on *Hockey Night in Canada.*

Nearly three decades later the image of Hec Gervais remains with me, but his presence has become much more intriguing upon reflection. I can now summon up the data, which tell me that Gervais rarely missed a shot and, in spite of his bulk, was blessed with what might easily be considered a gifted and delicate touch. He was, now that I am reminded of it, supremely talented at the game he played in spite of his average appearance. While he possessed none of the outward charisma or charm present in the other superstars I had seen, Gervais was able to perform theatrical acts.

In paying more attention to curling over the last little while, I have encountered many strange things, things that seem to defy explanation. In a minuscule place called Skull Creek, Saskatchewan, is one sheet of natural ice enclosed by a ramshackle shed. Annually most of the town's people—all those big enough to hurl a rock—go to the shed for what's called a bonspiel. For one week they curl around the clock, stopping only for sandwiches and tea prepared in the kitchen of the shed. Once a year the whole community lives in that rink, harboured from the biting cold of the forbidding prairie landscape. They cherish these seven days beyond all comprehension.

In the big cities of Canada, curling clings to our consciousness in the face of all the glitz and glitter. Fitness facilities, spas, indoor tennis courts, and golf domes provide almost endless competitive and recreational opportunities. Yet the sport continues to thrive in Canada's urban centres. The president of one of Toronto's most established downtown curling clubs has been playing for nineteen years and

she still curls competi-
tively. "I started curling in
Timmins," Sue Gillespie
beamed. "What else is
there to do in Timmins in
the winter?" But Toronto
is not Timmins, and yet
the membership of Sue's
club is on the rise.

There must be some
sort of mysterious thread
woven into the fabric of
the cable-knit sweaters
the curlers don as they
brave the cold, stale air of
their unpretentious ice-
houses. In the last several
months, I have talked to
curlers, watched curlers,

Prize night at the bonspiel, circa 1970

and, finally, even curled with curlers. I have come to
understand that it is combinations of things that define
what curling is all about. It's the circus-like atmosphere of
the enormous tournament where people from every walk
of life gather to hoot, holler, and watch a team from their
neck of the woods get its shot at glory. The dance of the
sweepers responding to the code of the skip's grunted
utterances is something to behold, especially when you're
up close. The grace of a forty-pound rock rubbing another
and finding its resting place nestled between two enemy
rocks is fascinating—particularly when you understand
that it was planned exactly that way all along.

Curling has no body-checking, jumping, dunking, or miraculous catches. There are no slap shots, and the speed is anything but blinding. Still, if you watch closely and search for it there is a magical quality to the game. You get a sense of it in the way the players observe the etiquette of the sport. Cursing is not a factor. Respect and honour dominate even the most bitter of rivalries. Beyond the combatants themselves, there are no referees on the field of play.

Bob Weeks of the *Globe and Mail* has written about curling for twenty years. He's been a witness to the impossible shots made by the great players and provided insightful commentary concerning all of the most important competitions in Canada and around the world. Weeks is a curler himself, hails from a curling family, and could easily qualify as one of the game's insiders though he bristles at the designation.

I ran into Bob Weeks at the 2002 Canadian Olympic Curling Trials in Regina when I was just beginning to define what it was that I was searching for in this game. We talked and he provided me with some good background information. Just before Weeks ran off to interview one of the skips whose Olympic dream had just ended on the Agridome's ice, he paused and then offered a final thought, as if it had just become clear to him.

"I think it says something about our country in the way we bond together around the game," Weeks began. "You are welcomed because you are a curler. It's almost fraternity-like, I guess. Or a secret handshake."

Out on the rink, the winners were shaking hands with the losers, just as they had done before the game began.

Curling: An open house

A plucky little rink (author is second from the right)

CHAPTER ONE

SCHOOL BOYS

IN EXPLORING THE PLACE OF CURLING IN CANADIAN life I have travelled from Halifax in the east to Kelowna in the west, up to Eagle Hill, Alberta, and down to Salt Lake City, and along the way I have journeyed back into my own memory as well. As surprising as it seems to me now, there are white Bauer curling shoes, beaver-tail brooms complete with noisemaking flaps, and checkered bell-bottom pants in my past. There are also memories of bitterly cold nights and the rush to convene at the Avonlea Curling Club on Railside Road, just behind the Esso car wash. It was there that we played a simple game and kept the company of our friends.

I attended the biggest high school in Metropolitan Toronto. In the mid-seventies Victoria Park Secondary School boasted 2,700 students, the North York Championship football team, a reputation for being an easy place to score drugs, and, rather oddly, the largest curling club of any student body in the city.

It was something of a personal victory that I was at V.P. in the first place. A newspaper article about the rampant drug problem at the school had caught the attention of my parents, and they held onto that erroneous information like a couple of dogs with a single bone between them. "It's Upper Canada College for you," my father boomed. "Discipline and a dress code is what's required, young man."

But all my friends were bound for Victoria Park and I dug in, determined not to be banished to a life of blue blazers, military striped ties, and grey flannel pants. Besides, if Victoria Park was good enough for my best buddy, Brian "Ace" Nicholls, who had scored 85 per cent or above on all his subjects in junior high, so earning his nickname, then surely it was good enough for me. It was, let me tell you, a hell of a fight, plenty of crying and screaming and dire predictions of a life spent in the ghettos of Toronto's seedy underbelly. But in the end I won, having promised that after four years of successful study at "the drug school," I would enter university as an Ontario scholar with first-class honours.

Things were different in those days. Teachers at Victoria Park were involved with the students on a number of levels. There was every kind of sports team and after-school club imaginable—from the football and gymnastics teams (bantam, junior, and senior) to the military history society and Mr. Arkwright's table tennis association.

Encouraged by the emphasis placed on extracurricular activities, Ace and I tried out for the bantam and then the junior basketball team in our first two years at school. Sadly, Ace, who was small for his age, was destined to be the last cut while I, at nearly six feet, somehow squeaked onto both squads. So as I was issued a school uniform of scarlet and gold, my chum signed up for the curling club, which met Friday afternoons at Avonlea. As I saw it at the time, curling was the consolation prize for guys like Ace, guys who couldn't make it on to a *real* school team. He, on the other hand, never complained, and I would see him rush out the front door, broom in hand, as the winter weekends began.

"Why don't you try it?" Ace asked me after a while. "It's a blast and I think I'm getting pretty good at it. Maybe you could be on my team." For those first couple of years I stubbornly resisted his invitation. I was fearful that an association with the curling types might be frowned upon by the other members of my basketball team and certainly by our coach, a disciplinarian by the name of Grant Heffernan, but whom we all called Heff (though not to his face, of course).

The first words of every 7 a.m. practice ring out to this day. "*Down and back!*" Heffernan would roar. Pushing off the rear gym wall we would all race to the other end, touch our fingers to the painted concrete, and desperately dash back. Heffernan resisted using a whistle and repeated his sharp command until all of our tongues were dragging on the floor. Bowlegged and dressed in a crisp white T-shirt and shorts, the coach would march before us with arms folded against his massive chest and chuckle to himself as we moaned in pain. "You little wieners have to learn to work harder," he muttered. "Damn it, that's the way it is—get used to it."

Originally a hard-ass farm boy from just outside Peterborough, Ontario, Heffernan drove a sharp, metallic-blue

Mercury Meteor, and his aura of influence extended well beyond those of us in his commercial studies classes or the members of his basketball squad. He had a swagger and with it came everyone's respect. Heff was the law in our school.

My next-door neighbour Danny, whose family had recently come to Canada from Indiana, showed up one day with a brand-new lacrosse stick and was twirling an Indian rubber ball in its pocket. "Whaddya got there?" I asked.

"I'm in Heff's law class this year and he's big into lacrosse," Danny drawled. "I guess it's Canada's national game and he actually plays on a pro team—I think they're called the Peterboro Lakers. The way I figure it, if I learn to play I'll get on Heff's good side real quick."

We all bought lacrosse sticks after that and watched Heff wage war on Wednesday nights in a short-lived pro league. The games were telecast on CHCH–TV, broadcasting from

Heff's Peterboro Lakers (Heff is in the middle row, fifth from the right)

Hamilton, Ontario, and featured the Toronto Shooting Stars, the Brampton Excelsiors, the Brantford Warriors, the Oshawa Green Gaels, and Grant Heffernan's Peterboro Lakers. I sat in slack-jawed wonder as I witnessed Heff, wearing number 15, storm around the arena cross-checking with alarming ferocity everything that moved. Not just tough, he was also very gifted, passing behind his back in full flight and then gyrating away from pursuers before snagging the rubber ball again, cradling it gently and ultimately firing it past the helpless goaltender in the opposing net. Heff was a star—one of the brightest in the pro game.

I hung on his every word from then on, both at basketball practice and in class where, more often than not, he would show up limping or sporting a vicious black eye. "Execution is the key," Heffernan would dictate. "I don't care if you have skill or not. Execute the plan, play with passion, and we'll beat them every time."

His legend grew and grew. Someone found out that Heff was also a hockey player of renown, having been an All-American while at Providence College. We discovered that he had set the school's scoring record while forcefully patrolling his centre ice position on the way to the Eastern Collegiate title in the United States.

So there you have it. The most popular, most macho teacher imaginable. There was no way that this guy would be caught dead near the Avonlea curling club on a Friday afternoon. I reassured myself that as the weekend approached Heff would invariably be busy lacing up his skates preparing to bash a few helpless beer leaguers into the boards during his weekly pickup match. With this in mind, I finally took the chance to hang with my pal Ace and joined a large group of my friends who ventured to the rink faithfully. This was, in many ways, an unfamiliar set of circumstances for a teenager who fancied himself a jock. Unlike the other extracurricular activities in which I was engaged, this one was distinctly co-educational. There were as many girls as there were guys on the bus that took us to Avonlea and the banter had a more polite, less profane tone to it.

Once inside Avonlea, I noticed that here people I knew less well at Victoria Park were stars in their own right. Bruce MacInnis, a powerfully built spark plug, raced from the bus to the playing surface where he began thrusting himself from the foot grips implanted in the ice at one end and sliding toward the other, perfectly balanced and in control. After reaching his destination, Bruce would scamper back as if sweeping a rock, his fabric broom echoing throughout the building. The sleeves of his V-neck sweater were rolled up over his elbows and he was making a ton of noise.

Ken Pearce was smooth. He was blond and lean, sporting a jet-black cardigan with a number of competitive crests stitched on either side of the buttons and his surname across the back. On the ice he was in complete command and delivered the rocks with a delicate touch and pinpoint accuracy.

Ken had come to Ontario from Winnipeg a few years back and was the only son of a curling family. His dad, Ross Pearce, had in fact been runner-up in the Manitoba provincials three times and suffered the same fate once in Ontario, losing his chance to go to the Brier on each occasion. Still, there was this feeling when you saw Ken, the undisputed skip, call the shots that his pedigree was impeccable. It was rumoured that he travelled around the city to various clubs teaching beginners how to curl. It was a part-time, minimum-wage job that Pearce never bragged about, yet even the whisper of it added to his mystique.

The president of our curling association was a fellow by the name of Rollie Hamar, and he was a year ahead of me academically. Hamar's favourite teacher was Heffernan, and in many ways he was as uncompromising, certainly as competitive as the basketball coach we all revered. Rollie wanted to win, badly, and it quickly became apparent that he was jealous of Ken Pearce's inevitable success not only in the mixed house league but as the school's representative in the Ontario Schoolboy playdowns.

"I think Rollie's trying to stack the teams," Ace muttered to me very near the beginning. "He just has to beat Ken once—he's obsessed."

Pearce would shake it off and accept the players he was dealt without complaint. It was, of course, Rollie who dominated the executive and so determined who played with whom. As I recall, Pearce got three greenhorns every time while Rollie ended up with veterans who brought relative experience and savvy to the ice. "Well, I guess we've got our work cut out for us," Ken would say with a smile as he accepted his new team list. "Let's see how it all comes out in the wash, shall we, Rollie?"

For his part, Ace was game for anything. A brilliant mathematical mind, he could figure the angles curling required. He could see every possible combination in a minefield of rocks. With an unorthodox shooting style that featured the occasional full frontal flop at the hog line, Ace unexpectedly became a skip to be reckoned with. His image as the plucky underdog was enhanced by his brutal sweeping efforts. Ace had the thinnest corn broom imaginable and only under rare circumstances did he venture into the house to help bring a rock in while awkwardly drawing the feathered blade between his legs and producing a feeble "Tap . . . tap . . . tap" sound in the process.

"We did it again, my friends," he would chuckle elatedly for the benefit of the spent sweepers. "My brains, your brawn." With that Ace would raise his skinny little stick to the successful shooter at the other end and slip-slide to his perch at the back wall to place the counting rock's score on the board.

Still, he developed leadership skills while winning hearts as the perpetual long shot. During a match that, if won, would take him deep into the Metropolitan Toronto finals, Ace avoided near disaster when a hothead member of his front end threw his broom in frustration and stormed off the ice. Faced with forfeiture, Ace summoned his vice-skip to hold the broom for the second's stones and scampered off to find his fuming teammate. I could see Ace up there in the lounge putting a consoling arm around the offender. It was a side of him that I had never witnessed, and it made me surprisingly proud.

Just in time, Ace returned to his squad with the deserter in tow and picked up where he had left off. On this occasion, my friend was, unfortunately, beaten by a powerful rival but I reckoned he had gained something at least as valuable in the process of playing the game.

"You have to be a team," Ace said philosophically over a hot chocolate in the lounge afterwards. "It's like dominoes. One goes down and we all fall. I guess that's what this game is all about." It was impossible to quibble.

Etiquette is a fundamental aspect of curling. I struggled with that from my first exposure to the Friday afternoon gatherings. There were handshakes after each game but also before. "Good curling" became a mantra as I greeted my opponents at the outset of every match. I wonder if I ever really meant it, or if it was like a rhetorical question to which one never gave a second thought.

There were no referees in sight. If you kicked a rock or had to call whose shot was closer to the button once the penultimate stone had been delivered, you convened a meeting to decide the outcome. Rarely was an aluminum measuring stick employed; players preferred to reach a consensus on who should be given the advantage.

"I figure he burned it but then again it may have picked up some straw," opposing skips would mumble. "Not that I want to draw this out, but getting the hammer is a big thing and shot rock here determines whether or not I'll freeze to that stone or try to wick off the guard and roll into the four foot." It was a language that would take some getting used to.

There were other strange rituals to be observed, which included placing our opposite number's stones beside the

Ace and his trademark flop

hack before each of our own deliveries, cleaning the bottom of his rocks with our brooms, sweeping the ice of any debris, chatting with counterparts on opposing teams while waiting for our respective bosses to make decisions at the other end, and remembering, without fail, to congratulate the enemy on his fine efforts. The whole confrontation was completely bereft of the antagonistic head-butting with which I was familiar.

Afterwards, we would convene in the lounge to dissect the match, winners buying the losers the first round of Cokes—frequently laced with a good measure of Bacardi White. We would comfortably linger into the evening and haggle over the problems of the Toronto Maple Leafs, who would often be hosting the hated Montreal Canadiens the following night at The Gardens. The next wave of games was being played on the other side of the glass, and we would marvel at the long, elegant slides of the best of the girls. It was hard to ignore tartan skirts and black leggings as they moved away from you in gymnastic form to the far end of the ice.

Some girls caught our eye

But ease with the game did not come all at once and the memory of that first rock thrown still conjures up feelings of overwhelming humility. Good old Bruce MacInnis and I were on Rollie Hamar's squad as he attempted to build a unit capable of knocking off Ken Pearce. My reputation as an athlete preceded me and so Rollie took a chance and picked me for his side, but I can recall my confidence and bravado evaporating as I sat crouched in the hack that day.

"Just draw the rock back easy," Bruce whispered, his powerful sweeping machine at the ready. "Slide out with your left foot forward but tucked underneath you, use your broom to balance, the rock will take you along for the ride. When you're good and steady, you just release and let it curl from your hand. Remember to keep your eyes focused on Rollie's broom at the other end. If you do all those things you'll never miss."

It all sounded and looked so simple. But as that first attempt slid past the point of no return, I knew I had made many miscalculations. The tight bell-bottom jeans were the first error—because of them I had trouble getting down low and my knee locked coming out. The rock was far heavier than I thought it was and I mistakenly, stupidly, tried to lift it on the back swing. My balance was immediately thrown off. I wobbled horribly right out of the gate and teetered on the brink of disaster as I tried to get the whiskers of the broom down to steady me. Then, split seconds into the delivery, the basketball sneakers aborted the mission. There was, to be honest, no slide to speak of. The soles of my shoes gripped the ice and I stopped dead in my tracks, just before collapsing. In an attempt to salvage something of this terrible mess, I pushed the stone wildly from my sweating palm. It spun like a top and whirled maybe fifteen feet before Bruce alertly lifted his foot and stopped it from crashing into another player's rock on the sheet of ice next door. I was laid flat out on my stomach, inches away from where I had started just moments before.

"Nice effort, bonehead." Bruce MacInnis erupted with laughter as he stood over my disgraced form. "It ain't as easy as it looks but you'll come around one of these days."

Down at the other end of the ice, Rollie tipped his broom, another point of etiquette in recognition of even the lousiest of shots. He rolled his eyes and looked skyward to the ceiling as if to say, "Here we go again!"

In the wake of these humble beginnings, I grew into the game and with time came to appreciate the skill required to gain a measure of competence. My parents resisted the temptation to say, "We told you so," and instructed me on the proper attire for success. (Parkas and running shoes were the beacons of a beginner or one among us who was not as serious as the rest.) There followed the purchase of stretchy slacks (checkered, of course), the correct footwear (white shoes with hard, black soles resembling those a bowler might wear), two tight gloves akin to a golfer's to help prevent blisters caused by rigorous sweeping.

Finally and critically, I obtained a contraption called a slider. This appeared in the form of a piece of slick, white floor tile cut to fit the front of my left shoe. It was fixed with a leather upper that enveloped the nose of the shoe and was held in place by a heavy black elastic band looped around the back of my heel. As my left foot led me out of the hack, the slider minimized my friction with the ice and ensured my survival. In those days the slider made possible the shooter's graceful, controlled delivery and provided the means by which the sweeping corps could keep up with speeding stones.

"*Hurry hard!*" Rollie might scream. The sweepers, who had been pushing off on their back feet and gliding forcefully over the ice, would begin to pound their brooms in an impressive dance. "*Off it now!*" was Rollie's next command. The workers would then rise in unison but continue along beside the rock, as escorts, until it reached its target and bumped the opposing object out of its position of importance.

In my penultimate year of high school curling things became a bit more serious for those of us who wanted to make a go of it as a bona fide sport. Again success was measured by the clothes we wore. We aimed to be part of a foursome who would all wear the same coloured sweaters. An added bonus was to have our names embroidered on the backs of those pullovers or cardigans. It was a badge of honour—a sign that you'd somehow made it. Rollie Hamar, on the advice of Bruce MacInnis, had accepted me on the team in the lead position, where I could do the least damage. (I would throw my rocks first and even if I missed completely there would be ample time for the three more accomplished curlers to recover.) My sweeping had improved considerably and I was not bad with the draw weight, although every takeout was still an adventure.

Sweeping action at Avonlea

Being somewhat near-sighted and too vain to wear my glasses during competition, I curled a bit cockeyed and found hitting the broom a nearly impossible challenge. Still, I did get the powder-blue sweater with "RUSSELL" proudly stitched on the back.

"We have to beat Ken Pearce," Rollie would plead with us before every match we played in that year, his final one as club president and our skip. "It's a must. I'll die if we can't make it happen."

Trouble was Ken had a good squad that included Ace Nicholls as the consistent and reliable vice-skip. Try as we might, we could not help but anticipate a confrontation with the smooth foursome, the only rival our leader cared about.

Rollie was a beautiful curler and came out of the hack with fiery determination on each delivery. His touch was delicate, and he could throw the big weight with unfailing accuracy and requisite power. Many were the occasions when our skip would rush from the back of the house to join us in an effort to sweep a dying rock into

The Victoria Park curling club gathered at Avonlea
Rollie Hamar (right)

the rings. His big fabric broom made explosive sounds throughout the arena, and more often than not the stone curled to the exact spot he had envisioned. We were a solid unit and with Doug Hinton acting as a steady vice to keep Rollie's genius and raging spirit focused, we won plenty of games.

But Pearce appeared to be unstoppable, and by the time we came to play his team they were heavy favourites brimming with confidence. "Good curling"—Rollie forced the words through clenched teeth as he swiftly shook Ken's hand. Pearce winked slyly at us all, turned on his heel, and slid regally to the other end.

For ten ends and with each of us throwing twenty stones, we battled in what proved to be as intense a competition as I had ever been part of. Rarely was a shot missed. I can remember a huge sense of accomplishment, almost elation, as I drew rock after rock into the house.

In curling, gratification and devastation both come instantly and are shared in equal measure by each member of the team. There is no better feeling in the world than releasing a rock just before the hog line after a long, controlled delivery. To watch it start out way to the outside and then gradually and deliberately find its path to the middle, evidence of an exacting in- or out-turn, can leave the shooter breathless. The rock will slip silently past the other team's guard, almost kissing it on the way by. Then it will rumble a little farther. "No . . . No . . . No . . . right off it," the skip will caution his sweepers in nothing more than a whisper. Without the whiff of a broom, the rock glides to its natural place, nestled behind the enemy and protected from imminent danger.

"Nice shot." "Great weight." "Good draw." "Perfect line." Everyone on the ice sheet has a compliment as you all gather to watch the next shooter. The skip points at you from the end, smiles, and raises his broom to signal his approval. For that one moment you are a marvel and enjoy the adulation of your team and the respect of your opponents. And just for that one moment it makes no matter that the shot you have so lovingly created will be erased by a wickedly thrown take-out seconds later.

But if you miss and your beautifully conceived draw sails right through the rings, wobbling to an awkward halt as it hits the hack at the other end, then there is a different kind of reaction. The skip doesn't bother to look at you, although he will grudgingly raise his broom to acknowledge your incompetence. The others won't say a word and will either look at their feet as you shuffle to your sweeping position or glance toward the lounge area beyond the glass where their girlfriends are waiting impatiently for the end of the game. You are left to suffer silently, alone in the hope that your opposite number will miss as badly as you did. When he makes the shot perfectly, you swallow your pride and conceal your sickening embarrassment. "Great shot," you say as he comes to join the group. Inside you hope you sound like you mean it.

We never were able to beat Ken Pearce's team and Rollie was almost destroyed by it. I can report with great conviction, though, that we did just about all we could do—made the draws, the takeouts, the raises, wicked in and out of the house and froze to his rocks at just the right time. We never burned a stone by kicking it and altering its path to the rings. We curled to our potential.

But at the end of the proceedings, we were left shaking our heads in amazement.

Pearce was like a sniper. He made shots that required multiple hits, impossible angles, and the precision of a master snooker player. Hunks of granite defied their outward appearance and gained an ethereal grace whenever we faced Ken Pearce. Each member of his team was uniformly flawless. Shot after shot they challenged us to be their equals, which, sadly, we were not.

"Great game, everybody." Ken Pearce was ever gracious in his frequent moments of victory. You could tell that he meant it too, that he valued the competition of a capable rival like Rollie Hamar.

"That's a real curler," our club's staff adviser, Mr. Elliot, used to observe. "He never celebrates too much." Guy Elliot, a youngish history teacher, had founded the curling club at Victoria Park Secondary School in the late sixties and had seen it grow, in a short period of time, to become one of the most popular school activities. No one could remember Elliot ever missing a Friday afternoon session. Wearing his familiar blue tam and watching from behind the glass, he took in thousands of meaningless games and witnessed the flourishing of some very talented champions like Ken Pearce.

For his part, Rollie was forced to bear yet another tough loss to the player he most wanted to overcome. As I remember it, like the good curler he was, he accepted his fate with class and never failed to wish his adversary well. He graduated after that curling season, and my brief fling as the lead on a team with a real shot at the schoolboy championship was over.

The final campaign of my high school curling career may have been the most memorable of all. The teachers in North York went on strike and we almost lost our Grade 13 year. With the labour strife, all school activities ground to a halt and those of us in senior matriculation feared that universities would not accept us in light of the missed academic time. That was worrisome. But what really hurt was the fact that the basketball team and the curling club were shut down while our beloved coaches walked the line.

This was the season in which Ken Pearce was touted to have a real chance at the Ontario Schoolboy championship. Undeterred by the strike, Pearce went about forming a super team, which would practise on its own, without Mr. Elliot's supervision, at the Avonlea Club. I remember when Ken regretfully told Ace that he was putting together a new side to challenge for the title.

"It's okay—I don't think I want to put in that much work anyway," Ace explained bravely. "I'll make my own team and, Scott, why don't you be on it?" It was an easy call. With Rollie's graduation, Bruce MacInnis and I had no place to go. Along with Ron White, we joined forces with Ace to form a plucky if not supremely talented foursome.

Joining Ken's contending team were Gary Keith as the smooth and lanky lead and Bob Cooper as a second who could throw booming takeout weight while possessing a broom to match. The vice-skip, Ace's replacement, was Cliff Phillips. He came from good bloodlines, being the son of Alfie Phillips Junior, a man who had won the Brier in the Centennial Year of 1967 and had gone on to narrowly lose the world championship to Chuck Hay of Scotland that same season.

It was a commonly held belief among the schoolboy curlers that Cliff Phillips's dad would do anything to win a match. "They say he smokes a cigar while holding the broom in the house," Ace told me. "If one of his rocks is coming in too fast, he just flicks an ash in front of it and it grinds to a halt right where he wants it!" There was never confirmation of this but the subterranean spreading of the tall tale through Avonlea gave curling an element of mystery.

The Pearce four breezed through the city playoffs and entered the provincial finals as a favoured group that season. It remained unknown to most that Mr. Elliot, in spite of the ongoing work stoppage, was making all the arrangements for the team and would accompany the delegation to Kitchener for the championships. We later learned that a group of teachers—very good curlers themselves—had provided the final opposition for the Toronto Schoolboy champs just before they headed west on the 401.

Our team stayed back but we were delighted to hear of Ken's win over the host club from Kitchener Westmount in the semifinal and then of their ultimate victory over a team from Etobicoke to claim the Ontario crown. As our group soldiered on in a less competitive but no less satisfying situation at Avonlea, we followed Ken's progress all the way to the Canadian final in Kapuskasing, where he narrowly missed the playoffs, finishing with seven wins and four losses.

Eventually the teachers came back to work. Dissatisfied with the settlement, many of them worked to rule so while life in the classroom returned to the normal grind, extracurricular activities remained in limbo. The senior basketball coach, for instance, said he couldn't field a squad that season, citing too much time lost over the course of the strike.

Heff, however, was willing to listen. We pleaded our case, all the juniors who had been with him for the last couple of years, asked if he would guide us one more time. Our favourite coach didn't take much convincing even though he already had a full slate of activities beyond his teaching duties. There was a junior lacrosse team he was involved with and hockey on the side but he took us on for good measure, reinstated early morning practices, and whipped us into shape. "You men deserve a chance," he would insist as he lined us up against the gymnasium wall. And then he'd holler that familiar refrain. "*Down and back!*"

Our basketball team was eliminated in the semifinals by a much more powerful group. But we had valiantly held our own and Heff had been proud of us. We in turn were thankful to him for giving us the chance.

School activities were drawing to a close, and many of us would be off to university in the fall. At Avonlea there was one last Friday of spring curling. The teachers were coming over from their Don Mills club to join us in a staff-student bonspiel. It was to be a celebratory final gathering of the club in which we had all learned so much, playing a game that had once belonged solely to our parents.

That's when I saw him on the ice for the first time. Grant Heffernan. Down and back he slid from end to end through his warmup. He wore checkered pants and a turtleneck under a bulky wool sweater not unlike mine. His delivery was the best I had ever seen. He got down so low on the ice and released the stone just a hair before the hog line. Heff was precise. Heff was powerful. His impressive forearms beat a blue fabric "Rink Rat" broom to thunderous effect. It occurred to me then that for all the rigours of our basketball schedule, all the early morning drills and after-school practices, Heff had never once scheduled play on a Friday afternoon. Looking at him, so at ease on the ice, I suspected I knew why.

Heff's was the only team we faced on that last day of my curling career. "Good curling, young man," the coach said, firmly shaking my hand just before I threw the first rock.

The Royals

CHAPTER TWO

THE PLACE

It was delivered to the mailbox late one summer. At first glance it appeared to be an annoying bit of junk mail, but something about this single white page with blue print caught my eye. I was being invited to attend an open house at the impressively named "Royal Canadian Curling Club."

Our home is set in a development within striking distance of downtown Toronto—part of what is fashionably called the "New Beach." We sit squarely on the spot where thoroughbreds once ran to distinction at the old Greenwood Racetrack. Now streets bearing names like Winner's Circle and Northern Dancer Boulevard are lined with brand-new three-storey homes. It's a place where the junk mail tends to be upscale—flyers for pedicures, women's fitness clubs, interior design consulting, heritage landscaping, that sort of thing. In this neighbourhood we receive solicitous telephone calls from fledgling golf courses offering their prospectuses with the assurance that initiation fees are in the "low thousands and really quite reasonable considering the amenities and the prestige that goes along with membership." That's why this lonely sheet of paper sent from the curling rink captured my attention. It seemed very real.

"Where Friendship is a Tradition," the flyer proclaimed at the side of a maple leaf flanked by crossed curling brooms. There weren't many details other than the time of the event and a few words about fees, $300 for the season and no mention of any lump sum to be paid up front. The invitation was welcoming and earnest. I really believed they wanted me there on that Friday in September.

The directions to the club were spelled out in a few simple words—"Broadview just north of Queen." If you know this area of Toronto, you know that it has a certain eclectic character to it. You are reminded of that when you try to elude the streetcar tracks that run past the Real Jerk restaurant, specializing in Jamaican food on one side of the road, and Dangerous Dan's hamburger joint on the other. If you continue west along Queen Street, you'll eventually wind up in the city's core. If you veer to the right, onto Broadview Avenue, you'll find Jilly's on the port side of your vehicle. It's a spot that advertises "Exotic Dancers" in neon lights and promises "The Best Party in Town." You can't drive too quickly up Broadview or you'll miss the curling club. Look carefully to your right and you'll find it, across from a squat white building that houses the Army, Navy and Airforce Veterans in Canada—Coronation Unit #259. The club is almost hidden, down a little alley with the front door tucked in between the Latvian Relief Society to the south and Ien Houng's Skin, Hair and Beauty Salon to the north.

"ROYALS" it reads above the faded blue building's front entrance. Also printed on the sign, a cartoon-like curling

The threshold on Broadview

rock reminiscent of the hockey folk hero Peter Puck and that familiar short phrase "Where Friendship is a Tradition." Open the door, take one sniff of the building's musty air, and time stops, so unexpected is this place, in this era, in this too busy city.

The first thing you see when you pass through the entrance is the most impressive trophy imaginable. Standing at least eight feet high and four feet in diameter at its base, protected by a wood and glass cabinet fit for a museum, the precious monstrosity would dwarf the Stanley Cup. The Dunlop Trophy has nothing to do with curling at all. It was awarded to the Royal Canadian Bicycle Club, racing champions eight of nine years beginning in 1894. "The old handlebar boys," as they were referred to, were the original incarnation of an athletic association that dates back to the end of the nineteenth century and that first established itself in a storefront and two upper floors on Broadview—the current site of The Royals—in 1906. It wasn't until 1928 that the six-sheet curling facility was attached to the building

The champion Royal Canadian Bicycle Club in 1894 with the Dunlop Trophy

and even then hockey players and figure skaters had the run of the ice while the "rock throwers" got on at off-peak hours.

By 1953, figure skating and hockey were dropped from The Royals program, and the premier pursuit became curling, although cribbage was played with fervour once all the sweeping was done. The six sheets of ice became the focal point of the club, and the old sand floor was replaced by a concrete floating ice bed that made the playing surface more consistent. "Extensive alterations and modernization followed," according to a brief history of the club that occupies a single page in present-day manager Bill McAnally's file drawer. "The latest in ice lighting, air conditioning, a bar, kitchens, snack room, dining room, two lounges and attractive furniture."

Owned by its members, the club operated from its early days in a democratic fashion with the active participants in sport required to sit on policy-making committees and to take turns serving on the board of directors. The members owned shares in the building and its facilities within an association inclined less toward profit than fellowship and sportsmanship.

The trophies and awards speak to the tradition of inclusivity fostered for decades at The Royals. Men, women, youth, and senior citizens from every walk of Toronto life have always been welcomed in the place. It was at this club that women who worked in the city's financial district found room to compete when, in 1962, The Royals launched Business Girls and held Ontario's first Business Girls championship. The club has always valued mixed curling, and from the very start games featuring teams made up of both sexes shared the spotlight with the competitive men's leagues. The men, building on the sporting success of the association, enjoyed a spectacular run in the mid-fifties and beginning in 1954 won an impressive five of six Metropolitan Toronto Curling Championships. On the panelled walls of the clubhouse, elaborate banners attest to the continued success of both men and women curlers from the club. Carol Thompson's foursome came out of this rink to represent Ontario at the Scott Tournament of Hearts (the Canadian women's championship) twice during the 1980s. The Ross Harrison- and Joe Gurowka-skipped teams from here won the Ontario Tankard in 1982. Jim Sharples and his foursome dominated senior curling in the province a decade ago and claimed the national title in 1992.

On the night of the open house I am greeted by a smiling woman who gently offers a "Hello My Name Is" sticker and hands me a glass of wine. Then she motions to the fine old Heintzman and Co. grand piano in the middle of the crowded room. Someone is playing and a delightful melody seeps into the air amid the lively chatter. Beyond the grandfather clock on the near wall is the bar where all kinds of folks are bellied up.

The ice doesn't go in at The Royals until just after Thanksgiving and so the open house is purely a social occasion. Tonight curling will take a back seat to chitchat. There are at least a hundred people gathered in the tight confines of the lounge under the umbrella of red, white, and blue

The timeless Heintzman still attacts a crowd at The Royals

balloons. They're eating french fries smothered in gravy and signing up for various leagues. The canteen opens onto the dining room, the serving window framed in the décor of a Lincoln Log cabin. Against another wall curling shoes are lined up in cubbyholes, and prospective members are trying them on for size.

"They come from every kind of background and every age group," Sue Gillespie tells me. She's about to enter her twentieth season as a curler and her second as president of The Royals. In recent years, she has seen the club struggle to hang on.

"Like any other club we were going through some rocky times financially. A hundred voter members were liable for the club. They were aging and had bought their memberships quite awhile ago. Many of them didn't curl anymore and their interests were elsewhere. They were concerned about getting their investment back and they didn't want any financial risk left to them. They wanted out."

By 1998 the club's membership had dropped to the point where fewer than a hundred people were curling with any regularity. "We were in danger of losing it," she says, shaking her head at the thought of this vibrant place fighting for its life. "What we did was band together. We raised some funds, bought enough shares to get the majority vote, and gained control. We've restructured so that sort of thing cannot happen again."

Five years later The Royals boasts a nearly full roster of 350 competitors who come in all ages, shapes, and sizes. In a storage room the granite rocks that will soon clutter the six sheets of ice lie in wait. Their red and yellow handles bear the names of The Royals families, the tangible results of a scheme in which members donated money to the club's flag-ging coffers in return for having their monikers carved in stone. The legendary Ed "The Wrench" Werenich, a former Brier and world champion, and his longtime lead Neil Harrison have been known to curl at the club, and I can see their support for it documented on a number of stones in the storeroom.

"We've had our competitive strength in the past," Sue says. "Now we've had turnover and there are a lot of new families moving into the downtown core and a lot of new teams are forming. These days I would say the strength of the club is mainly in the social aspect of things."

Sue's observations are reinforced by the gathering of people at the open house. The elders are here, clad in their more traditional garb—the men in sport jackets and ties, the women in tweed suits or pleated skirts. But there are others who might be considered less likely guests at such a function—kids, teenagers, funky-looking twenty-somethings with long hair and beards. I suspect some of those in attendance are from working-class backgrounds, while others appear to be employed as professionals. They mingle, free of the artificial barriers that might otherwise separate them.

"You don't really think of it as a Scottish game," Jeff Imai is telling me. Imai and his wife, Belinda, are both lawyers who spend their days in the city's downtown skyscrapers. She's originally from Newfoundland, and he's a first-generation Canadian of Japanese descent. On Friday nights they curl together in one of The Royals' mixed leagues, and midweek Jeff competes more seriously in the men's loop.

"I've always thought of curling as being a typically Canadian game," Jeff continues. Belinda nods in agreement.

The lounge looking toward the ice, circa 1970

"Anyone who walks in the door is welcome here," she stresses. "Even if you've never seen a curling stone in your life."

Belinda and Jeff have become ardent fans of the sport since joining The Royals. (The couple travelled to Ogden, Utah, last April to watch Belinda's nephew Brent Hamilton play for Brad Gushue's Team Canada at the World Junior Curling Championships.) Both curled in their relative youths, both have come back to the game in part because of the rink's proximity to their places of employment. And they've returned to curling because the sport affords them an opportunity.

"One of the attractions was that this was something we could do together," Jeff continues. "On a night out we didn't want to just go our separate ways."

Belinda windsurfs and Jeff plays hockey with his pals. "But we decided we both needed to get ourselves off the couch more," explains Belinda, whose family back in Newfoundland is crazy for curling. "We called up the club and asked what was going on. We just showed up on Friday night and that was it."

They are a charming couple and seem at ease in this environment. They beam at the chance to recount their shared experiences on the ice. They both boast of the simple joys curling brings into their lives. "I remember Jeff carting home all this meat after his rink had travelled to some small Ontario town or other to play in a bonspiel," Belinda chuckles. Jeff starts to laugh, knowing what she'll say next. "Yeah, that's the prize at most of the bonspiels we play in—meat!"

"I was dead asleep, it must have been well past midnight," Belinda continues. "Jeff woke me up and I opened my eyes to find him standing over the bed with this platter, telling me he'd won the bonspiel and wasn't it great!"

"That's right," Jeff jumps in, his eyes alight. "Here I was, champion of a 'spiel' held some small place near Kitchener, hovering over my wife's bed holding a platter of T-bone steaks as my prize."

There are no apologies from either of them when queried about the modesty of their current surroundings. They know the club is set in what some might call a seedier part of town; they just don't care. "That's how you tell people where it is," Jeff explains. "You ask them if they know where Jilly's strip club is. They know right away!" Not for one moment do Belinda and Jeff regret not being members of a fancy golf club—something well within their means. High-stakes competition and social status are not what draw the couple to curling.

"It's the people," Jeff assures me. "You go through four years of engineering school and three years of law school and you meet engineers and you meet lawyers and that's about it. Here you meet people from much different backgrounds. You find out there's more to life than just the law."

The key to good curling is the ice, and the man who makes it for The Royals is a reflection of the club itself. Modest to the point of being shy when considering his contribution, Mike Warren is a self-described "rink rat" and when I meet him a week before the season is to begin he is on his hands and knees covered in primary-coloured flecks.

"My back feels better already," the forty-five-year-old quips without looking up from his artistry. He's putting the finishing touches on the four-foot blue circle in the last of six target areas known as the houses, having finished the first five sheets of ice. Mike has painted all the bright red and blue rings by hand and covered the surrounding surface with three coats of white. It's a job that has obviously taken some time and a good measure of care.

"People want it to be as good as possible." He shrugs his shoulders as if to acknowledge that's what he'll deliver. For twenty-five years he's been the iceman at this curling rink and his beginnings in the craft are like everything else about him—understated. Mike was a printer by trade but confesses to hating every minute of it. "One day I went to Manpower and saw a posting on the wall," he says with a smile. "That's all there was to it. I came down here, did a quick interview, and started as an apprentice with the ice maker who was here at the time."

Mike learned while he was on the job and trained under the watchful eye of Horst Reichart, who was nearing retirement.

Knowing the ins and outs of good ice management became his hallmark and, eventually, he'll admit, his pride. The rocks—Ailsa Craigs in this case, named after the Scottish island they came from seventy-five years ago—weigh forty pounds and tend to wear out with age. Some rocks run straight, others are wild, it all depends on how ground down they are from their years of use. For a facility like The Royals the expense of buying new rocks—approximately a thousand dollars a pop—is prohibitive so the club makes do with the old ones. This inevitable effect of time, Reichart taught Mike, will guide the ice maker in doing his job.

"Rocks determine what your ice is going to run like," Mike says pointing to the ice surface with his paintbrush. He knows the rocks intimately and monitors how they change in minuscule measures season by season, committing these details to memory. Given the imprecise nature of the materials he is working with, Mike delights in providing consistency.

"For curling you want it as level as you possibly can get it—clean and quick and true. The rock, you hope, will do the same thing every time you throw it down and it hits a certain spot."

He snickers to himself and, in a kind way, reveals his exasperation with what actually happens most nights on the ice at the now busy club. "Some people will really enjoy a sheet of ice," he claims. "They'll have a great time. Then again, they've won the game. You get different opinions from the people who just got beaten on that sheet. I sit back here and laugh at people who just never seem to catch on. We know it's gonna run straight in a certain spot. They should know it too because they've thrown down there a couple of times before. Still they'll put the broom down like it's going to curl three feet."

The iceman: Mike Warren

Once he's finished painting, Mike will flood the ice and then, if need be, make it level with some vigorous scraping. Next he'll apply the pebble. He shuffles down each corridor with a tank of water strapped to his back, the small piece of hose attached to it resting gingerly in his hand. He waves the nozzle ever so slightly and the fluid sprinkles onto the ice, hardening the instant it lands. Run your hand over the resulting surface and you will feel a paradoxical texture, one that is bumpy and smooth at the same time.

It is, I judge, an artisan's life. Mike Warren is the formative individual in what is a sport of subtlety. There are evidently no shortcuts in this business and he prefers it that way. There is an impressive lack of technology to everything that will take place in the course of his day's work. There are no machines to drive and no computers with which to evaluate the temperature of the ice. All that

Mike creates is by feel—intuition enhanced by years of personal experience.

Each day, before the first game, Mike will engage in a ritual inconceivable in any modern hockey arena. He'll drag the heavy rocks over each sheet to work them in. "Put them in a box and drag them up and down to speed the ice up before that first game," Mike acknowledges. "People get upset if you don't drag the rocks for them. They'll go out there and try and throw a rock, they get it halfway down the sheet and it'll die. Ice is too heavy. You have to break it in for them."

Mike Warren doesn't curl much himself anymore. He was active in the game when he was growing up in North York and travelled the ice at the now extinct Parkway and Broom and Stone clubs. Like many Canadians of his generation he attended curling classes, offered as part of high school's physical education curriculum. He came back to the familiar sport a couple of decades ago and was a witness to the near-death of The Royals. Now he's encouraged by the flourishing of a new breed of curlers.

"They are getting younger every year," he figures. "When I first came back to the game twenty years ago, the average age in this club would have been between forty-five and seventy-five. Now you see a lot more people in their twenties and thirties. The game is opening up a little. Younger people are seen on TV playing the game at the national level. Younger people are therefore attracted to trying it." It's good news for Mike, who can see a future in the age-old practice of laying the ice at The Royals.

Like a groundskeeper who trims the grass and thrills to the symmetry of baseball's perfect red clay infield or the gifted and vigilant greenskeepers at golf's most revered courses, the ice maker in downtown Toronto is a nearly invisible part of the backdrop. The limelight is more likely reserved for the skilled participants of the game. It's the furthest concern from Mike Warren's mind.

"There is an emotional attachment to this place," he concludes. "I think what's kept me going here for so long is that I enjoy the people. The club seems to attract a lot of really decent people." His definitive statement made, Mike dips his brush in the bucket of blue paint and makes his last loving strokes. Time is running out, he has work to do, and opening day is fast approaching.

I made a third trip to The Royals just before the season began. I just had to see the results of the iceman's labour before the curlers crowded on to his masterpiece. When club manager Bill McAnally flicked on the huge overhead pot lights, the place came alive. The circles were concentric as if drawn with a mathematician's compass—not a drip of colour had gone awry. The lines were straight and true and the white was almost blinding. Rocks stood at attention, arranged row upon row, their handles coded by shade—fire engine red, the yellow of sunshine. At opposing ends the windows glistened, the scoreboards gleamed. Portraits of victorious teams from long past seasons adorned the outside walls. I took my shoes off and walked over the edge of the surface in stocking feet only to notice there wasn't a speck of dirt as residue. The ice maker had left no trace.

"I'll tell Mike those are your footprints out there," McAnally scolded as I returned to the warmth of the lounge.

"I guess he's pretty particular."

"Oooohhh, do you figure? It's something that he puts so much work into so I guess I understand where he's coming from. You know the old saying. 'If it wasn't for the curlers all the ice is perfect.' Every iceman will tell you that."

Mixed night at The Royals and it's early in the season, just barely into November. As I watch, a mismatch is developing on Sheet Number 4. It involves the favourites, a team skipped by Pat Corrigan, the political cartoonist for the *Toronto Star*, and his buddy Brian McAndrew, who writes on environmental issues for the same newspaper. Every once in a while Brian gets a chance to cover curling events like the Scott Tournament of Hearts because *The Star* doesn't have a full-time reporter for the sport.

"It's incredible, we get that much space," Brian told me, holding his fingers a millimetre apart. "Take a Prince Albert newspaper or whatever, they cover curling like *The Star* and *The Sun* cover the Leafs. Swarms of them. There's nothing too little for them to write about."

Back to the game and the two journalists are joined by

Friendly competition at The Royals

Sue-Ann Lewis and Anne Hewitt to form a smooth and efficient foursome. Their opponents on this night are not their equals but they are a spirited group nonetheless. I was drawn to this team because Sue Gillespie, the president of the club, curls second. She had told me about the lead, Michael Dobbs, a youngish guy, just turned thirty, who is curling to get in the good books of his prospective parents-in-law, Teresa "Terry" and her husband, Bere "Bear" Zbignew. Terry is the skip of Michael's team and Bear is the vice.

Michael recently arrived in Canada from Australia of all places. But with the exception of his Fosters Lager equipment bag, Mike looks pretty much like every other guy in the place when he's standing still—heavy sweater, turtleneck, stretch slacks, that sort of thing. Still, careful observation tells you that he's new at this game. Unlike Terry and Bear, Michael is a little rigid at times. During his delivery, he tends to draw his back leg in underneath him like a jetliner retracting its landing gear. As a result the Aussie comes out of the hack looking a bit like a cannonball.

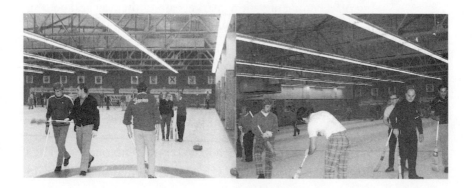

The delivery and release of the rock is a fascinating thing to watch. Some people ball themselves up, their bodies mimicking a fist as they shoot forward. Others remain quite upright, teetering back and forth as if they might tip over at any moment. More expert curlers get down very low, almost pasting themselves to the ice. Like cats on the prowl they lift their paws from the handle of each granite orb with great delicacy.

In spite of his awkwardness, Michael's not bad on the draw weight and he is also an extremely good sweeper or "brusher." Evidently he's got some athletic ability.

"He's somebody used to the 85-, 95-, 105-degree temperatures and no ice!" I can recall Sue pointing out Michael's obvious disadvantage before the match. All things considered, he's making it work and most times he's an effective lead, delivering the shot he's asked for by his soon-to-be mother-in-law. Still, they are being easily handled by Corrigan's team. As a group, they are missing ever so slightly and the superiority of the cartoonist's lineup is establishing itself over the course of a game scheduled to last eight ends.

In the fourth end Corrigan makes a nifty takeout, bouncing off a couple of yellow markers along the way and getting to his eventual target in pinball-like fashion. All of a sudden there are three red rocks left in the house, all of them closer to the button than any of Terry's counters. With this shot, Corrigan's side secures a 5–2 lead. Consistency is a huge advantage especially as the final ends approach.

I must admit it's quite a sight. Across the six sheets of ice the sweepers shuffle, slide, hop, and push with one foot. They dance around a minefield of rocks. As soon as one stone is in the house everyone hustles out of the way and the next group

The warmth of the clubhouse

takes its turn. One guy with black sweatpants has rolled up the sleeves of his sweater and left his purple shirttail hanging out. He's skipping up and down and all over the ice—unable to slide in his white tennis sneakers—obviously having a blast in what might be his first or second try at the game.

In addition to constant movement, there is incessant chatter. I can't hear it on my side of the glass wall in the viewing area but I know it's going on. And here's what's remarkable— on the Number 4 sheet the opposing skips seem to be going over strategy, working out where Terry should place the broom when calling for a critical shot in the fifth end. It's hard to figure out who's on whose team after a while, the lack of competitive tension almost off-putting.

In the sixth end a log-jam develops. Michael's team is in terrible trouble. The prime red rock is buried and the yellow ones, defeating their own purpose, are acting as guards. Terry will have difficulty making the takeout and she's already behind 6–2. A last noble effort but she's taken too much ice and the pick-off attempt rumbles through the house, leaving the red rock counting and giving Corrigan an impressive 7–2 lead. The teams shake hands. Terry's team has conceded the game and they all repair to the lounge for a drink.

"It changed twice during the game," a laughing Terry complains about the ice as she waits for the beer that the winning team will buy her. "Oh well, some days it's better than others." It's a good thing Mike Warren isn't around to hear that, I say to myself.

"Actually we were talking about ice conditions and which way it would curl," Pat Corrigan claims when asked about his fifth-end strategy session with Terry. "I played it one way, missed the broom, and actually made the shot because it did something completely different from what I thought it would. I came back after that and told her I was embarrassed having made the shot when I should have missed it by a mile."

In the background, Michael Dobbs is grinning as he takes it all in. Still a slightly puzzled observer, he strives to make sense of this festive post-game ritual. When it comes to curling, his fiancée, Sarah, has left him on his own. Sink or swim, he's taken up the challenge. Michael's originally from Melbourne and came to Canada by way of Chicago a couple of years ago in order to pursue a career as a mechanical engineer.

"I thought it was dead boring when I first saw it on TV," he confides in that Australian twang you just can't miss. "Curling's different when you're out there though. It's the ability to change the outcome of the game that attracts me."

Being piped in for the bonspiel

Michael decided to take up the sport the moment Sarah first introduced him to her parents. The Zbignews had been heading out the door on the way to the curling rink. Dobbs had played Australian Rules football as a youth and some soccer. He tried his hand at hockey once he got to Canada. He ultimately failed at this country's national sport because as an adult, learning to skate was troublesome and the speed of the game certainly beyond him.

"It's kind of nice to think of myself as an Australian curler," he figures. "I don't stop and think about it too often because I curl with a lot of other nationalities here. I've identified quite a few accents. I know I'm not the only foreigner who plays this game. But I do get a kick out of going back to Australia and telling everyone that I curl and they say, 'What's that?'"

If you let him, Michael Dobbs, the mechanical engineer, will slip into a discussion of the intricacies of curling. "As well as being a part of dynamics it's also a part of statics," he lectures. "The friction of the rock and the frost point of the ice. There is so much mathematics at play that you can't even begin to start working it out. You have to trust the other, more experienced curlers because by the time you finish your calculations you're beaten."

During the course of our conversation, Michael assures me that a fascination with physics has little to do with why an Australian has immersed himself in this game.

"I'm more Canadian than most Canadians who don't curl," he says in an attempt to put his finger on it. "Curling has brought me closer to Canada, I think."

Michael leans forward and looks over his shoulder at Terry and Bear as they buy another round for Pat Corrigan's winning group. "You've got to understand that I could have the worst night of curling in my life and I am still going to go home and sleep okay," he says. "This was a way to become a closer part of the family. It gives Sarah's father and me something to talk about. Of course, I'm dating his daughter and it can be an uncomfortable situation for many people. But we always have curling as a middle ground."

There's a lot of yelling going on for a Sunday afternoon. The atmosphere of the crackling, cool air is fractured by shouts of: "Yup yup. . . . Hurry!" Things are pretty serious mid-season at The Royals. By comparison to mixed night, the chatter is minimal, less given to pleasantry and confined to members of the same team. The sweeping is more forceful and the rocks are delivered with a striking purpose, colliding with solid-sounding thuds on frequent takeouts. It's the men's competitive session for the Riverdale League and all the curlers here today are gay.

Exclusively gay curling leagues have existed, even flourished, at this downtown Toronto club since 1983. From their quiet beginnings in 1962 when the old CN–CP railway leagues operated as unofficially gay—first at Avonlea in suburban North York, then at the Terrace Curling Club—gay curling leagues have come out of the closet and grown exponentially. At the outset there were a handful of members, maybe a couple of teams. Currently, the Rotators Curling League and the Riverdale Curling League boast a total of 150 participants and occupy two large blocks of time at The Royals, Wednesday evenings and Sunday afternoons. The Rotators' teams are geared for those who prefer recreational curling. Each season they field fourteen mixed teams made up of gay men and lesbians. The Riverdale League has a maximum of thirty recreational teams and a dozen more in the competitive loop. All the spots have been filled again for the duration of this curling calendar.

The network of gay curling in Canada is fairly substantial. The Royal Canadian Curling Club is acknowledged as the forerunner in the movement. Here all the players who take part on either Wednesday evenings or Sunday afternoons are attached to and pay their dues to either the Riverdale or Rotator leagues. They also enjoy associate membership at The Royals with full use of its facilities and access to its privileges.

Each of the two leagues sponsors and hosts an annual bonspiel at which gay curlers from across the country participate. The Survivor Spiel, the pride of The Rotators, is going into its fourth year. A kickoff classic for the gay season in this sport, it attracts twenty-four teams from coast to coast to "match wits and curling skills" over a guaranteed three games and a festive final banquet.

The Riverdale League has successfully staged fifteen annual bonspiels. "Do It on the Ice" features a different theme each March (it was "Taking Out Oscar" in 2003) and although it can accommodate forty-eight team entries, it generally has to turn people away. In addition, there are established gay curling tournaments in Edmonton (The Icebreaker), Montreal (La Quête du Roi), Vancouver (Pacific Rim Cup), and Calgary (Apollo Games—Western Cup 21). The opportunities for athletes in the gay community to participate in and excel at curling are many and varied.

As I watch the fierce rivalries play themselves out with intensity at the convening of the Riverdale League one Sunday afternoon, I am reminded that curling at this club is conducted in an atmosphere where the temptation to exclude is resisted. Everyone is welcome and that includes me. I take in the proceedings as an impartial spectator and draw little attention. I am not made to feel as if I am invading anyone's privacy. Unlike most minor hockey games I have attended, I do not have to pay admission to get in the door.

"It could be elitist," Don Kezima is telling me as he takes a break and grabs some warmth on the near side of the glass. "Where I came from the farmers didn't get a chance to play at the club." Kezima hails from the small Saskatchewan town of Verigan. It has a hundred people and a curling rink but, as he remembers it, only a select few enjoyed the benefits of the tiny club and its single sheet of ice. After attending the University of Calgary and then moving to Toronto, Kezima has found a much more open environment in which to enjoy the game. "We were all invited to a meat spiel in Uxbridge not long ago," he laughs. "I didn't even know where Uxbridge was. They gave us a big honking T-bone steak at the banquet and they did everything they possibly could to make us feel at home."

The web site operated nationally out of the Riverdale and Rotator leagues is called gaycurl.ca and it offers a basic understanding of how this association can feel comfortable in the curling world. "The off-ice atmosphere of cama-raderie is unmatched in other winter team sports," the web-master writes. "Integrity, a sense of fair play, and friendly competition are hallmarks of the sport. It's one of the few sports where men and women of all ages compete equally."

Having read this principled manifesto over a couple of times, I find myself subscribing to its basic decency. Still, there are more practical reasons gay curlers compete here at this ancient clubhouse. "'The Royals' is located minutes from downtown Toronto at 131 Broadview Avenue," the pitch goes, "offering a gay friendly atmosphere, a licensed lounge, restaurant, piano and large screen TV."

"It means that you're not in a gay bar," Murray Leaning, the president of the Riverdale and Rotator leagues explains, while sipping on a pint of beer. "You're not in a gay curling club. You are in a curling club that is very open and happy to have gay men and women there." Men and women are coming off the ice and lingering at the bar. Bill McAnally, the manager, is drawing pints and popping the caps off a squadron of beer bottles. One player is voicing a hint of displeasure with Mike Warren's ice. "It got more swoop as the game on the outside sheet went on," he complains.

"That's why they call it curling," Mike replies.

"I threw an out-turn and it really veered a lot," is the next criticism.

"So in other words, you missed your shot." The ice maker refuses to give an inch.

For his part, Murray Leaning feels at home here in the rink. A civil servant working in the Premier of Ontario's office, he is now entering his fifth season as president of the two leagues and he's proud of the diversity he sees on the ice. "There are youngish kids in their early twenties who also go out raving," Leaning offers. "We have mid-thirties professionals, business owners, people in government, people in corporate Canada, lawyers, and dentists. More than you can shake a stick at. Right up to the sixty-year-olds just about ready to retire. Something for everyone. You've got a bunch of people together socializing, drinking, and playing games. Sounds like gay life to me. The only thing missing is the dance music," he jokes.

Leaning is more circumspect when he seriously evaluates the reason for the continued success of his league. "Here's a place where you can come without any sexual overtones and just meet other people in the community. You hang out and chat and talk about something else you have in common like curling," he suggests. "I'm like all the other people here today. I came because a friend brought me here to try it. I liked it. I felt comfortable and I came back."

I too returned a final time to the Royal Canadian Curling Club on a grim January day more than two years after I had first visited the place. Perhaps it was the greyness of the sky that made the brown brick south wall of the club, covered with leafless vines, seem to have crumbled only slightly. The place was still standing but it looked older—weathered.

Down the alleyway entrance, I noticed that Peter Puck's curling cousin continued to beam from atop the doorway. But there was a huge scaffold erected at the threshold of The Royals bearing workmen who were banging away at the bricks. They looked to be chiselling out spaces where windows would soon be. One of the men dropped his hammer and it almost dinged me in the head as I reached for the latch to let myself in. "Sorry, buddy," he yelped. I felt fortunate to have escaped serious injury but a more urgent rush of anxiety took hold. It suddenly struck me that the presence of the construction crew might signal that the door would be closed, locked, that the open house was shut for good.

"No, she's open all right, pal," the worker continued apologetically. "You just have to tug a little, that thing's getting rusted pretty good." And there it was—relief and optimism all at once as I yanked the door and glimpsed the magnificent Dunlop Trophy in the spot where I had first encountered it.

In the lounge things had been altered drastically and a major renovation was in full swing. Where were the grand piano and the old grandfather clock? The canteen was nowhere to be found, and the cubbyholes where the curling shoes had once been so neatly arranged had also disappeared. In their place was a giant plywood wall hiding the major construction going on behind it. A familiar face, that of Bill McAnally, was still buzzing around answering the persistent phone that sat ringing on the countertop of the bar.

"Welcome back," Bill said, when he got a second. "Don't mind the mess—we're making a few changes around here. Had to lease out part of the building to make ends meet. They're putting in a daycare centre and we're losing our banquet room upstairs."

I wondered about the whereabouts of the piano. "Don't worry, it's in storage behind that wall," Bill chuckled. "We'll have it back in no time." He pointed to the ice surface where Mike Warren was dancing backwards down the middle sheet, deftly applying the pebble. "Not too much changes around here in spite of all this." Bill shook his head. They were getting ready for the late-afternoon session, the mixed league due in an hour. Registration numbers were up, the manager told me with no small measure of satisfaction as he hustled on to another chore.

Mike was glad to see me, and he hadn't changed a bit. The same spotless white sneakers on his feet. And in my uneducated estimation, the rink was perfect.

"It's been a little tough," the iceman sighed. "The dust and grime from all that work going on means I've got to pay special attention . . . I don't know." I assured him that his efforts had paid off, the place looked brand new in spite of itself. I wondered if I might take a picture of him while he was on task. Mike obliged and backed away from me down the next sheet of ice. His eyes gently told me to stay put on the sidelines so as not to scar his handiwork.

I lay on my belly and snapped a couple of shots of the ice maker making his sweep of the territory. "It's the greatest job in the world," he said, with a conviction that assures you it's genuine. "I just love the people."

The photos taken and Sheet Number 6 complete, I said

so long to Mike Warren as he was removing the little piece of carpet draped over the raised hack to protect it from the freezing spray he had just applied. "If you need anything else, we're here every day at this time," he said with a wave. "The door is always open." In a few words Mike had captured the essence of the Royal Canadian Curling Club, the very reason for its continued prosperity in a place where locking your door at night makes more than enough sense.

Colleen Jones: The grinder

CHAPTER THREE

KEEPING UP WITH JONES

EIGHT MINUTES TO SEVEN AND IT'S STILL DARK ON A mid-November's morning in Halifax. I'm down at the wharf by the museum, and the only evidence of life is a television camera parked beside an idling van, its lights fired up and pointed toward the narrows. There's a crackle in the air— make it a bone-chilling breeze that cuts right through you and the seagulls are screeching their sad song of protest.

Four minutes later there's some human activity. The van door opens and a thirty-something fellow sporting a ball cap and weather-appropriate parka springs to the pavement, slaps his gloves, and waves to someone approaching from up the hill. She doesn't notice him right away. Pink parka, pink sweater, brown porkpie hat, she's humming a little tune and fiddling with something she's trying to insert in her ear.

"What was that grin for?" Colleen Jones asks, flashing those enormous, gleaming white teeth. "I know, anyone else in the world would look at what I'm wearing and say, 'Man, is she overdressed!'"

Dawn on the docks of Halifax

In an instant Jones plugs in a cord, reveals a few sheets of notepaper, and assumes her position in front of Steve Lawrence's camera. A ferryboat slips from Dartmouth to Halifax—left to right—as if on cue.

"That's right, it's a gorgeous day," she announces, a few seconds after 7 a.m. "Forget the cold. Sun's coming up, I'm stripping down. Let's pretend it's August again!"

It's all in her delivery. Colleen Jones will present the weather and the sports on the national morning show for CBC with laughter, wit, and above all tremendous energy. She's done it for eight years now. For the mother of two hockey-playing boys who just happens to be the reigning world curling champion, this is just another busy day beginning.

Colleen Jones, at the time of writing, is forty-one years old and arguably one of the most accomplished curlers in

Canadian history. She has claimed three Canadian women's titles—all as the skip of her rink—and appeared at the national championships fifteen times. On all but one of those occasions she has thrown the last rock. Her victories span three separate decades and diverse regions of the country: the first was won in Regina, Saskatchewan, in 1982, the second in Charlottetown, P.E.I., in 1999, and the hat trick was turned in the winter of 2001 at the Sudbury Community Arena in the Ontario northland. The first championship came with two of her sisters alongside, the last couple with her existing foursome comprising lead Nancy Delahunt, second Mary-Anne Waye, and vice-skip Kim Kelly.

After failing to make the playoff round in 1982 at her first world championships in Geneva, Switzerland, she waited a long time for redemption. It came under ideal circumstances—the 1999 championship, staged at the gleaming new Harbour Station Arena in nearby Saint John, New Brunswick. The crowd was clearly a partisan one and Jones now had seventeen years of elite curling experience under her belt. But hope ended in disaster as the Canadian champions posted a sub-500 record in round-robin play and once again missed the chance to curl for the crown.

Undaunted, Jones kept her rink together, resisting the temptation to call it a day. After all, three of four on the team have demanding careers, and all four have young families to attend to. Jones, however, felt she had something to prove. She had her eye set on the ultimate prizes: a world championship and an Olympic gold medal.

Fuelling her fire further was the lingering notion harboured by some observers that Colleen Jones came from the wrong side of the tracks. The strength of women's curling in Canada is reputed to be in the west, particularly in Saskatchewan and Manitoba, from where champions like Sandra Schmirler, Connie Laliberte, and Vera Pezer have emerged to win three Canadian titles apiece. Doubters said Jones came from a weaker curling province and so was almost guaranteed to represent Nova Scotia at the Scott Tournament of Hearts every year. By a process of elimination and the sheer frequency of her chances, the skeptics argued, she would emerge as the winner every once in a while. She would never, however, be designated as the favourite from the start.

"Sometimes it enters into my psyche that maybe they could pick us just once," Jones says of her critics. "It's a bit like not being invited to the birthday party. It would be nice to get that invite once. Yet we've never had it so I don't get my hopes up. You automatically have an inferiority complex if you come from here—a curling province that is not big and not ever picked to win."

Jones fought back in 2001. After a miserable start—a sub-par record over seven matches—at the Scott Tournament of Hearts, Jones made her way to the final for the fifth time. She would face the reigning world champion Kelley Law and her formidable rink from British Columbia, who were favoured to win a second consecutive Canadian title.

The tenth end of the last game, Jones and the Nova Scotia foursome clung to a one-point lead but Law had the hammer and with it a chance at a long double-raise takeout for the win. To make the shot, the B.C. skip would have to knock back two of her own rocks to remove one of Nova Scotia's yellow stones, the one that was counting.

Kim Kelly could not watch, and so Nova Scotia's vice stood hidden behind the gum-chewing Colleen Jones, who was riveted to the action. Law executed the shot brilliantly and the thuds of the rocks echoed throughout the old hockey rink, otherwise silenced in appreciation of the tremendous curling on display. It all went as planned for Law with the exception of a solitary stone. Law needed two stones to stay in the rings for the win; instead one curled out of the house, helped along in no small measure by the brush of Nova Scotia's Nancy Delahunt. The game was now tied at 6. The 2001 Canadian championship would be decided in an extra end. Kelley Law's wide-eyed look told a story of both relief and fear: relief that she had survived for another end, fear that she had left the door open for the accomplished and fiercely competitive Colleen Jones.

In the extra end it was Jones who would have the final say, the last rock. There she was, the perennial underdog on the verge of a third national crown, wearing the blue of Nova Scotia and the black pleated skirt that had become her team's trademark and a reminder of curling's more formal past.

With the score tied and all the rocks but one thrown in the extra end, the Nova Scotia four held a conference to decide what shot Colleen Jones would execute for the win. The safest bet was to draw to the four-foot ring with an in-turn delivery. But Jones, wearing a microphone that made her deliberations audible for the television audience, opted not to try the draw. The decision and responsibility for the final shot lay ultimately with Jones, and she chose an out-turn takeout of the rock that was sitting second closest to the button. As she envisioned it, her yellow rock would then roll closer to the button than Law's remaining red marker, which was resting on the far side of the house.

"My out turn is my bread and butter," Colleen Jones has always claimed with conviction. "If that's not working, nothing is gonna work. That's got to be perfect."

After asking Nancy Delahunt to place the broom in just the right spot, Jones slid down toward the hack. She jumped up on the platform at the end of the ice and in front of a TV audience of well over a million she went fishing for something in her equipment bag. Jones emerged with a black woollen mitt and placed it on the foothold she would use to push off for her critical final delivery.

"That hack has been freezing up and I think she slipped on her last shot," said Mike Harris, the TV analyst. "I can't believe it," Joan McCusker, his broadcast partner and a former rival of Jones, responded incredulously.

Next the underdog set her jaw and came roaring out of the iron with her eyes blazing the path ahead. I noticed that her trailing shoe had silver duct tape plastered across the top of the toe and that it was not a curling shoe at all but a familiar summer sneaker known as a Skecher. Still, Jones hurled herself down the ice with a steadiness I had rarely witnessed. Steered by various sharp commands, "*Hurry*" and then "*No . . . No,*" which saw the sweepers rise and descend in harmony, the rock eventually whacked the target. Jones watched as the hit was nearly dead on and the roll very slight. Was it enough? Who was closer, red or yellow?

The naked eye couldn't answer the question being asked by every spectator in the rink, every viewer at home. The Jones rink locked arms while the official extracted the long silver contraption to measure the difference. Colleen, speechless for once, rested her head on Mary-Anne Waye's shoulder. Silence fell over the arena.

The signal was made. "*Yes . . . Yes . . . Yes . . .*" The frantic screams from the Nova Scotia foursome erupted. The underdogs would have their day. "I think Colleen's gonna hug everybody on the ice," quipped Don Wittman, the veteran play-by-play man. The sides shook hands and the defeated champions accepted a 7–6 extra-end result.

"At one point in this tournament we were three and four and the guts were ripped right out of us," Jones revealed to interviewer, Mark Lee. But she had refused to give up. "My son Zach said I should watch the movie *Gladiator* because he's a survivor and that's what I did. That's what I feel this team is. It's just remarkable."

She was back on top. At forty, she had won her third Canadian championship. Once again Colleen Jones had proven herself to be resilient. And modest. Lee pointed out to Jones that she now joined the late Sandra Schmirler and Vera Pezer, two other women who skipped their teams to three Canadian titles. "I've never considered myself in their league—ever. They were great curlers," the new champion said forcefully. Jones chose a different and more telling identity for her foursome that day. "Fighters, that's what we are."

As 11 a.m. Atlantic time approaches, Colleen Jones stands on some planks in front of the schooner *True North*. She is linked by the umbilical cord of technology to the mother ship show and its host, Mark Kelly, who sits in a comfy studio thousands of miles away in Toronto. She'll deliver her last word on the weather and then the Maritimes will give way to the centre of the country.

"Good morning, Mark!" she says, for what must be the hundredth time in her broadcast shift. "You know, we had such sunny skies at the day's outset—now it's turned to grey."

She's been up for six hours already. Colleen Jones rises at five in the morning, gathers her notes off the Internet in the comfort of her downtown Halifax home, makes a stop at the CBC to pick up extra copy on her way to the shoot location, and then does her job for four straight hours. She escapes the biting wind for only stolen moments, reading newspapers in the van with the heater at full blast. She admits to being tired all the time.

When it's 11 a.m. Colleen ditches the Telex cord and says her hurried goodbyes to Steve the cameraman. We make a mad dash to her green van and then it's on to the Mayflower Curling Club for her first practice session of the day. The vehicle is the definition of clutter—full of hockey sticks, Rollerblades, and the old Airwalk shoe she is taking to the cobbler for repair.

"No grip—I'm just shocked by it." She chatters constantly now while weaving across the lanes at a great clip. "You could walk across Antarctica on that but no grip. The duct tape is

Migration to the Mayflower, complete with sneakers and duct tape

there for resistance on my drag foot." Finally an explanation for the strange footwear I had seen at last year's tournament. "I used to have the mate to that and I curled in them but I got a pair of shoes that I liked better. I wear the left shoe of that pair and this one on my right foot," she continues.

We're picking up speed, racing toward the Mayflower. "It allows me to curl, working morning hours," Colleen says of her morning-show slot. "I've got all day to squeeze in curling as opposed to when I was working the supper-hour show. This way it gives me a chance to curl twice a day from now until the Olympic trials. I must admit, when I get too much time on my hands to think about curling it's bad. I love my job and it's a wonderful distraction for me."

Hurrying along, I think of Jones's life in comparison to champions of other sports. How many would work full time while pursuing their Olympic dream? And in addition to her television career, Colleen has familial responsibilities. She cooks meals for her husband and two active boys. She is a force in the fundraising effort for the local minor hockey league.

By 11:10 a.m. we have pulled into the parking lot of the Mayflower Curling Club. The sign above the glass doorway proclaims that this facility was established in 1905. Within its walls, the Mayflower houses six sheets of ice under a wooden ceiling, a living room with velour swivel rockers, an elaborate and ancient chalkboard that bears the schedule for days to come, and, in cowboy-style letters, a large banner that reads "Welcome Curlers."

The women's league is on the ice, but one sheet remains empty. Without much dilly-dallying or small talk, Jones makes her way to her practice area. There are no autograph seekers to herald the arrival of the champ. Strange, I note, considering she is the best in the world.

"It was always something I just did anonymously," Jones says of her competitive career. "Some people knew I curled but even though I had won a Canadian championship, it just didn't have the profile of what it is now. TSN wasn't around then. I remember Ernie Afaganis interviewing me back when I won in '82 in his orange jacket. That was a really big deal. Otherwise there was no television."

With absolutely no fuss, a world champion walks on to the ice in a fluffy pink sweater, a scarf draped around her neck, and starts throwing rocks to the other end.

"I sure am struggling these days," Jones laments. "The more you throw, the more you get in the groove." She begins to work on her game like a chess master might battle against himself. She sends a series of free shots to the target and then attacks her own rocks with bump backs, chips, and takeouts. In all Jones will deliver sixteen stones to the far end of the ice and another sixteen back. "The pressure on the knee wouldn't let you do much more than that," she explains. Having noticed how low she gets on each shot, I am certain she is right.

"I think I'm coming out of it, Scotty." Colleen's words are more infrequent as she concentrates on improving her form. The rocks seem to crackle by as they skim the surface of the pebbled ice. Gone is the vibrant smile she flashed with such frequency on the airwaves; it's been replaced by a fierce look of resolve. Her glaring eyes seem to pierce the heavy, cold air.

She has a stopwatch dangling from her midsection, which she uses to time each shot's progress to the house. It's the lone evidence of technology during the practice session. The rest comes down to intuition and personal judgement—Colleen Jones's continuous evaluation of where her game is.

"Not bad," she sighs, rising from her final effort, the forty-minute practice over. An observer might offer a more generous assessment. To the uneducated eye, Jones has missed very little—all thirty-two shots were on the mark. But curling is a game where millimetres can make the difference and errors are not expected or accepted at Jones's level.

"I've been having trouble with the out-turn," she says of her bread-and-butter shot. "I've been sliding out and off the broom. When you're in a slump, everything feels hard. I'm sure that's the way it is in all sports but when it gets like this you ask yourself, 'Where did the game go?'"

With a shake of her head and the sudden return of her smile, Colleen gathers what little equipment she has and we are running once again.

On the way to pick up her son Luke and his buddy Jesse for lunch, Jones chatters away. "Today it felt good. I must say, every time I practise, it feels good. It's almost a form of therapy or something." She sounds like she's trying to convince herself. "I should just relax and throw. But I start thinking too much and everything's got to be so automatic, the more you think the harder it is. It's got to be second nature all the time."

Having bounded into the van from Charles Tupper Public School, eight-year-old Luke and his chum shift the focus of our conversation. Curling gives way to more pressing matters.

"Fresh new-smelling pizza," the youngster exclaims, referring to the bright orange cardboard box he can't wait to rip open. "Today's the regular pizza day at the school," Colleen points out. "He doesn't have to have the ham sandwich he has every other day of his life."

We make our way to her house—Colleen, Luke, and Jesse and I. I am struck by how ordinary the whole scene is. "The kids and Scott [Scott Saunders, Jones's husband] do not care that I'm a world champion. They really don't," she says in an offhand way. "It's kind of frustrating sometimes, don't you think?"

I think that it must be. Jones comes from a family of nine—seven sisters and a single brother. She is one of Anne and Malachi Jones's middle daughters. Her father is a retired judge and the family is part of the Halifax establishment. Still, the three-time Canadian champion never thinks of herself as something special. Curling is just a way of life for her and her family.

"My mother saw the rink as a great place to send the kids on a Saturday morning," Colleen says, reflecting on her earliest visits to the Mayflower. "We'd wake up for a seven o'clock game and get there before Mr. McKinnon opened the door. I didn't understand the difference between in turns and out turns. I could never quite figure out how to put the handle on. It just confused me, and it was dumb luck that I actually found the right way."

Jones will claim that she is not the smoothest, not the most gifted, not the best curler in Canada. This is not false modesty on Colleen's part but a comment on her dogged determination and discipline. She will not be outworked. "When I was thirteen, I decided I wanted to be better than my sisters," she remarks. "I would go up to the Mayflower every day after school and practise on my own."

In 1979 Colleen played third for her sister at the first national championship she appeared in. Three years later when a foursome that included three of the Jones sisters won in Regina, Colleen was steering the ship. But in many ways, it was taken for granted that she would get to where she wanted to go if she worked hard enough. She would do what was expected of her.

The kids in the back of the van are laughing and playing a little game only they can decipher as we near our destination. Colleen looks in the rear-view mirror just to check on them. "I remember wanting to take my parents over to the world championships in Switzerland the first time I went," she recalls. "I told them a lot of other parents were going and that they could tour around and look at castles and

On the road and in uniform (Colleen is third from the right)

Early potential and plaid pants to boot (Colleen is far left, her sister Monica far right)

things like that. My mother said, 'No, we'll go the next time you make it.' I said, 'Are you crazy? There may never be a next time!'"

We steer into the driveway, and she shifts the van to park and the kids scramble out the sliding door. "It takes the pressure off that nobody cares," Colleen thinks aloud, as she gathers her stuff. "After a loss, it's nice to arrive home and have them say, 'Well, who cares?' I just figure, 'Oh well!' and go on to the next thing."

It's like stepping into the eye of a storm—the dog is barking, the kids are running, the phone is ringing. Preparing our lunch, Colleen moves back and forth between fridge and sink and every so often darts over to the window to lament the fate of her side yard. It's been paved over to accommodate a multi-season hockey pad (sneakers and tennis balls in the spring, summer, and fall—skates and pucks in the winter) and at present it's brimming with autumn's discarded foliage. "That's the trouble with me curling," Jones laughs. "The leaves from my beautiful rink don't get raked."

The kitchen cupboards have a hockey mural painted across their doors and a cabinet above the oven has stained-glassed windows in a curling motif—the red, white, and blue of the rings are adorned by the yellow of corn brooms. On the radiators, a hockey goalie's blocker and accompanying catching mitt dry. They likely belong to the teenaged son Zach. The icebox is completely hidden behind an extensive collage of family snapshots. Out of nowhere, sandwiches, a Greek salad, and tea appear. Colleen, sitting in front of me at the breakfast bar, motions me to dig in.

"The children were planned around the curling season," Colleen says between mouthfuls. "Luke was late. He was supposed to be born in the middle of October and back then, eight years ago, you didn't get ice until the middle of that month so I figured it would be no problem. He was three weeks late so I ended up curling in a bonspiel two days before giving birth. I curled two days after too. The little old ladies at the curling club told me that my uterus was gonna fall out. I didn't think that was true. But then I started to wonder if they were right. What if my uterus did fall out? In hindsight I would never do it again but I didn't think anything of it then. I had a season to get ready for."

Our lunch is interrupted by a number of short tours Colleen takes me on: one to the family washroom on the

upper floor to admire its *Hockey Night in Canada* theme—
a floor tiled like a sheet of ice complete with face-off circles,
players on shower curtains, pictures of wingers in full flight.

"Everything in this house works around the hockey and
curling seasons," Colleen says. "I said to my son Zach when
he was about ten years old that I thought I would quit curling. To him it was like saying that I would quit breathing.
He thought it was just a normal part of life. He thought that
every mum curled and you could go to the rink and watch
your mum play and you could hang around and she got you
french fries while she practised and off you go again."

Jones has built curling into her life as something that
benefits her personally as well as those around her. That she
competes at the highest levels of her sport does not dominate the lives of children, but rather enhances her ability to
be their mother. "If I know that their confidence is off or if
they are bothered about something, I am able to give good
advice," she reckons, "to tell them that they shouldn't beat
themselves up or that we are not great all the time. I'm able
to tell them those things and they understand that I know
what I'm talking about."

Jones remembers the loss at the 1999 world championships in Saint John as the most difficult of her career.
Having waited what seemed an eternity to prove herself on
the international stage, the Canadian champion failed to
deliver a performance that could erase the disappointment
of her appearance in Geneva seventeen years before.

"It was devastating to go there and lose. I hit rock bottom
feeling like I'd let another one slip by," she reflects. "But I
had to put on a brave face for my children. To tell them that
I would play again, that I would get to try again. Then they

see that you are playing because you love the game. That's what I hope they get out of all my losses."

Colleen went a long way toward dispelling doubts, her own and those of others, when she returned to the world stage in 2001 in Lausanne, Switzerland. Twenty years after getting to her first world championship, Jones had the final rock against Annette Norberg of Sweden in the tenth end. She also held a 4–2 lead. The Swedes had two red rocks in the eight-foot ring far enough apart that a double takeout was impossible. Jones was forced into a clear hit. A miss would open the door to yet another defeat. "So it will be an out-turn takeout attempt," Don Wittman announced to the national audience in Canada. The skip would go with her favourite shot to get a substantial piece of the rock and remove it from play. Finesse was not required. Precision and steadiness were.

In the sparsely filled stands at the arena in Lausanne, Scott Saunders and Colleen's two boys avoided the camera's eye. "How sweet will this be for Colleen Jones?" Joan McCusker asked from the broadcast booth as the last rock was thrown.

"Right on target and Colleen Jones is third time lucky. It will go into the books as a 5–2 Canadian victory." Wittman's call was understated and, with the exception of Nancy Delahunt's "Oh my God—yes!" clearly audible through the microphone she wore, so was the ensuing celebration. Jones shed a few tears, embraced her teammates, and then went to coax her hesitant husband and children out of the stands. As a world champion the Canadian skip finally, quietly, got her due.

"These guys came to see me win at the worlds in Lausanne, a beautiful place," Jones says of her kids' reaction that day. "They were sort of ambivalent about it because I really believe they think that every mum does this in her spare time. The good thing for them is to see their mother competing. I hope I'm sending the message that you don't have to stop playing whatever it is—gentlemen's hockey or running. Just because you turn into a grown-up doesn't mean you have to stop playing."

It's almost time for Luke and Jesse to return to school. Somehow, during our discussion, Colleen has managed to clean the dishes, clear the table, and corral Bruno into the basement for the afternoon. Following the drop-off at Sir Charles Tupper, Colleen's got another practice session. This time, her teammates—Nancy Delahunt, Mary-Anne Waye, and Kim Kelly—will be waiting for her at the Mayflower.

The side will meet to practise, having returned empty-handed from a Vancouver Skins Game this past weekend. The designed-for-television event saw Sherry Middaugh, one of the great curlers from Ontario, take home $72,000.

"That was all that was on the line, money." She shakes her head, emerging for the last time from her basement and hushing Bruno's whimpering yelps. "I'm not so used to playing for money. Once I started thinking I could get the basement finished if I won, I was focused on the end result as opposed to playing. Stop thinking about what's on the line and you'll be fine."

"Luke! Hello! Time to go to school!" The boys groan and it takes a while before the television finally gets switched off.

"If not money, then what?" I ask.

"What you play for is not a million-dollar contract," she begins. "Far from it. It's a totally intangible thing that is nothing you can actually hold onto. It's just something you know in your heart you've got. You're playing for the camaraderie and the friendships and the love of the game more than anything else. And the mental escape of it. The rhythm of throwing rocks is just that. It's something I have done since I was thirteen every single day of the curling season. I have always lived five minutes from the club. I would get there quick. I've always done it. I don't know what I would do without it now . . . it's just a natural part of what I do."

It's a couple of minutes past the bottom of the clock. They convene for practice every day at 1:30 p.m. Already hard at it are the three others. Holding the broom at the far end and running the show is Nancy Delahunt. Tall and with a shock of curly hair held back by an old-fashioned head band, Delahunt is a full-time homemaker with two kids under the age of ten. She was a high school rival of Jones but first came on side in 1991 when she was the team's substitute player at the Scott Tournament of Hearts. Since then she's accompanied Colleen to six Canadian championships and has qualified for another still to come.

"Definitely I am a friend for Colleen in and out of curling," Delahunt says, when she has a few moments. "We laugh that she'll be pushing my wheelchair when I'm eighty. We have a great relationship on the ice."

They have known each other for a long time, and it's Delahunt who helps keep the skip in line both literally and figuratively. She not only manages the team's finances and makes all the travel arrangements during the course of the competitive season, she also holds the broom when Colleen throws. Normally this would be the job of the vice-skip but on Jones's rink Kim Kelly gives way to Nancy Delahunt. "We have known each other for our entire curling careers," the lead says of her boss. "She's quite a player."

On the ice Jones is curling head-to-head in a mock competition with Kim Kelly. "We're playing for the championship of the world," Jones calls out.

"And we get to do it until Colleen wins!" Kelly is only half joking in her response.

Practice is essential for this team. Given their family commitments, they do not compete very often on what's known as the Cashspiel Circuit. "The reality of it is those other teams are out there more," Delahunt emphasizes. "They are up there on top of the cash leader boards and that does make them more visible than our team. We do not go to Manitoba and Saskatchewan to play a lot and we're not going to start doing that."

So they practise. "As a group we are not motivated by the cashspiel." Nancy Delahunt shakes her head. "It's more intense to curl for a championship." And for that, she's convinced this squad is eminently qualified. "We're like an old

Mary-Anne Waye (left); Colleen Jones

jalopy. Blow up our tires, patch it up and off we go—fight, fight, fight, grind, grind, grind."

On the ice, Colleen's closing in on Kim Kelly. Those eyes are glaring and the teeth are clenched. Jones doesn't care much for details; she'll freely tell you she's not sure how far it is from the hack to the house. Her competitors are just that, people to beat on the way to the championship. Making friends with them has never been a priority. "Usually I go out and try not to think about who I am playing. Sometimes I can talk myself out of a win instead of trying to win."

Colleen will concede that she changes her demeanour in the heat of the battle, becoming much less jovial. Local folklore has it that she has been challenged to half a dozen fist-fights on the rink. Supposedly she's mellowed over time.

"I think the way her competitiveness manifests itself has changed," Mary-Anne Waye tells me. She's the team's second and has finished her practice early today. Her four-year-old daughter, Lauren, is tugging at her coat wanting to get french fries. Mary-Anne is a massage therapist and works three days a week. Wednesdays and Thursdays she

Nancy Delahunt (left), Kim Kelly

89

brings Lauren to practice and the ladies at the club baby-sit while Mary-Anne hones her game. She curled for Colleen Jones in 1993 and then, after an absence, came back into the fold in 1998.

Mary-Anne Waye is leaving the session early because she has to take care of Lauren. No questions are asked and her teammates do not challenge her to stay longer, even though the Olympic Trials are just a few weeks away. "Obviously our families come first," Waye admits. "If we couldn't curl, then we couldn't curl. If there was something in our family that demanded that we couldn't curl, then that would be the end of it. The Olympics are everything only as far as curling goes."

Kim Kelly defeated Colleen Jones in a game of one-on-one. Her last draw was perfect and came to rest right on the button. For now she's the undisputed champion of the world. She'll have a day to bask in the glory of it all and then tomorrow she and her skip will go head-to-head yet again.

"I've been with Colleen for eleven years, since 1991," Kim brags. "I'm the longest serving. I have the record."

Together she and Jones have won two Canadian titles and a world championship and have reigned supreme in Nova Scotia for years. Kim is a mother of two children—both preteens—and works a dozen days a month as a pharmacist. For now she's a spark plug for Team Jones and the one the others count on to keep spirits high no matter what the situation.

In competitions past I have seen Kim Kelly wear her emotions on her sleeve. In the huddle, she's the voice that urges calm or intensity, depending on the circumstances.

"It's a passion. I've always looked at it that way," Kim

says. "I know the game is changing and there have been strides to put it on the professional level. But ever since I was a little girl I've seen it as a game that I love to play."

"The three girls that I curl with have become a very important part of my life," Kelly adds. "That is the part that I cherish the most. I don't know that every woman with a family gets to go and hang out with her friends—leave her kids with the husband. We eat, we sleep, we curl, and we do the things we love to do.

"The most interesting and fun thing I've learned is how to win," Kelly says of her ten-plus years with Jones. "She's a person who knows how to compete and I believe that you can learn that."

It's nearly three in the afternoon and there are kids to be picked up, jobs to get back to, domestic duties beyond escape. The last off the ice is Colleen. There's a long way to go yet in this day of hers. Luke will be collected from school and she'll go home to make an early supper. She's volunteered to sew the name tabs into the hockey jerseys of all the players on Luke's team. Laundry is piling up, and the house needs tidying. Zach has to be ready to leave tonight for a hockey tournament in Moncton, New Brunswick. After all that she'll go to the gym to work with a personal trainer. Physical fitness has become an obsession that she suspects is lengthening her curling career. Her workout complete, she'll attend a meeting of the minor hockey committee to help plan a charity auction to raise thousands of dollars so the boys can travel to tournaments. Each parent donates five hundred dollars and thirty hours of time. The world champion of curling is no different than the rest. By ten in the evening Colleen hopes to have lights out so she can be up at five tomorrow morning to do it all again. But before moving on, she has time to lovingly reflect on her teammates.

"It's the right chemistry. It's amazing that you can find four people that click," she says. "A lot of my curling career we had people on the team who either weren't compatible or couldn't get along. You're out there too much together to not actually enjoy the people you are with. It's just been lucky that we've found each other and now we just kind of hold on. You know that you're not going to find that again, the magic of four people."

Even at this juncture, Colleen Jones is not considered the most accomplished of curlers in the women's field. Three Canadian titles to her credit, secured in three different decades, Colleen Jones has spanned generations at the top of her game, yet even she will not rest on her laurels. She feels she still needs to do more and prove herself over and over again. At the root of her unrest is a competitive instinct that has at times distanced her from others in the "friendly" curling world.

"I wish I could mellow and I don't," she says, almost apologetically. "There are some things that I'm more managed about in terms of being able to control myself a little better. You know I can go up and have a drink if I lose. I never used to be able to do that. I smile through gritted teeth but I couldn't do that before. I'm a little better at it but not much. I still have sleepless nights over losing games. It drives me crazy if I don't play well," she sighs. "I wish I wasn't like that. I always thought that I wouldn't be like that now. And yet I'm the same as I always was. I have a feeling that if you were born wanting to kill your mother for a win—you can't fight what you are."

She's got her two curling shoes—the one with the duct tape slapped across the toe and the other that doesn't match—tied together and slung over her shoulder. Her broom is in her other hand as she heads out into the gloom of the late afternoon. The Olympic Trials are but a few days away and she has so much to get done.

"The family and the boys are head and shoulders above everything else," Colleen Jones tells me. "Yet curling is such a part of who we are. It's just the same way as others look at breathing and drinking water. We curl. It's part of what we weave into a life."

Four months and untold disappointments later, Colleen Jones was at it again. She was playing a somewhat familiar role—the Maritime outsider curling for the national title in the sport's western heartland. Members of her Halifax rink were clad in the colours of Team Canada at the Keystone Centre in Brandon, Manitoba, but Sherry Anderson of Delisle, Saskatchewan, was the favourite.

Jones's trip to the final had been a difficult one. Struggling from the start, she had to scramble in the late rounds of the tournament. Along the way she had lost twice to Anderson. But she battled to a narrow 8–6 victory over Ontario's Sherry Middaugh in the semifinal, giving her rink a chance for their third Canadian title in four years—a record rarely matched in Canadian curling. Jones herself was vying for a fourth national victory. Success would stand as a landmark in the women's game.

Midway into the match Team Canada led 3–2. "Don't get me talking about any routines now, I'm just trying to have fun here," Jones told interviewer Mark Lee at a crucial point in the play. "There's no place I'd rather be than right here . . . except maybe at home with my kids."

In the sixth end, Jones delivered a knockout punch to Sherry Anderson. The Saskatchewan skip missed with her final stone, leaving three of Team Canada's rocks in the house to count. The score was suddenly 6–2 in favour of the defending champions. "Ten days' work gone in one shot," Anderson could be heard saying. How quickly the tide can turn in a game of inches.

Colleen Jones went about the business of protecting her lead. Her smile was back, but when she threw her rocks she glared. She, Nancy Delahunt, Mary-Anne Waye, and Kim Kelly picked off Saskatchewan's vulnerable rocks one by one and built an 8–5 lead going to the tenth and final end.

The statistics spoke favourably of Colleen Jones. She was curling at a 98 per cent success rate and her team was exceptional in their support of her. The lead, Nancy Delahunt, had curled with 91 per cent effectiveness throughout the gruelling tournament. Still, the Nova Scotia four had not garnered the unqualified respect of those witnessing the historic run. "You hate to see a championship decided on a missed shot," Don Wittman said of the Anderson mistake in the sixth end.

Colleen held the broom for her friend and longest-serving ally, Kim Kelly, as the long-shot champions dispatched the challengers from Saskatchewan. Jones had run Anderson out of rocks and the last takeout was complete.

Scott Saunders ran down the stands to embrace his wife and then Colleen disappeared in the huddle of her team. I couldn't see her but I could make out her voice. "I love you guys," she was telling them.

They gathered at the trophy for the third time as a group and there Jones stood—somebody's mother in the spotlight, waiting to say what it was like to go into the record books. In less than twelve hours she would be behind another microphone and on the air, back at work as if nothing had happened.

"It feels a bit surreal. It's been a wonderful ride for this team. We loved coming to Brandon. The ice was perfect. The important thing was to win this one game. I'm a bit like Gordie Howe. I'm old and I keep going."

"Congratulations, Colleen," the CBC's Mark Lee said. "You are the enduring image of a champion in women's curling."

Not bad for a grinder from the wrong side of the tracks, I thought. It may prove to be an entirely futile ambition—keeping up with Jones, that is.

The distinctive roar of Russ Howard

CHAPTER FOUR

TRIALS AND TRIBULATIONS

I'M AT THE BONSPIEL. ACCORDING TO THE *Canadian Oxford Dictionary*, bonspiel is a noun meaning "a curling tournament . . . 16th century perhaps from Low German." The 1964 edition of *The Concise Oxford Dictionary* defines bonspiel as "a curling match, usually between clubs." It is classified as part of Scottish vocabulary and there is speculation that bonspiel derives from two Dutch words, *bond* (league) and *spel* (game).

Regardless of its mysterious origins, bonspiel has acquired an almost exclusively Canadian connotation and is one of the most frequently used words in the curling lexicon. It is the all-encompassing term that describes any form of competition in this sport. A bonspiel is a tournament, gathering, final, championship, match, celebration. On this day I'm in the stands at the Agridome in Regina, Saskatchewan, to see one of the most important bonspiels of all. These are the Olympic Trials and midweek, early in the afternoon, the fans are crammed in like sardines.

I had flown in that morning. Left the December drizzle and 14-degree temperatures of Toronto for the frozen prairies and the hunt for Olympic glory. There hadn't been much about it in the newspapers back home. *The Star* had a few inches of type on the back page—a soft piece about Heather Fowlie of Calgary being a rather jolly fan favourite. The *Globe and Mail* was more generous. Bob Weeks, their regular curling columnist, wrote about Sherry Anderson of Delisle, Saskatchewan, "skipping along toward the Olympics." It wasn't much, nothing to suggest this was the biggest bonspiel in years.

"I'd rather have needles shoved in my eye than cover this thing," said the veteran Toronto sportswriter sitting next to me on the plane. The Trials for the 1998 Nagano Games had been held in another curling hotbed, Brandon, Manitoba. "At least there I could go to the casino," he grumbled. As a neophyte to the big bonspiel experience, I felt my heart and my expectations sink. "Minus eight for our arrival in Regina," the captain said just before landing. Curling weather, I thought.

The smell of the Agridome is one I remember from the midway at the Canadian National Exhibition—cotton candy mixed with roasted peanuts. There's an old guy draped in a green apron patrolling the stands. He's selling the 50–50 tickets and he's making a killing. This is draw thirteen of the Trials. I'm one of 6,700 at the bonspiel. The place is jumping and I'm getting a rush. The men will soon take to the ice over what will be five sheets of play. In all there are ten teams made up of the world's very best curlers.

The Grade Sixes and Sevens of Connaught Elementary School sing the national anthem. Their rendition is beautiful, and they look crisp and clean in starched white shirts and black slacks. They're all wearing Santa Claus hats, and after receiving the polite applause of the anxious crowd they rush to the section reserved for them. Enter the bagpipers in their traditional kilts and big headdresses. The music is louder and somehow more melodious than I thought it would be. Everyone around me is sitting up a little straighter now and all at once they slide to the edge of their flimsy grandstand seats and begin clapping in unison. The curlers all wave to the fans. Some throw souvenir rubber balls into the stands. Everybody's smiling.

The big event, the one the television cameras will focus on, is the match between Kevin Martin of Alberta and Russ Howard, who now curls out of Moncton, New Brunswick. It's a clash of titans. Martin, the younger man, is recognized

The biggest bonspiel: Inside the Agridome 2001

as one of the most skilled curlers in the game's history. A two-time Canadian champion, he's regarded as a sort of professional curler and has been instrumental in forming a breakaway league that competes for big money. Howard is originally from Penetanguishene, Ontario, and has also captured two Brier titles, the most recent in 1993. I've been told he's very vocal when he takes to the ice, and legend has it that he once yelled so much during a bonspiel that he became hoarse. At the subsequent Canadian championships, Howard attempted to outfit his sweepers with earphones while wearing a wireless microphone himself, hoping he could thus call the sweeping instructions in the whisper that was left to him. In an arena full of television equipment, the plan wouldn't fly and on that one occasion Howard's roar became a squeak.

The curlers all shake hands. Then without warning—no horn, whistle, or buzzer of any kind—they're away. Like five jets on the runways at Pearson International, the lead curlers and their rocks rumble forth. Ready to analyze every shot, the crowd settles back under the red cardboard maple leaves and snowflakes that dangle from the steel rafters of the arena's ceiling. The draw has begun.

"Right from day one they've been making all their shots," a voice behind me says of Martin and Howard. I turn to see a teenager under a John Deere hat guzzling Coca-Cola from a huge cardboard container. "It's like they'd been here all week," the kid proclaims before scurrying away to his seat.

"*Only if it bites.*" A booming voice calls me back to the action on the ice. It's Russ Howard, nearly plastered to the surface, well past the hog line.

"*Haaaaaaaaarrrrd.*" One word from Russ Howard's

mouth and it's heard throughout the old arena. The crowd cheers as if it's the sound they've all been waiting for. Howard makes the shot, only just, but he smiles and raises his broom to the faithful nonetheless.

The very next rock belongs to Kevin Martin. The skip, who is about the same size as a good power forward in hockey, doesn't take much time. He brushes the bottom of his rock and then lets fly. The stone hurtles to the other end at an amazing speed. There is no sweeping required and in mere seconds it erases Howard's finely crafted effort from the field of play. Once again the crowd roars its approval and Martin nods his head.

"Kevin Martin's a favourite here." Edmund Genoway states the obvious. "He let her rip here yesterday. Musta cleared four rocks outta the house. The sweepers were running after it!"

Genoway's thirty-one years old and drives a truck that delivers medical oxygen to most of the hospitals in Saskatchewan. He is taking time off to watch the curling because a bonspiel of this magnitude doesn't come to town all that often. "I told my partner that I'd work mornings. He could sleep in and I'd come here in the afternoon." Each day of the competition Edmund will meet up with his older brother Roger to catch all

The boys from Rama: Roger and Edmund Genoway

the action. Roger runs a dairy farm of about a hundred Holstein cattle two and a half hours outside of Regina in Rama. "We used to curl like the dickens there," the older Genoway confirms. "I sure hope Russ Howard wins because if he does he'll give the Americans a dose of real Canadian curling. He and his brother yell pretty good."

Out on the ice, Howard and his brother Glenn, who plays third, are screaming at their stones, trying to coax them into the desired positions. It's working, and after the seventh end they have a 3–1 lead over Martin. It's late in the Trials and the two men are battling for top spot in the standings. The Genoway brothers nod their heads in appreciation of the finely played match that's developing before them.

Roger tells me that the crowd is relatively quiet compared to other big bonspiels he's attended. "This is not like the Brier," he claims. "This is pretty serious business. Usually the provinces are fighting each other. Here people don't know who to cheer for because whoever wins will play for Canada." The elder Genoway claims to have attended almost every big event that Saskatchewan curlers have participated in and only regrets missing his "buddy" Gerald Shymko at the 1999 Brier in Edmonton. Shymko, trying to put an end to nearly two decades of defeat for Saskatchewan's men's teams, lost to Guy Hemmings of Quebec in the semifinal. Perhaps things would have turned out differently if the Genoway brothers had been there. "Too bad we had to go to our uncle's funeral instead," Roger grunts.

"Wow," an older man behind us murmurs as the young John Morris of Ontario makes a great shot to knock off his provincial rival and the heavy favourite Wayne Middaugh. Omar Heggestad sits clutching a book about the Canadian

Omar Heggestad: In the same spot for every draw

Rockies and a neatly folded paper bag, which not so long ago held his lunch. He has thin grey hair and sad, watery eyes. According to the Genoway brothers, Omar has attended every draw of the Trials and been in the same seat all week long.

"I love coming down here because it helps me cope," Omar says. "My wife Donna died a couple of months ago. She was in hospital. I come down here and stay with her cousin so I can watch the curling."

Omar is sixty-seven years old. He's from Frontier, Saskatchewan, about four hours outside of Regina, where he used to operate a general store that's been in his family for nearly a century. There are 395 people in Frontier and curling was an essential part of Heggestad's childhood there. "In those days you had to have your own rocks," Omar recalls. "I bought some that were like tea kettles. They had a really wide base. We'd cut ice blocks from outside and melt it to make the perfect water for pebbling. Every school kid curled and the teachers made sure you got time off for bonspiels."

"Yeah, we used to go to Phys. Ed. over at the curling rink in Rama," Edmund Genoway pipes up. "But they'd never let you out of school for that now."

"I love the game," Omar says with a gleam. "The first year we curled was in Weyburn. It was a nice rink but the concrete floors made it really noisy. Every rock rumbled so much. The Massey bonspiels were big in those days. The best prize you could win was a garden tractor. Back then it was quite a thing."

He settles back into his chair. The match between Morris and Middaugh complete, he turns his attention to the Martin and Howard showdown. Like the old men who occupy the bleachers at a baseball game or the one-time inhabitants of the nosebleed sections in Maple Leaf Gardens, Omar Heggestad seems perfectly connected to, an essential part of, the game he is watching.

"Here comes the haymaker," Edmund warns. Kevin Martin delivers another takeout to get some action and lie one in the eighth end. After Russ Howard throws up a guard, Martin draws impossibly past it and gets another rock close to the centre of the smallest circle. The game is tied at three with two ends left. "Like splitting hairs." Roger Genoway whistles and rolls his eyes.

Away from the play, young John Morris is surrounded by a group of grey-haired men. Their microphones bear the flashes of radio stations from Saskatoon, Yorkton, Fort Qu'appelle, Estevan, Ottawa, and Kelowna. Soon word will go out across curling country that Morris, the kid, the former world junior champion, is a contender for the chance to represent Canada at the Olympics.

Back on the near sheet, Martin and Howard have the undivided attention of a full house at the Agridome. Theirs is the only match still underway and it's strangely silent in the big barn of an arena. In the ninth end Kevin Martin steals two points and the place begins to buzz.

"What a game!" Martin engages Edmund and Roger Genoway in conversation. Remarkable. Arguably the game's biggest name, on the verge of a huge victory, is chatting with a couple of guys from Rama, Saskatchewan, who have scurried down to the boards while Martin takes a break.

"Tight?" Roger asks with a knowing grin.

"Way too tight!" gasps the skip from Edmonton before waving and pushing off to the final end.

In an atmosphere so intimate, the devoted followers mingle with the acknowledged stars as an accepted and welcomed part of the game. I look up at Omar Heggestad clutching that book, his eyes fixed on the ice and I know why he comes here to cope with his wife's death. These people might as well be family.

Backstage, Russ Howard is all smiles. He lost 5–3 to Kevin Martin, and his edge at the Olympic Trials is waning. Still, the man with the big voice is delighted with what's transpired. "That was the best game of the week. I'd like to prove myself one more time," the forty-five-year-old New Brunswick skip muses. "It's all about your résumé at the end of the day. What have you done?"

Russ Howard has done a great deal. Originally from the southern shores of Georgian Bay, Howard grew up a curler. Rather than flooding the backyard for outdoor hockey, his father created a homemade curling rink instead. Russ and his younger brother Glenn spent hours on end perfecting the takeout. Later Russ was able to accommodate his obsession for curling by folding the seasonal game into his career as a professional golfer. It was granite in the winter, green turf in the summer.

"Golf is the only other game that I can use as a comparison," Howard says of curling. "I think that the shot making is the most exciting thing. I made two or three today and even though I lost the game they were really hard shots and I made them. It's like hitting that one-iron six feet from the hole. It doesn't happen very often so it's very exciting."

These are the small but vital pleasures of a consummate competitor. Heading into the Olympic Trials, Howard has been to the Brier ten times as a skip and has twice been the winner. He's represented both New Brunswick and Ontario and has won more games in his career than any other curler who has appeared at the Canadian championships. He has captured two world championships, the first in 1987 in Vancouver and the second in 1993 in Geneva, Switzerland. Russ Howard has been a force to be reckoned with for close to twenty years and still he craves the unpredictability of the sport he loves.

"There's no possible way the top three teams here this week would be the top three if we held it next week. It's unfortunate in some ways but you don't have a Gretzky who will win every event—it's close!"

Although he has, at times, dominated the leader boards, Howard has never been to the Olympics. He had two previous tries at it—once before the Calgary Games in 1988 and then ten years later before the Nagano Games—but he failed on both attempts "I'd love to go to the Olympics," he acknowledges. "I've been lucky to strap the Maple Leaf on my back twice at the world championships and it was incredibly special to win for Canada." Still, he is not counting on anything, least of all a trip to Salt Lake City.

Though he hails from central Canada and now represents New Brunswick, Howard is quick to admit these Saskatchewan crowds ignite him. "People out here know what they are talking about and that makes it more fun as a competitor," he says. "I've been in other parts of the country where you are trying to blank an end or hit and roll out and you nail it dead on. They clap because you scored one and that wasn't the intent at all. Nothing against the east but the western crowds are very knowledgeable curling fans and that makes it interesting."

Once the young hot shot, Howard is quickly becoming the senior statesman of the men's loop. To find himself at or near the top after all these years is a satisfying personal victory for him. It speaks to the values of the game that wisdom and experience are still prized in the face of charging youth. Russ Howard's ambitions have changed over time but what binds him to the roaring game has not.

"Naw, naw, this will never be professional for me." He rebuffs any suggestion he could make a living as a full-time curler. "I get more motivation out of winning and staying at this level. It's partly because I'm getting older. I think I end up measuring myself all the time because I'm forty-five years old. If I can help my team and contribute to winning and if I can continue to play with these guys then that's what I want to do.

"You need to keep these memories," he says confidently and with a measure of pride. "The unfortunate part of playing this game is that, as a human being, the only shots you remember are the ones you miss. That loss was the best game of my year and I missed a shot in the ninth end. I'll never forget it. I guess with experience you learn to have a beer and get over it."

The link between beer and the big bonspiel is ever present and even at the Olympic Trials the tradition of mixing social time with raging competition works to great effect. My trip to the Roar Inn takes me on a path through the dusty innards of the Agridome. I'm heading to the immense pub on the other side of the concourse to fill the hours between the men's afternoon draw, just complete, and the women's action in the evening. The band is playing loudly as I pass by what appears to be a curling trade show housed in the guts of the building. One fellow sits at a table hovering over his thousands of pins, ready to make a swap. United Van Lines has a booth in case you're planning a move to the prairies, and right next door the Saskatchewan Curling Association is waiting to sign you up. The RCMP Musical Ride is represented as is WestJet and there is a display for the upcoming Scott Tournament of Hearts in Brandon. Everyone is eager to extol curling in the west, and people from across the country are there to listen.

In the Roar Inn at least a thousand fans are drinking beer out of plastic cups at long tables covered with plastic sheets. On huge TV screens coverage of the men's games is being replayed. Some of the afternoon's participants are watching intently as their missed draws and takeouts are scrutinized by wise fans who munch on back bacon sandwiches and fries smothered in gravy. The Newfoundlanders lining up to buy beer tokens have their arms around British Columbians, and there is much laughter in the queue. Over in the back corner, a rock'n'roll band is belting out familiar tunes. People are dancing. It is noisy and festive.

A youngish guy holding two cups of beer comes over and introduces himself as Shannon England. I recognize the name. He's the husband of the late Sandra Schmirler, Saskatchewan's favourite daughter. "Here, take this." England thrusts one of the cool ones into my hand. "Drink it fast though, buddy. You've got to get out there because the women are lining up." I thank England and guzzle the beer, anxious not to miss a moment of play from the would-be heirs to Schmirler's Olympic legacy.

The women are already into the fourteenth draw, each team playing its eighth game of the bonspiel. Some squads have a playoff spot secured. Others including, surprisingly, the world champions, Colleen Jones's rink from Halifax, cling to life and must win their final two matches to stay in contention. Still others are set to play the role of spoilers. The cowbells and air horns greet every good shot and the members of the capacity crowd, fortified no doubt by their trip to the Roar Inn, are in good spirits.

As I survey the crowd, I begin to distinguish what sets these spectators apart from those who might attend a professional sporting event in this country. The people here are not just fans of the game, but ardent, even moral, supporters of the players themselves. The banners draping the facades of the concrete stands identify several small blocks of allegiance. "Attack—Fowlie—Attack" is a reference to the popular Heather Fowlie of Calgary who fared well in the early going but is starting to fade. "Holland Rocks" is written boldly on a white sheet bearing a picture of a giant windmill. The twenty-seven-year-old local hope, Amber Holland, waves to the faithful who hold the sign in her corner. There are countless other public declarations of support in the bleachers. Not a single placard bears a negative message.

Keith Lawes has lived in Toronto, Quebec City, and Newfoundland, and now makes his home in Winnipeg. From over my shoulder he's talking about his daughter Andrea who's playing for the Sherry Middaugh rink from Coldwater, Ontario. With four wins and three losses they can't afford to drop another game. "This fall they've been working very hard," he says of his favourite team. "At this time they're the top money winners on the ladies' tour. They've come in here anticipating a lot of tough competition, which they've met."

Keith's daughter lives and works in Whitby, Ontario, and he doesn't get to see her all that often. Still he is reluctant to get in her way at such a critical time. "I know that she's tense and so I've stayed clear of her on purpose," Lawes stresses. "We wave, we wish them good luck, we're not staying at the same hotel and that makes a difference. We try not to interfere one bit. We don't want to create any more tension. There's enough tension for a parent sitting in the stands."

These days the elder Lawes spends a lot of his time watching curling. Kaitlyn, his thirteen-year-old daughter by a second marriage, is with him to witness her half-sister take a run at an Olympic medal. Kaitlyn's also collecting the signatures of as many competitors as she can. She too aspires to great things in the sport. "The curlers like her delivery. They always comment on that when they sign an autograph," Lawes boasts, as he flashes an action shot of Kaitlyn. "Whenever she has time off school we go curling.

Within five or ten minutes of my house in Winnipeg there are five or six rinks and we can always find a sheet of ice to practise on."

Curling, even at its highest levels, is refreshingly accessible for fans of all ages. Single tickets for this event will set you back a few dollars but most people buy packages that allow them to see dozens of games over the course of the entire bonspiel. The best seats in the house for twenty-two draws or sessions, including the opening and medal ceremonies, cost $360. For that the avid fan is guaranteed not to miss a moment of the best curling to be had anywhere. Three hundred and sixty dollars, probably what you'd pay for one good seat at the Air Canada Centre to see the Toronto Maple Leafs host the Columbus Blue Jackets.

Colleen Jones is sputtering along in her penultimate round-robin game against the Sherry Fraser rink from Richmond, British Columbia. Fraser is ahead 3–2 after six ends and Jones can't find much room to establish her game. And time is evaporating for the world champion.

In one of the end zones, a group of bizarrely costumed men are gathered. They look like circus clowns with noses painted blue, hair dyed the same colour, sporting vests and trousers hemmed with the Nova Scotia tartan. They come armed with yellow sou'westers and wave the flag of their home province—a lion at the centre of the yellow coat of arms embossed over the white field and dominant blue of the St. Andrew's cross. John Murphy, the team's sponsor, is here. The company he represents has come up with some cash so that Team Jones can travel to bonspiels like this. Jonathan Waye is cheering on his wife, Mary-Anne. David Delahunt is doing the same for Nancy. Colleen Jones's

The bluenosers in Colleen's corner

husband, Scott Saunders, prefers the quiet solitude a few rows up from his more demonstrative compatriots. Only Kim Kelly's husband, Mike, is absent. "Can you imagine? He's a liquor representative. How does a liquor representative not get time off in December to come to a curling tournament?" David Delahunt asks incredulously.

The husbands of Team Jones wouldn't miss an event of this magnitude. All of them have travelled across the country and around the world in pursuit of their wives' dreams. Questions of role reversal don't even register with the Nova Scotians. All of them gladly take time off from their careers to support their spouses and each is vocal in defence of their team's chances here in the heart of curling country. The Bluenosers are the most visible supporters of any of the teams. With their colourful garb and antics, they have endeared themselves to the crowd, but there is a slight suggestion that they are viewed as a harmless novelty by the westerners, that the Nova Scotia rink is thought of as the underdog, yet again.

Delahunt is fiercely loyal to the Jones rink. "What she's done for the sport is phenomenal. I think the fact that they are never favourites is human nature. The four of them are a wonderful team and they can keep up with the best of them."

David Delahunt and the faithful from Nova Scotia are having a good day. The Jones rink has responded to their devotion by scoring two in the seventh end to take the lead over Sherry Fraser. I notice, before making my way to the other end of the rink, that Sherry Middaugh has lost her match and falls to a record of 4 and 4. Looks like her rink, the last of the hopefuls from central Canada, will not make it to the playoffs. The guy with the fire-engine red hair walks by me now with a freshly painted blue beak. David Delahunt flashes a knowing grin. The Bluenosers have added a new recruit to their camp.

Don't be fooled—curling is not all fun and games. This is a sport, and even in the carnival atmosphere of the Agridome, you can feel the pressure building. Smiles are less frequent. There is stress written on the faces of the skips who are confronted with key decisions on every shot. Though they seem to spend endless minutes agonizing with their teammates over the challenges at hand, a game clock runs on each sheet ensuring that no match goes over time. Exceed the limit and your team will be penalized.

Ken Bagnell sits directly behind the sheet of ice where the Jones team is facing Sherry Fraser's group. Fraser is hanging tough in the eighth end, down by a single point.

Bagnell is part of a growing group that functions within what is becoming a more specialized sport. He's been hired to act as the Jones team's psychologist, to help Colleen and her foursome keep their focus on the ice. Bagnell is a graduate of the sports psychology program at Michigan State University and spends most of his time at the National Sports Centre's Atlantic Division in Halifax. Given how the Jones team struggled in 1999 in Saint John, Bagnell was brought into the fold for the world championships in Lausanne two years later.

Ken Bagnell had left his seat next to Laine Peters, the team's fifth and alternate player, in the fifth end for his one chance to consult with the squad during the course of the match. They were down by a point and while the British Columbians appeared at ease, the Jones foursome seemed

Talking things through: Kim Kelly, Colleen Jones, Mary-Anne Waye

troubled. However, the world champions emerged from their brief huddle with Bagnell looking refreshed, imbued with an obvious confidence. The match turned following the simple but effective discussion.

"It's a matter of respect," Bagnell confided in me. "They have to respect themselves. The lack of respect from others sometimes rubs off on them and on Colleen in particular. They must understand that they deserve to be here in this field and they deserve to be in the thick of things. They are never the favourites coming into any competition but they are comfortable with that now. It allows them to sneak up on the field."

When a team is on the ice it must be there alone. There are no line changes, no shirking of duty. All stones count in curling and every miss is public—there's no hiding a botched takeout attempt. While the sport requires flawless team play, each player performs his or her task in isolation on twenty occasions during the course of the match. No wonder then that some form of counselling is needed to overcome the ever-present fear of failure in this charged environment.

Looking out at the Jones team as it takes control of the match in the late ends, I wonder how they handle this with all the other things they have

The delivery: Jones right on target

in their lives. The same is true of many players attending these Olympic Trials. For a tiny minority, curling is full-time work at which they can make a living. For the rest it's a chance to step out of everyday life and for a fleeting moment aim for the world stage. When it's over, most will return to relative anonymity, in the truest approximation of amateur athletic status remaining in Canada.

"All these players are so exact in what they do." Bob Weeks sweeps his hand across the arena's deck spread out below him. "And yet there is no perfection in it, no way of knowing what is going to happen. After every shot the entire slate changes again. Every time someone throws a rock there are a whole new set of parameters, a whole new set of possibilities." In a country where there are more than a million registered curlers, where national television audiences for curling events can on occasion rival those of *Hockey Night in Canada*, that there is only one national newspaper columnist for the sport is astounding. Bob Weeks has written about curling for the *Globe and Mail* for the last fifteen years, has authored a history of the Brier, and is the editor of the *Ontario Curling Report*. His is a voice frequently heard by curling's faithful followers.

He grew up in Montreal and Toronto and shares his family's curling heritage. Weeks's father, when he was living abroad, once lost the final game of the German championships, narrowly missing the right to curl for the Silver Broom, as the world title was then known. Too small for hockey, too competitive to sit on the sidelines, Bob Weeks went to the rink with his dad and took to curling immediately. Many times he would find himself alone, in the dark empty arena, throwing rock after rock in pursuit of the perfect draw weight. He knocked around the competitive circuit for a while and played at the Weston Golf Club in Metropolitan Toronto until he decided to mix business and sport and forge a career writing about his obsession.

"Curlers are so different from the athletes I have covered in other sports," he points out. "First of all they don't have agents and there are no contracts so there is a real genuine feeling about who they are. Very generally speaking, we are an open society and we don't have a lot of class distinctions. In curling you may have a plumber playing against a Member of Parliament. I've seen lawyers playing with hydro linemen. That, to me, says a lot about curling and Canada."

Weeks might just as easily be referring to the demographics of those currently on the ice. Colleen Jones is a broadcaster from Halifax competing at the highest level against Sherry Fraser, who works as an administrative assistant in a Richmond, B.C., office building. Jones is eight years older than Fraser and her team is made up of three other mothers, two of whom also have careers. Fraser's squad is, with one exception, made up of single women. There is a building code consultant, an accounting manager at a lumberyard, and a computer software salesperson. Their ages range from twenty-seven to forty-eight. It's quite a mix.

While he admires this diversity, Weeks worries that it has some drawbacks as well. "One of the big problems that curling faces in growing as a sport is the fact that its very best players are still curling at clubs down the street. You don't go down to the local arena and see Mario Lemieux skating around. If you are really going to develop the sport you have to have a separation of the club curler and the top curler. It goes hand in hand. You don't yet have these idols that kids look up to because you don't have a bona fide structure of professional players."

Although there is conviction evident in his words, I can tell that Bob Weeks is somewhat ambivalent about the major turn that curling seems poised to take. He obviously loves the intimacy of the old ways and yet is resigned to the changes that will push the game to become less colloquial, and maybe even more accessible than it already is.

"There is still the mystery of how you start playing if you're an older person," Weeks continues. "Curling is seen as almost hereditary, you curl because your parents curl. The Olympics will change that outside of Canada, especially in the United States, and you are already seeing it in Denmark. There are a lot of European countries where they are starting to build facilities and where there is now money available to start programs. In Australia as well as Korea we're opening new doors. That is where the Olympics will have a really big impact. It could have a bigger impact in Canada if we wanted it to."

Colleen Jones has beaten Sherry Fraser. She now has one game left to breathe life into her Olympic dream. Tomorrow she will face the youngest and most inexperienced skip in the field, twenty-two-year-old Marie-France Larouche, of Quebec. To date, Larouche has been misfiring and has won only one of the eight games she has played. Still, few doubt her ability to pull off a dramatic victory against Jones. It is a part of the beauty of curling.

"You never know what's going to happen," Bob Weeks grants, as he hurries down the stands to interview Jones.

"It's unlike any other sport. In hockey you've always got the puck on your stick. In football the ball is in the air for only a couple of seconds. Here for almost half a minute you've got this rock coming down and for those thirty seconds you can see the possibilities. Once the rock is played, you start thinking about the next set of possibilities that have presented themselves."

Downstairs in the Agridome Colleen Jones greets her inquisitors with relief and patience, joking about her competitive nature. "I've mellowed this much." She demonstrates by holding the index finger and thumb of her right hand a millimetre apart. "I think it's human nature after a bad game to believe that you can't curl anymore, can't do this, can't do that, you beat yourself up. Comparatively speaking I'm a little better at it but I still act like it's the end of the world when I lose."

As I listen in on the scrum of writers and radio broadcasters firing questions at Jones, I can't help but wonder why she's in this position in the first place. As the reigning world champion it seems only fitting that she should automatically be the Canadian representative at the Olympic Games. It doesn't work that way in curling. As Bob Weeks reminded me, nothing is a given in curling. Without exception, when the best are involved, curling is literally a crapshoot. In this wildly unpredictable sport, there is much truth to the often used phrase "On any given day, anyone can beat anyone else."

"Is it going to be any easier waking up tomorrow than it was any other day this week?" the *Globe and Mail* columnist asks Jones.

"I'm trying to enjoy it and not fear playing in another game," she says with a wry smile. "If this is my only kick at the Olympic can then I've got to make it the best kick I've got. I don't think being scared or being fearful is the way that I want to approach it."

As she walks away from the scurrying reporters who will file their stories to eager fans across the prairies and the rest of Canada, she's whistling a little tune and has her broom over her shoulder. She saunters down the old grey hallway of the Agridome to meet the girls in the locker room. They'll go back to the hotel together to relax. The game they absolutely have to win tomorrow will be far from their minds as they gather, four grown women set free from their husbands and their families. "This is their little vacation to come and get all stressed out watching us," Jones snickers, without stopping.

The Roar Inn is hopping. Flags of all the provinces are flying amid the swell of the crowd. Far from stressed out, the Nova Scotia supporters remain resplendent in their regalia—still campaigning with threatening tubes of lipstick in hand. A growing number of people from the dry-land regions of the country are now sporting blue noses. The husbands' efforts have obviously been buoyed by Jones's gutsy victory over the Sherry Fraser rink and recruitment is in full swing.

In a corner, only slightly removed from the jubilant gathering, is a large fellow with glasses, carefully nursing a beer while making sideline observations. Mike Harris is unassuming by design and, for the most part, escapes recognition. He's the man who curled for Canada in Nagano almost four years ago. The overwhelming favourites to win the gold medal, Harris and his rink sailed through the Games and wound up in first place after preliminary play. And then, on the last day of competition, Harris woke up sick with the flu. He got behind early and was trounced 9–3 by Patrick Hürlimann of Switzerland in the final. His silver medal was viewed with disappointment in the Canadian curling world, where expectations are invariably high and failure is met with polite disapproval.

"There isn't a day that goes by that I don't think about it," Harris admits. "I feel it was entirely my fault. As a skip that's part of the deal. I was so sick. I feel this great disappointment in letting my teammates down."

He still curls, competitively when he can, but in addition to his growing family and golf business, Harris has become an astute television analyst for curling. Now he marvels at the longevity of skips like Russ Howard and Colleen Jones, understands the commitment they've made to remain at the top. "I should feel like I miss it more than I do, but I have a real life now. I curl a little bit but I have a wife and family and kids. I see these others who combine all that along with top-level curling and it's very impressive."

Harris will admit that the bug comes back when he attends a bonspiel like this. It's the feeling of being on a team that attracts him. "There is not one shot that gets made in curling that isn't a four-player shot at this level," he states. "Not every curling fan can appreciate it until they've been in the arena. All four players are in constant communication and that separates teams that win from teams that don't."

One day, he says, he'll go back to take another shot at the Olympics. "You get so much more out of the Olympics than you do at a regular curling event," Harris begins. "You get

to become a part of the great Canadian team. That feeling
was so satisfying that I've found it hard to focus since then.
I won't play unless I think I can be competitive. The reason
I tried to compete at the top level was personal," he concludes. "You get to an event like this and you want to know
if you've got what it takes to win. You are always trying to
win respect from your peers. You try to feel like you belong
at this level."

The bonspiel only has a couple of nights left and so the
revelry is turned up a notch. The music is a little louder and
the skips who have been eliminated are enjoying a few cool
ones with their supporters. Everyone I encounter claims the
festivities will be even better at the Brier in Calgary where
all the provinces will be represented. Edmund Genoway, the
truck driver, strolls by to say hello. He says his brother
Roger has driven back to Rama because come morning
there will be chores to do on the farm. Edmund also confirms that Omar Heggestad is planning to be in the same
seat again tomorrow to catch all the action. "Old fella just
sorta belongs there," Edmund sighs. He raises his beer to
salute me and then joins some of his other buddies across
the vast and swarming hall.

A sense of belonging is revealing itself to be at the centre
of curling's heart. The players talk about belonging at the
top—fighting constantly to prove they have a place among
the best. The fans belong to the players, empowered by the
ordinary people they see excelling on the ice. Everyone and
everything seems to fit this scene where crucial competition
and frivolity are huddled under one roof, safe from the
vicious bite of a Saskatchewan winter.

As the night wears on, I've celebrated with people from

Winnipeg, Kamloops, and Kitchener. I may have had one too many because the guy from Cornerbrook was offering. The next thing I know, David Delahunt is painting my nose blue and I am officially welcomed into the Nova Scotia fold. Not one member of the assembled crowd seems to mind. Even some of the fans of Kelley Law's B.C. rink have joined the fun and become "Bluenosers" too.

For now, we all feel like we belong at the bonspiel.

Looming over Salt Lake: Curling centre stage at the Olympics

CHAPTER FIVE

THE SHOW

At the Olympic Center in Salt Lake City, Utah, there's more than a whisper of the Wild West. The city is an arid place surrounded by the peaks of jagged mountains. The streets are wide and even in midwinter they are wind-whipped by a gritty brown dust. The sign on the city's tallest edifice bears the name, in old-style cowboy letters, of the stagecoach company that helped build this settlement, Wells Fargo. On a huge cloth mural, draped over the curve of an office tower's corner, is an enormous picture of a female curler—a blond Amazon releasing a blue-handled rock. It's a not too subtle reminder that a Canadian game will take centre stage when the global showcase of winter sport begins in just a few days.

Curling has drawn significant television audiences in Canada for decades and has been a fixture at the Canadian Broadcasting Corporation since the sixties. In recent years specialty channels have capitalized on the game's popularity among viewers across the country, and especially in the west. Every year the Scott Tournament of Hearts, the Brier, the Canadian junior championships, and the world championships command stem-to-stern cable coverage. Events from the World Curling Tour and the Grand Slam of Curling are increasingly finding airtime as well as a loyal TV following. Throughout Canada, local cable stations now air their provincial playdowns.

Over time, the broadcasting of curling has become more sophisticated, with coverage approximating, if not equalling, the level of production expertise once reserved for hockey. While *Hockey Night in Canada* may expect an average audience of over a million viewers for its Saturday night telecasts, on select dates during the competitive season curling can rival those numbers. The Canadian women's championship final between Colleen Jones and Kelley Law late in the winter of 2001—a match that went to an extra end—drew more than a million Canadians to their television sets.

Curling reached its televising zenith during the live broadcast of the gold-medal contest between Canada's Sandra Schmirler and Norway's Helena Blach-Lavrsen at the 1998 Olympics in Nagano. At the actual venue, an hour and a half outside of Nagano in the municipality of Karuizawa, the size of the grandstand gathering was average. The faithful, including Wayne Gretzky and other members of the men's hockey team that had already finished out of the medals, were there in full force to catch the game's dramatic end, a 7–5 victory for Schmirler's small-town Saskatchewan rink. Despite time differences that made viewing the live telecast of the match inconvenient, to say the least, Canadians flocked to their TV sets to witness the biggest event in international curling history. Two million three hundred thousand pairs of eyes watched with jubilation as Schmirler's team salvaged what had turned out to be a disappointing Olympics for Canada.

Through three Canadian and world championship titles Sandra Schmirler had developed a devoted audience, but the Olympic victory turned her into a national icon. Television executives had not found the hero of the Nagano Games among the gods of hockey as they had expected. Yet when a mum from Biggar, Saskatchewan went to the podium and won the hearts of a nation, they got something at least as good. Curling had stolen the show and solidified the sport's place near the core of the Canadian consciousness.

The fit between the Olympics and curling, however, has not always been an easy one. Curling was a demonstration sport at the first Winter Games in Chamonix, France, in

Proclaiming her legacy: Biggar's pride is Sandra Schmirler

1924. Only three countries curled in the open-air venue and Great Britain was the class of the field, winning 18-end games over France and Sweden by scores of 46–4 and 38–7 respectively. Eight years later in Lake Placid, only delegations from Canada and the United States participated. The two countries each iced four teams representing various regions of the continent. Manitoba, Ontario, and Quebec were the top three finishers in a competition limited to male participants.

The opportunity for curling to take a shot at full medal status presented itself at 1988 Calgary Games. There, in the game's heartland, eight teams in both the men's and women's divisions curled for medals, though still on a demonstration basis. This time Europe, Scandinavia, Canada, and the United States were represented. And though there was a ticketing foul-up that resulted in less than capacity crowds for most matches, Canada's Linda Moore did win the gold while Albertan Ed Lukowich took the bronze medal on the other side of the draw. It was the Norwegian team that captured the men's championship in Wild Rose country.

Yet while the two other demonstration sports, short-track speed skating and freestyle skiing, attracted Asian nations into the competitive field, curling appeared much more parochial. For a sport to be granted full medal status, twenty-five countries from a minimum of three continents are required to officially participate in the sport on an ongoing basis. Curling came up short, even after the Calgary experience.

In Albertville, France, four years later, with curling still considered a demonstration sport, Canada's Julie Sutton won a bronze medal while Germany claimed gold in the women's division. A bright young star from Edmonton,

Kevin Martin, had a frustrating time, losing the bronze-medal match by a score of 9–2 to Tim Somerville of the United States. Somerville's father, Bud, considered a pioneer of curling in the United States, had won two world championships, in 1965 and 1974. The native of Superior, Wisconsin, having battled back from heart problems that had plagued him throughout his career, curled second for his son in Albertville. In the French Alps, though, it was Urs Dick from neighbouring Switzerland who would win the gold medal in men's curling.

The relegation of curling to the demonstration level at the Albertville Games did not sit well with the sport's international officials, who had done a tremendous amount of work to develop the game in places like New Zealand, Korea, Japan, Mexico, and even the crumbling Soviet Union. Despite their efforts, in the lead-up to the Games there had been a movement within the International Olympic Committee that resisted the inclusion of curling as an equal partner at the elite gathering of amateur athletes. And it was the IOC's program commission that was responsible for filtering the applications of sports to full medal status. Prior to Albertville, that body had passed over curling, claiming that it was not a sport at all but a pastime requiring little or no athletic ability. To make matters worse, some former Canadian athletes sitting on the IOC had questioned the readiness of curling's stable of participating countries, many of which were seen to have formal administrations but very few competitive curlers.

Dick Pound of Montreal, the first vice-president of the International Olympic Committee at the time and the man responsible for the broadcasting revenue the Games generate, had come to the rescue. The son of a former president of the Montreal Thistle Club and a curler himself, Pound forced a further examination of the application by the program commission. A decision on curling would be reserved until the summer after the Olympics in France were complete.

In July 1992 curling was officially granted full medal credentials, though not for the 1994 Games in Lillehammer, Norway, but for the 1998 Games in Nagano, Japan. In retrospect, the failure to have an emerging curling nation like Norway host the biggest bonspiel in the sport's history did deprive the game of much-needed exposure. The Norwegian fans are notoriously boisterous in their partisanship. The enormous crowds attending ski jumping, speed skating, and hockey would surely have translated to a curling venue, most especially because Norway would have boasted medal contenders in both the men's and women's divisions.

Still, the unconditional acceptance of the sport at Nagano was welcome news to everyone involved with curling in Canada. The victory had been close and won largely because the Japanese had promised that a facility suitable for the sport would be ready in time for the Games. Unfortunately, the Kazakoshi Park Arena in Karuizawa was well removed from the Olympic Center, and while it was an idyllic setting, it drew few spectators to the matches themselves. Thus, while Sandra Schmirler's win and Mike Harris's narrow miss delighted the fans of Canadian curling, it was like preaching to the converted. The 1998 Games then only confirmed the perception of curling as a sport understood by a lot of people in the country north of the forty-ninth parallel and by very few others around the world.

The decision of the major broadcaster at the 1998 Games, CBS, to do all that it could to avoid curling, refusing to air anything beyond the occasional highlight to its tens of millions of viewers back in the United States, further isolated the sport. A Canadian production and technical crew provided the pictures and sound from the curling site in Japan but few Americans would see or hear anything of the "roaring game."

"As you know, at Nagano CBS did not do curling," Don Duguid, twice a world champion and the analyst on the Canadian telecasts, recalled. The Winnipeg native who has broadcast twenty-nine Briers and now works for NBC believes that CBS, in overlooking the inspiring story of Sandra Schmirler's victory, missed an opportunity. It was a mistake the broadcaster of the Salt Lake City Olympics would not repeat. "NBC stuck their necks out on curling," the sixty-seven-year-old former skip noted. "It took a guy like Dick Ebersol [the head of NBC's sports programming] to notice the big numbers they get in Canada for curling and to give it a shot."

Don Duguid: Former Brier and world champion, curling's veteran analyst

Curling entered the 2002 Games with a renewed sense of optimism. With a commitment from NBC to give curling airtime and with a more viewer-friendly schedule, curling seemed poised to break through to American audiences. "The best thing possible would be for the Americans to win a medal," Mike Harris had speculated. "They may not say it openly but everyone in Canadian curling agrees that it would give the sport so much exposure."

The Americans do not readily give up the right to produce pictures for the rest of the globe when the Games are on their home soil. It's a matter of economics and of pride, as broadcasting giants CBS, ABC, and NBC have always believed themselves to be the leaders in sports television. Still, when it came to curling, they sought the help of the experts to make sure they got it right.

Freelance producer Pam McNair, who had been part of the production team for curling in Nagano, got the first assignment. Under contract to USA Curling, the association that oversees the sport in America, McNair produced a primer on the game to air prior to the Olympics giving Americans some sense of the sport—what to look for and how to understand it. "Rock Stars—The World of Curling," an hour-long documentary/infomercial, was televised on Outdoor Life Network and MSNBC. Appearing in the low-budget production (it cost $75,000 to complete) were recognizable Canadian actors Paul Gross and Leslie Neilsen as well as the reigning women's world champion, Colleen Jones. McNair drafted American Olympians from other sports who had never curled before and some of the 100 or so registered curlers in the state of Utah to her cause.

"The purpose was to increase the interest in curling for the Americans so when the Olympics came they'd have a little better understanding of what it is and they'd be sparked to go out and actually see it and then follow it on TV," McNair explains.

The campy opening sequence, accompanied by the theme music from the hit movie *Jaws*, features a point-of-view camera mounted on a curling rock as it pursues a horrified-looking Neilsen down the ice. What follows is a light-hearted fool's guide to the basics of curling. "I didn't want to get too much into the whole competitive part of it," McNair says of her limited intentions. "I tried to stay away from a Canadian or American angle. I wanted to show that it was more of an international sport."

Paul Gross, the onetime co-star of the popular sitcom *Due South*, and Leslie Neilsen, best know for his starring role in the Naked Gun comedies, were featured heavily in McNair's production. (The two actors would also star in the 2002 feature film *Men with Brooms*.) Neither had any curling experience, though both were reared in Canadian hotbeds of the sport. During the shooting of "Rock Stars," Neilsen and Gross insisted that they be shown throwing their own rocks. While their style was not perfect, it was at least a style and served McNair's purposes well.

"I asked myself how we could show that curling is fun but also difficult. I wanted to show that there is sportsmanship involved. If you show curling being played by non-curlers as well as those in the game then you can show a comparison between the two. It shows good, healthy looking people having fun out there. They look hilarious but they're having fun. So the message is twofold. It's okay to be goofy and it's a hard sport to be good at."

While filming the primer in Utah, McNair discovered a willing but almost entirely ignorant potential audience for

Olympic curling. "I didn't make a lot of money on this project considering the amount of time I put into it. I love curling. I think it's a sport that needs some oomph," she admits. "The people in Ogden were so nice. They only have something like a hundred curlers in the area. Our production crew from home was laughing because they all seemed so much like Canadians."

To call the play-by-play for major curling matches is to be in an exalted position within the Canadian television industry. The numbers don't lie. When millions of people watch the Brier final or the Scott Tournament of Hearts, an on-air personality's exposure to the public is immense. In the early days of the sport's broadcasting history, Don Chevrier was the face and voice of curling. Chevrier, I can recall clearly, had a booming but soothing voice. Whether it was Alberta's Hec Gervais or Ron Northcott holding the advantage, or Jim Ursel of Quebec, or Jack MacDuff of Newfoundland, Chevrier called the play with an understated, impartial passion. His even-handed approach no doubt paved the way for Chevrier to become a steady broadcaster of baseball and eventually a fixture on the major American networks covering boxing events throughout the United States and the world.

These days TSN's Vic Rauter is the man who calls the most curling in Canada. "I'd say several hundred, maybe even as many as a thousand games," Rauter responded when I asked him how many matches had come under his watchful eye. "It's seventeen years' worth, that's all I know."

Though he did not play the game prior to broadcasting it, he has formed an easy and enduring affection for it, an attachment no doubt deepened by the fact that he met his wife while hosting a dinner at a curling club. Over an impressive broadcasting career, Rauter has provided commentary on every major professional sport, but curling has become a passion that rises above the status of just another game to call. "Absolutely I have become a fan," he acknowledges. "[Watching] hockey you usually have to concentrate for two and a half to three hours because you don't want to miss anything. Curling you can sort of go away and wander back," he goes on to explain. "It keeps you company. Much like baseball once did on radio. Curling is like that. It keeps you company."

The game, he says, is simple and straightforward, unencumbered by a subjective element that makes winning and losing difficult to determine. "That's what the Olympics liked about this sport. When they thought of its acceptance, they liked that it had a conclusion to it," Rauter states with certainty. "There is no judging involved. You start. You have a finish."

Ironically, the same cannot be said for the set of circumstances under which Vic Rauter broadcasts the game he has come to love. Although he bears the bulk of the workload during the course of all major bonspiels and has done so for close to two decades, when the final game is played TSN, his cable employer, steps aside so that the CBC can air the championship matches nationally. "Selfishly, sure, I wish I could call the big game," the familiar voice of curling admits. "But I learned something very early. If you are on cable, you are not going to do it. It comes back to what is Canadian. Cable only has so much reach. You have to give every Canadian the possibility of seeing it. If you are on some rural farm, even in rural Ontario, the only chance to see it is over the air and that means the CBC."

Commendably and without complaint, Vic Rauter reported on freestyle skiing in Salt Lake City, while Don Wittman, the dean of curling commentators, took his place at the microphone. Wittman, a Manitoba resident, has covered the Brier as both a host and, following Don Chevrier, the play-by-play man, thirty-one times. He is a member of the Canadian Curling Hall of Fame and is revered for his no-nonsense approach to the sport. Also a member of the Canadian Football League Hall of Fame, Wittman is authoritative yet sparing in his commentary and allows the analysts—the experts—to shine. "It's a sport where anything is possible for one game," Wittman remarks. "It makes us a great television event. I have a lot of friends who have never curled but they enjoy watching it. They walk by the television set and they see five rocks in play and they just have to watch."

Wittman credits a simple innovation in the coverage of curling with sparking interest in the sport outside of its hardcore fans. Along with a producer named Hugh Carruthers, Wittman came up with the idea that curlers could wear wireless microphones during the course of all critical matches. Prior to the 1983 Brier final in Sudbury, Ontario, Wittman and Carruthers convinced Ed Lukowich of Alberta and Ed Werenich of Ontario to clip on the microphones to spectacular effect.

"It was when Werenich was getting set to throw his final stone," Wittman remembers back twenty years. "He said to Neil Harrison and John Kawaja, [Werenich's men with brooms], 'I'm just gonna throw this and you guys sweep the piss out of it.' He dragged it right into the four-foot and Lukowich had no shot. They cut to Lukowich and he was standing in the house and trying to figure out what he could play and he says, 'Guys, looks like Ontario just won the Brier.' I remember the *Globe and Mail* had an article on the Monday, which said that the CBC had overstepped its bounds with these wireless mikes because the guys are swearing and so forth. But I believe wireless mikes have made the game. I had a hand in that and I'm proud of it. We have those microphones all the time now." Wittman rightly celebrates the Canadian innovation that will make the coverage of Olympic curling uniquely compelling. Even for the uninitiated, it will be like eavesdropping on a private strategy session, the microphones allowing spectators to place themselves onto the field of play.

On the cell phone I can barely hear Geoff Johnson over the shrill of screeching bagpipes in the background. "I'm sitting at ice level just watching them figure out what they're going to do for the opening ceremony today," says the executive producer of television's curling coverage for the Olympics in Salt Lake City. "This sport is so based in tradition. When you figure that in Nagano four years ago they still piped the curlers onto the ice, you realize how steeped in its origins it is."

Johnson and his crew of sixty technical and production personnel will send around the globe pictures and sound from four sheets of ice and over twelve days of competition. The vast majority of the group travelled to Utah from Canada—most of them from west of Ontario and veterans of broadcasting the sport. "We said that we would train enough Americans here so they could do curling on their own when we left," Johnson says with pride.

Johnson was born in Regina and lived in Toronto and Ottawa before settling in Winnipeg fifteen years ago. During his tenure with the CBC, he has become one of the premier directors of curling coverage and feels remarkably privileged to call the shots for the vast Olympic audience. Only one other group of sports—the Nordic skiing events—has someone other than an American in charge at these games. As Canadians do with curling, Finns have a long and distinguished broadcasting tradition in cross-country skiing, ski jumping, and the biathlon, so their expertise takes over.

Billed as a state-of-the-art training centre, the Ice Sheet in the small urban centre of Ogden will house the 2002 curling showcase. At the Ice Sheet all the athletes will wear microphones while competing. Action from all four sheets will be

The showcase venue: The ice house in Ogden, Utah

covered at all times. Eight overhead robotic cameras will be employed to make curling one of the most television-friendly sports at the games. Every angle will be seen, every strategy heard by every viewer and in several languages. Four mobile trucks, two Canadian and two American, will fall under Johnson's aegis. The American hosts have become willing students of the masters from north of the border. "They were very happy in the beginning because they understood that we knew the sport and they felt they could trust us for advice," Johnson says. "This is the curling crew. This is the crew that does every event in Canada."

This is Johnson's first crack at running the show. In Nagano four years ago, he and Richard Wells of TSN had been truck directors under the leadership of the late Joan Mead. Mead, born an American, came to Canada as a young woman and began her television career in Newfoundland en route to becoming a pioneering sports producer at the CBC. Mead died in January 2000 at the age of fifty-seven. "She's the reason that curling has become this popular." Johnson is unequivocal in his estimation of Mead's contribution, which spanned two decades. "Joan is the one who developed so much of the shooting style of the sport. She loved it and its competitors. I have never seen a producer who has worked for that length of time on one sport every year be able to look at it with fresh eyes."

Mead understood that overhead camera angles at both ends of the ice would allow the audience to decipher the ever-increasing complexities of the field of play. She fought for more resources, and curling became one of the best equipped sports productions in Canada. Her commitment was rewarded by large and devoted viewerships for both men's and women's events of the highest level. "She would never just go to the pattern," Johnson says, reflecting on Mead's style. "She would never say we're going to do it just like we've always done it. To her, the game would drive a change in the coverage of the sport. Her passion was such that if you put one shot on the air that she didn't like she would be all over it. She had tremendously high standards."

One person who never failed to reach the mark set by Joan Mead is cameraman Len Dubyts of Winnipeg, and he's here as part of the production team at Salt Lake City. Over the course of thirty-one years, Len has worked for several television networks, broadcasting all the major curling competitions in Canada and around the world. Like Johnson, Len is a disciple of Mead's. As she revolutionized curling coverage, Mead relied heavily upon Len's expertise and loyalty. Len Dubyts does know the game inside and out. There's no room for error in his line of work, no second chances when each shot is televised live.

"I try to shoot it so that the viewers can decide for themselves what kind of shot the curler will make next. When the curler knows what shot he or she will deliver, I listen to the microphones they are wearing. That helps me out a lot. I can hear the strategy. Is it going to be a takeout? Is it going to be a hit and roll? I will know and tailor my shot to show what is coming into the house. For instance, I may be a little wider for a takeout to show the action in the house.

"The finesse shots," he says, almost lovingly, "you watch them do a hit and roll behind cover. You look at the angle. You say to yourself they've got to be pretty darn good to make a rock curl 150 feet and make it do that at the very end of its course. It's just so nice to watch and you know it's not a fluke but a planned shot."

Geoff Johnson says he and his production group will fashion the equivalent of four baseball games per day until the gold-medal winners are declared. The process will be exhausting and the margin for error nil. Millions will be watching curling this time, and their numbers will go far beyond the faithful back home. Canadians will be the favourites on the ice but the reputations of standard-bearers like Len Dubyts and Geoff Johnson will be on the line behind the scenes as well.

"It's a long haul," Johnson estimates. "There aren't many indoor events at the Winter Olympics. This one ends up getting a lot of coverage whenever the outdoor venues have weather problems and cancellations." That said, Johnson knows he's got a lot to live up to in every respect. "We all know that this event would have been the last before Joan's retirement. She will be the extra producer on our shoulders and we are cognizant that we cannot let our standards drop. We are going to do Joan Mead's farewell show. We'll do Joan's style. We'll do Joan's shoot. This will be Joan's show."

The International Broadcast Center in the core of Salt Lake City is teeming with people from exotic and far-flung locales. Many languages exist at the confluence of the Olympic Games and the common bond is sport. Ski jackets present a rainbow of colour as reporters, hosts, technicians, sponsors, and dignitaries swarm the place that delivers the action to homes around the globe. There is constant noise, and the rush to meet deadlines is unremitting. On mammoth video screens throughout the acres of the renovated convention centre known as The Salt Palace, huge crowds are seen thrilling to the rush of the alpine skiers at nearby Park City. From the panorama of Soldier Hollow, the cross-country skiers are exhorted by the vocal Scandinavians as they engage in a gruelling marathon. The short-track speed skaters whiz around the Delta Center, the downtown arena, as the excitement of onlookers builds to a ferocious crescendo. Just up the highway, legions of partisans are packed in, standing room only, to wonder at the skill of the best professional hockey players on the face of the earth.

The smaller television monitors positioned at regular intervals along the endless hallway that all the broadcasters must travel are almost like oases. These screens reflect something calm amid the frenzy. In reserved tones, the commentators draw unwitting spectators into curling. People from Korea and Slovenia pause on their way by the security gate to catch a glimpse of this foreign game. Curling is different, even a bit mysterious for most. It is intimate and complex when compared to all the racing and jumping going on at the other venues.

The Ice Sheet is the smallest indoor arena in operation at the Games with a capacity of only 2,000. Ogden is, conservatively speaking, an hour's drive from downtown Salt Lake. With the traffic, travel time has only increased since the Games got underway. Still the television screens show crowds huddled at the curling sheets, crowds that deserve recognition not only for the fever pitch they can achieve but for the deathly silence that often descends on them. At most points in a match, the only voices heard are those of the athletes. Confidence, resolve, self-doubt, and indecision are all plain to see. The players mutter, dictate, and plead in a host of mother tongues. Even in the absence of translation, the will of the participants is obvious and readily understood.

I suspect those of us who linger at the screens in the International Broadcast Center, watching draws expertly delivered and the execution of booming takeouts, do so, in part, because we recognize ourselves on the ice. As a group the curlers are, on average, the oldest of the athletes at the Olympics. Some are carrying too much weight, others wheeze whenever they push the broom, more than a few are peering from behind eyeglasses. In short, the curlers look a lot like us.

Perhaps too there is a fascination with curling as a game of strategy. In the midst of all the pumped-up warriors on display, the masters of guile and execution have carved out a spot for themselves. The Olympic credo has always been "Faster—Higher—Stronger." But with the rise of curling here, "Smarter" might well find inclusion in the vocabulary of the Games.

The voices we listen to at the International Broadcast Center are those of veteran broadcasters Don Duguid and Don Chevrier, and the network is MSNBC, an American cable giant. The commentary is expert and sparing, precise but unencumbered by too much technical talk. "They asked me to do it because they felt I had a lot of spirit for the game," Don Duguid says, relating the way NBC approached him to become the Olympic voice of curling.

Duguid started competing at the age of eight playing at the Winnipeg Granite Club, in one of the fiercest curling environments in Canada. A diminutive man, he developed an uncanny ability to read varying and often unpredictable ice conditions and came to possess a subtle knack for always throwing the right weight at exactly the right time. Duguid was almost peerless from the mid-sixties to the early seventies, an era that saw him win three Canadian championships (two as a skip, one as a third). In addition, he led his Manitoba rink to consecutive world championships in 1970 and 1971. Following his retreat from the hotly contested ice wars, Duguid remained active in the sport recreationally and as a coach; he also signed on with the CBC to become the most recognized curling analyst in the country for almost three decades.

Duguid had teamed with Colleen Jones to broadcast curling as a demonstration sport at the 1992 Albertville Games. Six years later in Nagano he was back with his familiar partner, Don Wittman, to tell the story of Sandra Schmirler. In Salt Lake City, the challenges for Don Duguid, arguably the most listened to curling analyst of all time, would be very different and perhaps much tougher. His audience is in the United States and he would have to make sense of something regarded as almost exclusively Canadian.

"Everyone in Canada knows and understands curling," Duguid claims. "I just set the table for them. The viewers sit back and because they've been curlers or associated with curlers for a lot of their lives they understand exactly the difficulty the shot presents." As Duguid sees it, curling is almost second nature in Canada. "Somebody's curled somewhere along the line and somebody in their family has been associated with curling for a lot of years," he says of Canadian curling fans. "They kind of grew up with the game.

Curling's elite broadcasters: Don Wittman, Colleen Jones,
Don Duguid

"You've got eight people at your house and you're having a few drinks," Duguid continues. "You start arguing and joking around and the next thing you know you're down at the curling club. You can't say to someone, 'Listen, why don't we go rent a luge?'

"Broadcasting to Americans . . . it's curling 101," he chuckles. When Duguid's play-by-play partner, Don Chevrier, came down with laryngitis in the middle of the Games and was lost for three days, NBC executives asked Duguid to handle the commentary solo for one session while they sought out an emergency replacement. He struggled along until the network delivered Bob Poppa, the voice of the New York Giants pro football team. "He knew nothing," Duguid recalls with glee. "He had never seen a curling rock and he said I was going to have to lead him by the nose. I told him not to worry about it."

The two commentators developed an endearing rapport as the naïve Poppa asked the sage a series of obvious questions on live-action television. "He was like the average viewer in the United States," Duguid figures. "He knew nothing about the length of the ice sheet, the pebble, the rock or anything else. He just asked me questions and it worked out absolutely fantastically. We got more phone calls from people saying it was the best show they had watched in a long time." Good thing too, as MSNBC was relying on curling to provide anchor content for its round-the-clock coverage of the Olympics.

Duguid and Chevrier, who recovered to call the medal games, were at the Ice Sheet in Ogden from seven in the morning to eleven in the evening. They're not exactly sure how many hours they were on the air, but in Duguid's estimation "it was substantial." As one of curling's disciples, he takes considerable pleasure in the fact that audiences for MSNBC were dramatically increased whenever his sport got to the airwaves. "Dick Ebersol stuck his neck out, he went with a gut feeling and it paid off," Duguid says with pride. "Ebersol said it was a new venture for everyone, and he told us that the only thing that can ruin a perfect sport is bad commentary. No pressure at all!"

From the outset of the Salt Lake City Games, there was huge competitive pressure placed on the shoulders of Canadian curlers. Kelley Law, a thirty-six-year-old full-time mother from New Westminster, British Columbia, had won the world championship two years earlier in Glasgow, Scotland. Despite their dramatic loss to Colleen Jones's team at the 2001 Scott Tournament of Hearts in Sudbury, Law's foursome had been hyped as the hottest team in Canada and the natural successors to Sandra Schmirler's Olympic title.

In Ogden, Kelley Law cruised through preliminary play, losing just one of nine matches. As the first-place finisher in the round robin, the Canadian skip drew the fourth-ranked squad, Rhona Martin and her teammates from the Greenacres Curling Club in Renfrewshire, Scotland, for the semifinal. It turned out to be an excruciatingly close match with Martin forced into a near-perfect draw on her last rock. She made the shot and thus eliminated the overwhelming favourite. She would go on to win the gold medal in handy fashion—a 9–3 dismissal of Switzerland's Luzia Ebnother. Law had to settle for the bronze medal with a 9–5 victory over Kari Erikson of Bemidjii, Minnesota.

For the United States and Great Britain, the results yielded substantial curling rewards. The American Erikson's respectable fourth-place finish awakened interest in the game in many parts of the host country. In Scotland, the historic cradle of the sport, there was much anticipation preceding Rhona Martin's triumph and an unprecedented wave of celebration in its wake. "BBC told us they had the largest television audience they've ever had for the Winter Olympics that night Rhona Martin played for the gold medal," Don Wittman reveals. "Forty-nine per cent of all television sets in the United Kingdom were tuned in. That's big. That's better than our numbers!"

While Kelley Law fell short of a second consecutive gold medal in women's play, the Canadian men were exceedingly positive about their chances at the top prize. The man leading the charge was Kevin Martin. Martin is always confident, never more so than when he executed a surgically conceived draw to the four-foot ring at the Olympic Trials in Regina, defeating the former world champion Kerry Burtnyk of Winnipeg. Martin, as I recall, flashed a little grin as his sweepers ushered the rock to its final resting place and the ticket to Salt Lake City that came with it. He looked like a man who could beat the world, hands down.

Martin's, however, has not been a story of great international success. He was heralded as the boy wonder upon his arrival as a skip on the Canadian scene. The captor of a national junior crown at the age of nineteen, he finished second at the world championships in Dartmouth, Nova Scotia, later that season. Martin also failed to win internationally following his two Brier victories—finishing second at the 1991 world's and fourth in 1997. Sandwiched in

Maybe the greatest: Olympic silver medallist Kevin Martin

between was a disappointing fourth-place result at the 1992 Olympic demonstration event in Albertville.

As I kept an eye on his progress throughout the Games, I drifted back to Kevin Martin's inspiring battle with Russ Howard at the Trials in Regina. I remembered that Howard had called it one of the best games he had ever played, how Martin had chatted with fans in the crowd and how he had marvelled at the closeness of the contest. At the Olympics, Kevin Martin disposed of rivals far less qualified than Russ Howard and countless other Canadian teams, in short order. He went through the first round of play with a record of eight wins and a single loss—some games were, to be charitable, lopsided in Martin's favour. It was a little closer in the semifinal but the Canadians still managed to get by Peter Lindholm of Sweden by a margin of 6 to 4.

Things were looking good as the skip from Edmonton headed into his gold-medal confrontation with Norway's Paal Trulsen.

I had an eerie feeling as I checked into the match on television. In the ninth end with only a couple of rocks left for each team, the Canadians held on to a 5–4 advantage. Tuning in at that point, all a viewer could see and hear, besides the score displayed on the screen, were the Canadian team members discussing one of their final shots. For more than a couple of minutes the commentators remained silent as Kevin Martin, Don Walchuk, Carter Rycroft, and Don Bartlett calmly debated the course of action. At times, the discussion became heated, and there was obvious dissent within the ranks. All the while, the capacity crowd sat hushed. It was like they were all listening in on a tapped telephone conversation. Trulsen and his Norwegian squad were listening too. The moment was electric.

Finally the shot was delivered and the mission of the Canadian team accomplished. The Norwegians would take a point to tie the game with one end remaining. Martin would deliver the final stone—the hammer—for the gold medal. Martin seemed strangely relieved, and yet, as an outsider, I could not imagine why he would be, having permitted the tally to be evened in the eleventh hour.

The first ends of the game had seemed much less momentous. Now each shot was critical. I couldn't bear to take my eyes off the screen or to look, in equal measures. It came down to the last throw. As anticipated, to win gold Martin would have to make a delicate draw to the centre of the ice. "He's not cocky but he's extremely confident," the CBC's Don Wittman had told me. "He has confidence that he can make every shot and that his team can too. He's not afraid to play any shot."

So it was that Martin quickly assessed the situation and without a moment's delay instructed his third to place the broom on target. It was, as Wittman pointed out, and the work of Geoff Johnson and his television crew reinforced, a starkly similar shot to the one that had got Martin here in the first place—the shot that had elicited that magnificent, knowing smile and sent Kerry Burtnyk packing on a December day in Regina.

"There are always such great expectations for Canadian teams whenever they go into international play in curling," Don Wittman commented as Martin made his way to the end of the ice. "Now Kevin Martin has a chance to rid himself of the international demons that have blemished his résumé."

It was all that needed to be said. There would be no blow-by-blow of what was to happen next. Martin was just the best curler in the world forced to deliver a perfect shot with no room to spare. A team game hinging on one player's brilliance. The Norwegians had two yellow stones in play. The one that mattered, the one Martin needed to better, was in the white, eight-foot ring. The other was out front and in the middle of the ice, just kissing the blue circle of paint. The Canadian skip released the red handle of his final stone quickly and with conviction. "Now a chance to seize the moment," Wittman mused.

"We need a piece!" The sweepers and Martin realized immediately that the rock was a touch heavy. Frantically, they would try to rub the front Norwegian stone ever so slightly and then curl into position. The four members of the team yelled instructions with sharp clarity and no small measure of panic. Then they watched as their rock hugged the Norwegian but kept sliding. When it finally ground to a halt, it was a fraction farther from the centre than the yellow one it was trying to improve upon. Martin had accomplished the unexpected, to be sure. He had missed the gold medal by a hair. For a second or so, everyone, including the victorious Norwegians, was left in stunned silence.

Immediately, the CBC went to a commercial break and returned with action from the semifinal hockey game between the United States and Russia. Still, on a Friday afternoon, 2.5 million Canadians, the largest audience for a televised curling game in the country's history, had tuned in to see Kevin Martin go down 6–5 to Paal Trulsen of Norway. The attention of tens of millions more around the world had been caught by the closest of finishes. Martin graciously accepted runner-up status, shaking hands without hesitation. Don Bartlett, Martin's lead, hugged his Norwegian counterpart and there was no bitterness. Once transfixed, the crowd at the Ice Sheet erupted with appreciation.

The CBC broke away from the hockey game to join an interview with the vanquished Canadian skip. "Yeah, it was about an inch, I guess," Martin told Don Wittman, with the slightest of shrugs. "I feel bad for the guys. You have a shot to win. I hate it when I'm the one that misses it."

"It was devastating for Kevin," Wittman told me later. "This was the one shot that I suppose he had always dreamed of throwing to win a world championship or an Olympic gold medal. Unfortunately it was just a little too heavy."

It had been an exhilarating, unexpectedly thrilling match to watch. The sparing and timely interjections of the commentators had helped make it so. The Canadian television crew didn't miss a beat. Every nuance was captured in the weaving together of a great tale—a duel worthy of the frontier setting.

All in all, the show could not have asked for a better script. More people than ever had taken curling in, igniting interest in the sport in places where it once was ignored. The last shot had rung out resoundingly from the Olympic Games. And yet, for all that Canadians had brought to the table in Utah, they left without the gold medals they were expected to claim. The magic of curling. Anything can happen and ultimately that is what makes the show worth watching.

The champion: Alberta's Randy Ferbey

CHAPTER SIX

THE BIG TOP: THE BRIER

THERE WERE FOUR SPORTS EVENTS WATCHED RELI-
giously in our household. Each rolled around once a year,
each dominated our thoughts and our hearts for hours on
end. Things became emotional when favoured teams or
individuals struggled. Many a time we ate our meals in front
of the television set for fear of missing a dramatic or decid-
ing moment. Trips to the washroom were reserved for commercial breaks and conducted in a panicked frenzy.

The Stanley Cup final was a must. In the early spring we
would find ourselves glued to the action, which in those
days usually involved the two original Canadian teams. The
the Maple Leafs' rare victory in 1967 seems forever sweet.
George Armstrong's shot hitting the empty net with less
than a minute left, sinking the despised Habs in six sensual
games remains a landmark of unbridled joy for me. We
locked arms and danced around the room.

On the other hand, the calamitous fumble by the
Argonauts' Leon McQuay during the 1971 Grey Cup game

made me shed more than a few embarrassed angry tears. I just couldn't bear it as the Calgary Stampeders and their sinister middle linebacker, Wayne Harris, swaggered over the frozen turf with the biggest prize in Canadian football. Even my folks and their neighbours who had gathered to watch the game sustained by a crock of chile con carne and a case of Labatt 50 stared at the screen in disbelief. The Argos had somehow blown it again.

Then there was the Royal Agricultural Winter Fair. A strange one, I'll admit, but my dad was fascinated by jumping horses and equestrian competitions. As I drifted by the television on certain Sunday afternoons in the late fall, I was drawn to the majesty of the animals under the control of skilled riders like Jim Elder, Tom Gayford, and Jim Day. Inserts during the course of the telecast featured the prize Hereford cattle owned by hockey superstar Bobby Hull, portly pigs, and the bizarre sheep-shearing finals. I didn't think of it back then, but the Royal smacked of something that was uniquely Canadian.

The Brier was like that, and in our house it was mandatory viewing. The Canadian men's curling championship brought together teams from each of the ten provinces plus another two squads that represented the Yukon/Northwest Territories and Northern Ontario. By virtue of our clan's traditional homestead in the environs of the automotive city of Oshawa and our recent move to suburban Toronto, everything outside of Ontario seemed exotic to me. For a young person who had travelled no farther west than Thunder Bay and had yet to embark on a jetliner, there was a mysterious vastness to our country. Very early in my life, the Brier became a window on Canada's rich complexity.

Contested in places as diverse as Charlottetown, Brandon, Kelowna, and Quebec City, the Brier held my attention because so many things were going on at once. The TV coverage would skip from game to game—something I had not seen in any other sport. The players wore bulky sweaters and the combatants from rival provinces soon became as recognizable as, say, the Leafs or Canadiens in their traditional uniforms of blue and red respectively. Provincial coats of arms were crested on the back of the curlers' sweaters, but the colours became a more vivid reminder of who was from where. Alberta bundled in blue, Ontario for some reason was light brown, Saskatchewan always wore green.

At the Brier, we ended up cheering for the best the sport had to offer and unlike the baseball or football games that crowded our consciousness at other times, the major players in curling were all Canadians. So it was that the sweepers who banged the big straw brooms so noisily and the meticulous skips guiding the rocks to impossible places had the power to fascinate. Men like the cigar-smoking Alfie Phillips Junior of Ontario and Ron Northcott of Calgary became household names. Jack MacDuff ventured all the way from St. John's to win in Regina—the only time that Newfoundland has been victorious. There was Jim Ursel, a transplanted Manitoban, bearing the fleur-de-lis in the Montreal Brier of 1977 and finally winning for Quebec.

Orest Meleschuk of Fort Rouge also won, as did Hector Gervais of St. Albert and Ed Lukowich of Medicine Hat. I wondered, as I watched, where those places were, what people who came from there were like. My dad always made note of the fact that Gervais was actually a French Canadian from Alberta. I was amazed as I had always thought that all francophones in this country lived in the province of Quebec. I first gained an appreciation for the smallness of places like Prince Edward Island as I watched the Brier. The Islanders were the constant underdogs and scrambled mightily as they faced the much heftier provinces. The men from the Territories had come from a place known to me only through the Klondike Gold Rush an eternity ago. Northern Ontario was a force, and it seemed strange that they would even have a team—wasn't one per province good enough? My dad explained that Ontario was a huge place measured not only by its population but also by its physical dimensions. So it was that Bill Tetley of Fort William at the head of Lake Superior had to venture far afield to win in Fredericton, New Brunswick. Al Hackner, another curler from Northern Ontario, was dubbed the "Iceman," adding depth and intrigue to the game's lore.

The rivalries, unlike in hockey, were not forged between cities or clubs but between provinces. For one week every year, Canada was engaged in a friendly civil war. Fans were vocal and passionate in the cause of their provincial squads and yet their hearts went out to the long shots from Nova Scotia and New Brunswick, as did mine. It always struck me that the people on television never talked about a country other than Canada during the course of the competition—it was a given that the winner of this event would be the best. It's assumed that the finest curlers in the world are found by searching within our borders. This is the enduring prestige of the tournament and I promised myself, if ever I got the chance, that some-day I'd get to the Brier.

Mid-March and the spring thaw is already on. In central Canada, where the myopic believe that anything of any importance in this country just naturally happens, winter is in full retreat. As I scramble to gather my gloves when the cab pulls up to the airport terminal, the driver chuckles confidently. "You won't need those today, sir," he offers.

"I will where I'm going," I huff back. The newspaper forecast bears me out. With temperatures ranging from minus 10 to minus 16 centigrade, in Alberta the frozen season has not yet receded.

I'm making my way to Calgary and what they are saying is, at least with respect to attendance, the biggest Brier of all time. I'll get to the Saddledome by way of Edmonton, where in 1999 nearly 250,000 fans watched nine days of curling at the Skyreach Centre. This year the NHL's Calgary Flames are struggling to make the playoffs for the first time in six years but won't play at home until the curling is over. The Brier is a significantly bigger draw, and so the hockey idols have embarked on a nine-game road trip—a rare hardship these days.

At the Avis car-rental kiosk in Edmonton, the attendant advises me that in spite of the recent buildup of snow, Highway 2 is clear heading south, though there could be a little black ice, the temperature having dipped below minus 20 overnight. "I'm a curling fan too," she says with a wink. "I've never actually played but I love to look at it and when the Brier was here in Edmonton a couple of years ago I took my husband to watch. He liked it so much that he got tickets for us to go to the final this year in Calgary." She hands me the key to my mid-size and says she might see me at the Saddledome on Sunday.

Curling country is wide open, and the first road sign for Calgary proclaims the Stampede City to be a mere 294 kilometres down what can be a mean stretch of road if the weather turns nasty. I'll pass by or through the communities of Leduc, Ponoka, Lacombe, Sylvan Lake, Red Deer, Innisfail, Olds, Didsbury, Carstairs, Crossfield, and Airdrie before reaching the main event. All these places have at least one curling club, a reflection of how deeply rooted in the soil of western Canada the game is.

The cattle wandering the snow-covered fields don't seem to notice as my car skitters among the transport trucks past the combine machinery left to winter in the desolate-looking fields. A quick flip of the radio dial brings in a country music station and Kenny Chesney singing "When We Were Young." Agricultural news dominates the airwaves. "Steers were a dollar eleven to a dollar sixteen midweight and grass calves were fully steady and fleshing on feeder cattle," the announcer states in what could be a foreign language. There's talk of beef prices, barley seed, and the fact that this is Farm Safety Week across the country.

On the all-sports radio station, The Team, the scores from the Brier are updated every fifteen minutes. "Manitoba squeaked out two in the tenth to beat P.E.I.," the voice recounts. "Ontario crushed Northern Ontario 9–3. With the win, Ontario has improved to eight and two second only to Alberta at eight and one. B.C. is alone in third place with a record of six and four."

It seems the home team is in the driver's seat again at this year's Brier. Alberta is represented by a rink from Edmonton and has come to the event as the defending champion. Randy Ferbey, the skip from the Ottewell Curling Club, is enjoying a tremendous run of success even though he finished fourth at last year's world championships in Switzerland. Still Ferbey, who won an additional two Briers playing as a third for the stoic Pat Ryan, comes by his favoured status honestly. His major challenger is a twenty-three-year-old representing Ontario by the name of John Morris. Morris, a former two-time winner of the World Junior Curling Championships, is appearing at his first Brier. A kinesiology student who attends Wilfrid Laurier University in Waterloo, the Ontario skip will surely get an awakening once the elimination rounds begin. This is, after all, a game where experience counts.

The closer I get to Calgary, the lighter the sky becomes. It opens up to become a brilliant canvas, and huge white clouds roll across its expanse. There are more horses than cattle roaming the fields now, and the landscape, once flat, has become gently rolling. I can see the mountains in the distance, hovering beyond a substantial cluster of skyscrapers. Maybe I won't need those gloves after all. Then again, as they say of the weather in these parts, if you don't like it, just wait five minutes and things will change.

The name of the tournament comes from a brand of tobacco once produced by the Macdonald Company. Brier was reputed to be the most popular smoke with Canadian men in the twenties and thirties, and over time the Dominion Curling Championship for the Macdonald's Brier Tankard came to be known simply as the Brier. The tournament was held for the first time in 1927 at the Granite

Club in Toronto and featured a foursome from that city as well as rivals from Montreal and Saskatchewan, the only western Canadian representative. The Brier's scope developed quickly, and in 1928 three western teams, including Joe Heartwell's foursome from Rosetown, Saskatchewan, which had entered and won the Alberta playdowns, made the field five strong. City representation was soon dropped and championship teams from the provinces were entered starting in 1932. By 1936, Prince Edward Island and British Columbia stepped into the fray. The Brier was becoming a truly national event.

The tradition that the national curling championships should move around the country was established early on. Eager Canadian cities vied for the honour of hosting curlers from across the land as well as the passionate fans that came along with them. By 1940, when Winnipeg became the first city other than Toronto to host the national party, the Brier was well on its way to becoming a unique and sought after extravaganza. Manitoba had already distinguished itself as a powerhouse curling province as Gordon Hudson's rink from Winnipeg's Strathcona Curling Club captured back-to-back championships in 1928 and 1929.

Since 1940 the Brier has pitched its tent in Victoria, British Columbia, St. John's, Newfoundland, and many places in between. The national men's championship returned to Toronto only once after its original departure, in 1941 when Howard Palmer's rink from Calgary captured the title. Smaller centres such as Brandon, Manitoba, and Moncton, New Brunswick, warmed to the arrival of the tournament and delivered substantial audiences for it. Figures go back as far as 1946, and in Saskatoon that year

22,000 Canadians took in the Brier first hand, many having come from far afield. Western Canadian cities proved to be the bastions of curling—32,000 through the gates in Edmonton in 1954; Regina packed in 51,725 a year later, a mark nearly equalled by Calgary in 1961. It's startling to note that, as early as 1963, a modestly populated city like Brandon was able to attract more than 42,000 fans to a curling tournament.

The filling out of the field seemed to trace the growth of the country. Newfoundland arrived at the Canadian curling table in 1951, two years after its entry into Confederation. By 1975, the Territories had made their debut, and a dozen teams came to contest the coveted crown at the most inclusive of the national championships. Where the Grey Cup involved Canadian football teams, it also featured a large number of American players. Hockey's Stanley Cup has more often than not been fought over by one or more clubs based in the United States. This in spite of the fact that the overwhelming majority of the National Hockey League's stars have hailed from this country. The Brier is 100 per cent Canadian and has been throughout its history. Every province is represented and every combatant is a citizen of the place he battles for.

Throughout the history of the Brier, both the provinces and their individual stars have made their marks. Manitoba has become the Montreal Canadiens of men's curling. That province has claimed victory in twenty-six of seventy-three Briers, and one of its early stars, Ken Watson of the Strathcona Club in Winnipeg, became the first three-time winner as he triumphed in 1936, 1942, and 1949. The Richardson brothers of Regina created a curling family dynasty. Representing the Civil Service Curling Club, skip Ernie and his siblings Arnold, Garnet, and Wes dominated and won the Brier three times in the late fifties and very early sixties. Ernie Richardson directed another Brier victory for Saskatchewan in 1963 thus becoming the first and, to date, the only four-time winning skip.

There have been other stars. Garnett Campbell of the Avonlea Curling Club in Saskatchewan first started as a sixteen-year-old at the 1947 Brier in Saint John, New Brunswick, and when he finished his career had appeared at ten national championships. The bespectacled Bernie Sparkes of B.C., who also curled with the Calgary rink of Ron Northcott, competed in a dozen Briers and Northcott himself won three titles in the mid to late sixties. Hec Gervais, the immense man with the delicate touch from St. Albert, Alberta, won titles thirteen years apart—the first in Calgary in 1961 and the second in London, Ontario, in 1974. Hec Gervais's legacy is indeed one that can be attributed to curling in general. Experience counts in this sport.

Charismatic figures have also taken centre stage at the Brier. Ed "The Wrench" Werenich, a Toronto fireman, produced a star-studded team and claimed Canadian championships for Ontario in 1983 and 1990. Werenich was known for his no-nonsense approach to the game. The fans warmed to him as a street fighter in what had been considered a somewhat sedate sport before his arrival. In 1981 in Halifax, Kerry Burtnyk of Winnipeg proved you didn't have to be one of the game's elders to win. As a twenty-two-year-old, Burtnyk skipped his Assiniboine Memorial Curling Club rink to an 8 and 3 round-robin record and then won dramatic matches over Saskatchewan and Northern Ontario to hoist what had become the Labatt Tankard the year before when Macdonald cigarettes gave way to beer. Members of Burtnyk's squad, with an average age of twenty-two, were just barely legal when it came time to drink from the new mug, which stood five feet high and weighed 150 pounds.

Fans have developed an affinity for certain characters over the years. Russ Howard, who originally represented Ontario and who won championships with his Penetanguishene Curling Club foursome in 1987 and 1993, is revered for his tremendous roar when calling at his sweepers. Paul Gowsell, a double winner of the world junior championships, shocked fans and rivals alike at the 1980 Brier in Calgary. In what is known as a game of tradition, Gowsell, wearing the blue sweater of Alberta, showed up with a scraggly beard and unkempt hair that dangled to his shoulders. He and his foursome, renowned for hard partying and barnstorming on the cash circuit, displayed a swashbuckling style and while shattering many accepted practices came close to winning that year. Guy Hemmings of Quebec played to huge western Canadian crowds while reaching Brier finals in Winnipeg and Edmonton in successive years in the late nineties. Though Hemmings and his team were dramatic underdogs, the flamboyant skip stole hearts as he joked in two languages and flirted with women in the crowd. It was not an easy trick to turn for a French Quebecker in the heart of the west.

In recent years, over the course of competition, the Brier has attracted crowds in excess of 200,000. Calgary, Edmonton, and Saskatoon closed the last millennium by consistently filling NHL-sized arenas and bringing curling to the big stage. Television audiences hit new heights and while cable stations attracted hundreds of thousands of viewers during mid-week play, the finals were gobbled up by millions of fans watching the CBC on the weekends in the comfort of their living and recreation rooms across the country. In 2000 the Brier got a new sponsor as Nokia replaced Labatt as the title supporter of the national championships. A new trophy, which is actually the original Brier tankard after a $10,000 refurbishment, was unveiled to the Canadian Curling Association. It now embodies hand-engraved silver hearts bearing the names of all the curlers who have won the cherished championship since 1927. The replacement value of the trophy is reputed to be $30,000 but to most curlers it is priceless.

The Thursday I arrive is the last day of the round robin and most of the playoff spots are already decided. It is the sixteenth draw or session and amid the dangling banners that drape the cavernous Pengrowth Saddledome the fans are "Rockin the Rockies." At least ten thousand strong, they are here to see the boys from home, wherever that may be. A guy with a Yukon Territories flag poked into his ball cap is bellowing to his favourite. "Let's go now, Jonathon," he screams. "You the man, buddy. You the man!"

Jon Solberg, a thirty-year-old skip who works in the pharmacy lab at the Whitehorse General Hospital, has his hands full. He's skipping the team from the Yukon/NWT against New Brunswick's Russ Howard. Solberg knows that since first appearing in 1975, the Yukon/NWT has rarely come close to winning. The best showing was that inaugural year when Don Twa and his team finished second with a record of eight wins and three losses. In two of the last three

years, Yukon/NWT has gone winless at the Brier with a
final tally of 0–11. On the other hand Howard, who makes
his living as a professional golfer, is also aware that his
adopted province has yet to field a champion too. This
could be his chance to make a little history, if only he can
solidify his playoff position with a win over Solberg.

After nine ends, youth and ambition have taken the
upper hand, and Solberg and his soldiers lead 7–6. Even
though Russ Howard manages to take a point in the tenth
and final end of regulation play, the underdog from the
north will have the hammer coming into the first extra
frame. Howard, the wily veteran, puts a bunch of rocks in
the house, forcing Solberg's hand. Just watching, you can
tell that the pressure is getting to the underdog. He sees a
double takeout chance with the first of his two remaining
stones but proceeds to throw a clear miss. "I wouldn't be
doing that with Russ Howard in the house," the Yukon/
NWT fan grunts. Solberg then miscalculates with his
final draw and the favourites from New Brunswick pre-
vail. Howard embraces his younger rival and shakes his
head as if to say he survived only by the skin of his teeth,
and the fans enthusiastically welcome both teams coming
off the ice.

Now just one game is being played out there, and
Saskatchewan is fighting for its life against Northern
Ontario. In spite of its almost mystical connection to curling, the breadbasket province has not produced a Canadian
champion in men's play since 1980 when Rick Folk and his
foursome from the Nutana Curling Club in Saskatoon won
in Calgary. Saskatchewan has seven Brier victories in all,
fourth on the all-time list that's led by Manitoba with

twenty-six, Alberta with nineteen, and Ontario with eight, but they've rarely had a sniff since their last win.

This time, however, Scott Bitz has a chance. If he can finish up with wins over both Ontario teams, he will make it into the playoffs. It's Bitz's first Brier appearance and he is guiding a veteran outfit from the curling-mad province. The proximity of this year's site in Calgary to neighbouring Saskatchewan means that folks from just east of here have come in large numbers. They got a moment of inspiration the other day when Bitz, a chiropractor from Regina, laid down his broom in the middle of a game and rushed into the stands. He proceeded to perform CPR on a fan felled by a heart attack. Bitz then returned to the ice to finish his match.

Three wins in a row have given the Saskatchewan four a boost of confidence and even though they've been pushed to an extra end by Tim Phillips, a bartender from Sudbury, they keep their hopes alive with a 6–5 win. "Only one thing would make me happier," Joan McCusker says, as she leaps from her seat. "That's another Saskatchewan win tonight when they play Ontario." McCusker is a three-time world champion who also won the Olympic gold medal in 1998 while playing on the team skipped by Saskatchewan's Sandra Schmirler. McCusker's husband, Brian, is curling second for Scott Bitz. But should her home province make it to the final of this year, Joan is one fan who will have to keep her partisan feelings in check. McCusker happens to be one of the commentators for CBC's curling coverage, and cheering over the airwaves just won't do. It will be a struggle. "Our team always said that they could dress us up in red and white but our blood runs green and it always will," she chuckles. "Down deep we are from Saskatchewan and we are very proud of that."

With that McCusker is off and running, urging me to follow her to the Brier Patch, the watering hole set up in the Stampede Centre directly across the road. She's making an appearance there in between the draw just complete and this evening's action. "Answer a few questions, sign a couple of autographs," she says, with a smile. I think to myself that it might not be too crowded late on a Thursday afternoon. People will want to get home and have their supper. Besides, the only game that is going to mean anything in the evening session will be the one involving Saskatchewan—unlikely the stands will be full for that.

It is a revelation. The gathering at the Brier Patch is immense, at least two thousand people sitting at long tables eating burgers and conservatively sipping on beers. They're trying to remain alert for the seventeenth and last draw of round-robin action, which, despite its anti-climactic billing, they wouldn't miss. These are the fans of curling, and many of them have come a long way to cheer on their favourite province—faithful travellers who have become inseparable from the game they love.

It seems that everyone knows everyone else in this huge crowd. Then the lights go down. A chance to listen to Joan McCusker, Don Wittman, and Mike Harris of the recently arrived CBC crew. The three have the undivided attention of the audience as they regale them with curling stories. "Ten reasons why curling is better than sex." McCusker gets things rolling. "Number one. There are only four positions to learn and you just have to be good at one." The crowd erupts with laughter and the tone is set. Whether they are

The play-by-play team: Don Wittman, Joan McCusker, Mike Harris

from the east or the west, whether they are French- or English-speaking, everyone gets onto the Brier bandwagon. Wittman is the revered voice of the game, and he's fielding questions about the upstart Grand Slam of Curling series operated by the World Curling Tour. The series prevented some of the better players from contesting their provincial playdowns and so from getting to the national championships. It's caused some controversy and challenged the Brier's reputation as the most prestigious of events.

"It's a national championship," Wittman says in answer to one of the queries. "I always compare it to golf. People can identify the Masters winner, the U.S. Open winner, the British Open winner but ask them who won the Westchester

Classic or the Greater Honda Classic or any of the other tournaments and they have no idea. The same is true of curling. People know who wins the Brier. They can probably tell you what the score was in a given year. Ask them who won the World Tour championship and they don't know."

TSN's Vic Rauter echoes Wittman's contention. He believes the Brier's universal appeal is found in its connection to the grassroots of the game. Each provincial representative must emerge from a system of qualification that involves more Canadian communities, large and small, than any other sporting spectacle, professional or amateur. "John McEnroe, when he won the U.S. Open in tennis, would you see him playing at some club working his way out?" Rauter asks me. "Of course not. And no pro hockey player is playing in the beer league on Saturday morning either. On the other hand, you know that Russ Howard next year is going to be at the Beaver Curling Club in Moncton and somebody like you or me is going to be playing against him. These people—and I hate to say ordinary Canadians because that sounds silly—are just ordinary folk!"

Wittman alludes to Howard as well when he states his case for the continued reverence for the historic national championship of men's curling. "Russ Howard said it best when he said this week, 'The Brier makes curlers. Curlers don't make the Brier.'" On the subject of major prize money, or rather the lack of it, Wittman has an easy retort. "There is no interest in that. That's the way it is. There is a title on the line. Until they win the Brier they may have been recognized as good curlers. Then they win the Brier and they become great curlers." The crowd roars its approval and it's quite clear that the man who will soon be inducted into the

Curling Hall of Fame is preaching to the converted. As I glance around the room, I wonder how many of these so-called ordinary Canadians have aspired to greatness themselves. They are obviously stakeholders in a truly national championship that, unlike other sports, is in no way beyond their reach.

Things have changed mightily in the few short hours since I arrived at the Brier. As I emerge from the Stampede Centre and head back to see the prime-time action at the Saddledome, I am blasted by driving snow. A late winter storm in the foothills has, in the space of forty-five minutes, blanketed the sandy brown terrain with an inch or more of fresh, white ground cover. Visibility is next to nothing, it's windy, and the temperature has dropped at least 10 degrees centigrade. The exhibition grounds that surround the Saddledome are jammed with traffic—headlights boring through the blizzard as droves of fans arrive for more of "The Roaring Game."

Thankfully, the big arena provides shelter from the elements, the same way so many tiny curling rinks do throughout rural Canada. With only one game of any importance on the docket, the cavernous building is now teeming with raucous fans. The place holds 17,000 for curling and there are at least 15,000 who have paid their way through the turnstiles. It's like the midway at the fair and there is a constant din.

At the far end of the ice and through the window of one of the Saddledome's private boxes, which patrons pay heavily for in order to watch a hockey game, Vic Rauter's on the air and setting up the show. Alongside are his analysts,

Linda Moore, a former Canadian champion, and Manitoban Ray Turnbull, who won a Brier himself back in 1965. "Now the ice is going to swing a little bit this way," Ray is writing on the telestrator, offering fans a visual demonstration of how rocks will react when thrown to a certain section of the ice. It's like the old practice of divining undertaken by so-called water witches. Still, Ray Turnbull's been getting it right for years, and when it comes to reading a curling match he's the best.

The bagpipes, an institution since the very first Brier in 1927, have ushered in the eight rinks that will occupy the four sheets of ice over the next couple of hours. Sounds like "Scotland the Brave," and the fans clap in unison as the pipers, in their tartan and tweed, lead the way. Suddenly, amid the clanging bells and horns, things are underway. Flags wave, the rising sun of British Columbia, the St. Andrew's cross of Nova Scotia, and the green and gold symbolizing the magnificent prairie of Saskatchewan.

In Draw 17 all the matchups provide, if not life and death implications, at least a measure of intrigue. Alberta's Randy Ferbey faces Pat Ryan of British Columbia. Ferbey used to curl third for Ryan when both were representing the Ottewell Curling Club in Edmonton. Together they won back-to-back championships in 1988 and 1989. On this occasion the one-time lieutenant is a favourite, whereas Ryan is out of the running. Russ Howard's New Brunswick foursome will get to the playoffs but want to finish strong against their traditional rivals from Quebec. Francois Roberge of Ste. Foy has been a disappointment. He finished third at the 2000 Brier in Saskatoon but has stumbled in the round robin this time.

Rules of the road at the Big Top

I notice that in the early moments of the match, Howard hurries off the ice and reappears about a minute later. "Just had a pee break," he tells the fans closest to the boards when he gets back. Something that could never be envisioned in any other sporting event of this stature somehow fits in curling, it feeds the atmosphere of normalcy here. Not unlike the handwritten cardboard sign at the threshold to the ice. "All Players Must Use Boot Boys," it blares, warning curlers to clean their feet and not dirty the pristine playing surface. It comes off a bit like someone's mother or father demanding that your shoes be wiped before entering the living room.

In the stands, I find my place beside Joan McCusker. She has a shock of dark, curly hair and a voice reminiscent of Peppermint Patty's; she smiles all the time and has opinions—plenty of them. McCusker has become one of the most popular and listened-to people in curling. Highly visible as the second on the team of the late Sandra Schmirler, McCusker won three Canadian championships and just as many world titles as an integral part of the intrepid foursome. She is a sought-after speaker, and it is her story of Olympic gold that continues to fascinate and inspire so many Canadians. McCusker has turned her cachet into a spot in the CBC's broadcast booth, becoming an astute analyst of the game she continues to play. Dreams of getting back to the world championships or to the Olympics with a rink from Saskatchewan are still vivid in Joan McCusker's mind.

Joan McCusker: Just a fan from Saskatchewan who grew up on a one-sheeter

"When people start curling, they don't do it for the money," McCusker says, without taking her eyes from the ice. The Saskatchewan men's team is trying to survive to play one more game at this year's Brier and needs to beat young John Morris to do it. "They don't do it because they think they are going to be rich. They do it to represent their province at a national championship," she continues. "This is the pinnacle. There are bragging rights at stake."

Joan McCusker grew up on a farm not far from Yorkton, Saskatchewan, which is in the southeast corner of the flat land. She flourished in one-sheet rinks and, like every other kid in curling's heartland, had to ride the bus to get there. Curling was never a pastime for Joan, nor was it a ticket to a richer life. She already had that.

Saskatchewan's team in front of a packed house

"Oh what a shot!" Joan rises from her seat to applaud with the thousands who surround her. Scott Bitz has just completed what's known as a raise takeout—a complicated removal of one of the Ontario stones. Bitz is therefore able to count in the early ends against the strong team that sits in second place and has already been assured of a shot in the playoffs. "Oh, they needed that one," she says, gushing with relief.

"It's all about what we become and not what we get," McCusker figures, as she zeroes in on her husband. He's a farm credit manager and hasn't been to the Brier for nine years. Brian McCusker played third for the Randy Woytowich team that missed the playoffs in the 1993 Brier and before that came very close to winning in the 1991 Hamilton event. Saskatchewan lost in the final to a young Kevin Martin of rival Alberta, and the team in green has been scrambling to get close ever since.

"I've wished this for Brian for a lot of years," Joan sighs. "You know, he hasn't been here since 1993. To work that hard and to be at such a fantastic event—I wish him the best experience and that's winning. I'm here as support. I'm here as the mother of our children who need me here to watch their father at the Brier." There is a reverence to McCusker's words that stays with me. Her thoughts on the Brier are passionate but not over the top.

"As a kid I can remember being taught the right things to do in the game," Joan begins. "Being dragged off the ice and told not to laugh or joke or smirk when the opposition misses. There is deep-rooted stuff in curling that there isn't in any other sport. You are taught to be good people in curling. Good curlers tell the other team that they made a great

shot. It's emotional, and the drive and the competitiveness
are huge but you have to be able to turn it on and off, and
I think that the people of Saskatchewan raise their sons and
daughters well in this game."

The Brier, according to McCusker, is something Canada
can always count on. "You don't need big names to draw a
crowd when Saskatchewan plays Manitoba or Ontario plays
Alberta." She spreads her arms to demonstrate. The congregation in front of us is enormous. "These are the great
matchups of the week but they are the same ones which
happen year after year. It's province against province, area
against area, and you cannot recreate that in any other
event. There is a tradition of people coming from those
provinces every year to wherever the Brier is and cheering
on their province. Then they get reacquainted with people
from other provinces that they have met who have done the
same thing. It is this friendly rivalry, and it's something
which does not happen in any other men's curling event that
we have going."

Things are looking up for Saskatchewan. Maybe John
Morris and the youngsters from Ontario are resting on their
laurels just a touch. Their place in the elimination round is
secure. Still the squad from Regina is playing with conviction and showing why they are about to win their fifth game
in a row. Takeouts, draws, rollbacks, everything is working
and the crowd loves it. Maybe, just maybe, they'll get to see
a traditional favourite fight for the title.

As I look over at Joan McCusker I wonder why her
celebrity has not translated into a swarm of people seeking
her wisdom, her acknowledgement, her autograph. She is
a star of the sport and the arena is full. If she were a hockey

player, even of modest renown, she wouldn't have a moment's peace in a setting like this. But the Olympic gold medallist shakes her head when I bring my query to her attention. It's not that way at the Brier. The people on the ice are the stars and their fame lasts only as long as they are in the spotlight. Once removed, they recover their everyday lives.

"I can't describe to you what it's like to be playing out there with 12,000 people in the stands," McCusker admits. "They're calling to you softly and they won't cheer for your misses," she almost whispers. "They will applaud your smallest effort. It's the closest thing that you can get to that feeling of celebrity. People like me and they come to see my team. You get a tiny taste of fame and then you go back to being your ordinary self. You don't have to give up a lot of your privacy. It's just that little fifteen minutes of fame that everyone talks about. If I could just have a little shot at it."

Brian McCusker and the rest of his Saskatchewan team survive to continue the hunt for the province's first Brier championship since 1980. John Morris has given way in the last draw, and Ontario will go into the playoffs as the second most successful group after round-robin play. Randy Ferbey's defending champions from Edmonton have been supremely steady and have nailed down top spot so far. Morris and Ferbey are separated by nineteen years, a couple of thousand kilometres, and not much else. Somehow, at the Brier, they have both found their place.

John Morris's young team includes three university students. Only the vice-skip, Joe Frans, is employed full-time, as a golf course superintendent. Frans is also the

Ontario's hot shot: Two-time world junior champion John Morris

oldest member of the group, a comparatively ancient twenty-six years of age. Together the foursome has been tearing it up at their first Brier, both on and off the ice. Making the good shots hasn't been a problem for the rookies, and neither has their relationship with the partisan crowd. Morris, in particular, has proven to be gregarious, and even the Alberta fans who are firmly planted in Ferbey's corner have taken a liking to the kinesiology student who shows up to play sporting several days' growth of beard. It's also well known that Morris and his associates have, following the conclusion of each day's play, indulged in a few beverages at the Brier Patch.

"This might be the only time we're ever here so let's enjoy ourselves." Morris is blunt in revealing his team's strategy. "We'll have a couple of beers, we'll enjoy the atmosphere, and we aren't on a strict schedule. You know, we just want to be on an even keel and do what we normally do in life. It worked for us the first time we won the world juniors."

Morris is highly approachable and there is no pretence about him. He talks with anyone who walks by. If the truth is told, he only ever looks nervous when the media scrums form around him at the end of each match and he's asked to speak about his team's fortunes. It's a task one might expect to be less stressful than holding his own against the likes of Pat Ryan, Randy Ferbey, and Russ Howard. "Maybe about three or four years ago when I was eighteen and I was playing these guys for the first time, I was a little nervous," he concedes. "But I think that motivates me now because playing against them is such a great challenge. It feels great to beat them. They are good guys and they are legends but I'm definitely not awestruck right now. I'm just not that type of guy."

Morris faces the scrum

I recall now that Morris had been a factor for a while at the Olympic Trials in Regina a couple of months ago. He finished with a respectable record of 5–4 and at times looked to be capable of carrying Canada's curling hopes onto the world stage in Salt Lake City. He says he likes the feel of the Brier better. "If you told me I'd win three or four Briers in my life and not an Olympic gold medal, I don't think I'd be too disappointed. It would be great to win [the Olympic medal] but it is very stressful. You have to play your guts out all the time. Here you come and it's a lot more enjoyable. The fans are great, the players are great, and you just have a good time. That's why I play this game."

It's a stark contrast that John Morris presents to the many professional athletes I have encountered. He appears to play for the highest stakes with modest expectations of what victory can mean. "When you're on the ice, you play your butt off, and when you're off the ice you have a good time and let the chips fall where they may," the boy wonder from Ontario figures. "I really enjoy playing this game but I really couldn't see myself doing this as the only thing in life. There are a lot of other things that I enjoy. I'd love to travel and I've sort of missed out on some of the social life at school because of my curling. I get good enough marks but if I put more effort and time into my studies I could probably improve quite a bit. There are a lot of other things in life to look at. You can't take this game too seriously or you'll get grey hairs really early."

That message delivered, the Ontario skip concludes his day at the Brier. So far Morris has handled veterans and relative newcomers with flair and determination. His dad has been in the crowd and he's gained many supporters. Now

Morris disappears down the tunnel knowing that to unseat the reigning champion, Randy Ferbey, he'll have to knock off a sentimental favourite or perhaps a boyhood idol. Saskatchewan is still in it. So is Russ Howard. On the eve of his most important day in curling, John Morris is gone in a flash. He's off to the Brier Patch and a couple of cool ones before hitting the hay.

Randy Ferbey is a bit of an unlikely hero. He's smallish, not very imposing—looks like an average guy. He speaks quickly and with a raspy voice that engages you. There are no booming proclamations from the champion, the commander of arguably the best curling team in the world.

"We're all regular Joes," he insists.

A quick glance at his team roster confirms Ferbey's assertion in one way, destroys it in another. Each member of the squad obviously has the ability to juggle a big life with substantial curling talent. David Nedohin, the man who plays third, is employed in the field of geo-environmental engineering. He was born in Winnipeg and has been curling part-time for nearly twenty years. Regarded as one of the most precise shot makers in the game, Nedohin throws the final stones for the Alberta rink even though Ferbey retains the skip's title. Scott Pfeiffer plays second and at twenty-five is the youngest member of the foursome. He works as a hydro-geologist and won a world junior championship in 1994. Pfeiffer is the only player to throw left-handed on the Alberta side, one of only five southpaws in the field of forty-eight players. Lead Marcel Roque is a teacher at a junior high school in St. Paul, Alberta, and had to find his own teaching substitute for the length of the Brier. For good measure, Roque had

All the answers: Randy Ferbey, the favourite again

to forfeit a fraction of his salary during this absence from his teaching duties. These are not professional curlers, even though they have been successful in winning some prize money on the cashspiel tour.

"We personally want to play for Canada and money is not an issue," Ferbey reiterates. "Would I walk away from the Brier in order to play for more money? Not in a million years."

Ferbey's frankness has, at times, got him into hot water. Other teams have suggested that the Brier is no longer able to attract the best curlers in the world because some of the more successful barnstorming foursomes are busy playing for cash instead of in the arduous provincial elimination rounds that the Brier historically requires. Ferbey scoffs at these arguments, saying he's had a lucrative cashspiel season and made it to the Brier just the same. "The decisions have to be made, right or wrong," he says in answer to his detractors. "Would I like to be playing for money during the year at certain times? Absolutely! Maybe I want the best of both worlds."

Randy Ferbey, at the time of this Brier, is well on his way to setting records but at forty-two years of age he wants nothing more beyond the satisfaction that the Canadian championship can offer. He'll do anything, within reason and the boundaries of what is acceptable, to win a match. If that includes letting Dave Nedohin have the final say when it comes to throwing the last rocks and in turn relinquishing a few accolades if it all works out as planned, so be it. It's simple as far as Randy Ferbey is concerned. The Brier makes no allowances for prima donnas.

"It's a gentleman's game," he's quick to point out. "There is no room for jealousy. This is a team game and that's what makes champions in any sport. I'm not jealous of Dave and he's not jealous of me. Everyone knows their role on this team because they belong on this team. We're not looking to make a trade to get this guy or that guy on the team. We are four individuals who enjoy each other's company on and off the ice and it will be like that forever."

Ferbey fields a bunch more questions from the hungry scribes and radio reporters. There are more than a few TV cameras here now and the champ agrees to do a one-on-one interview for anybody who desires such a thing. The crews from Calgary and Edmonton are particularly eager to get a couple of words of wisdom from the Alberta skip who now knows that the up and comer John Morris, old rival Russ Howard, and Scott Bitz of Saskatchewan remain as challengers to his title. He looks at ease in the glare of the lights.

The Brier champion represents the Ottewell, a large curling club in a suburban section of Edmonton that has spawned a bevy of Brier celebrants, including two-time winners Pat Ryan and Kevin Martin. In the past decade the curling club's reputation has grown tremendously and all things being equal, if Martin contested the provincial playdowns every year, Ferbey might be hard pressed to get out of his own club. Still, that's the way he likes it. Travelling the full route to get to the destination is important to Randy Ferbey, as it must be to all the other competitors seduced by the Brier's lure. Maybe it's about paying your dues and avoiding short cuts that could weaken your resolve. "It's a long year," Ferbey reckons. "We curl against these guys the whole year, and that's the way it has to be because it makes the end result a whole lot more enjoyable."

The Brier will soon be seventy-five, and only for a couple of years over the course of World War Two did the men's curling championship skip a beat. Once reserved for a very small portion of the country, it has evolved into a championship that paints the broadest of strokes across the land. Any man who curls has, on paper, a chance to get to the big top. I'm left with the understanding that, in curling, the major leagues embody the brilliance of far-flung and sometimes unheralded locales. That's what I witnessed when I watched the Brier all those years ago. I saw people who were somebody's neighbours shining in front of a national audience. Small places . . . huge ambitions.

"There's probably a one-sheeter nearby that you should go and see." Randy Ferbey is at my ear and reading my mind. "I'll ask around and get a name for you. Don't worry." I'm not worried. In fact, I'm certain the Brier champ is pointing me in exactly the right direction. It's all starting to seem so familiar.

Hallowed house in a one-horse town: The Foothills Curling Club in Eagle Hill, Alberta

CHAPTER SEVEN

LITTLE WHITE HOUSES

THE BRIER IS THE MOST IMPRESSIVE OF ALL THE bonspiels. Calgary's Pengrowth Saddledome exists in the heart of a city populated by 800,000 Canadians, and the arena's capacity for a single session of curling is 18,761 fans. When all is said and done at the seventy-third Brier, upwards of a quarter of a million people will have seen the action first-hand from the grandstands. An additional million or more will have tuned into network television to watch Edmonton's Randy Ferbey defeat the Brier rookie John Morris of Ontario in the final match. By any measure, the game has clearly become big-time.

More remarkable, however, is the determination of the participants as well as the onlookers to honour the grassroots of the sport. They constantly remind one another that the genesis of curling has been significantly more modest. The goal is to arrive under the glare of the spotlights on a big stage, but the starting place is almost always more humble.

The barn in Biggar, Saskatchewan: Sandra Schmirler's home rink

"The first time I curled was in a one-sheeter in Rokeby, Saskatchewan," Joan McCusker hastened to point out from her perch in the Brier's bleachers. Rokeby is a tiny spot, barely visible on the road map, not far from Yorkton in the southeast corner of the province. "It had natural ice," she continued. "The building was wooden and was eventually condemned because it was so dilapidated. The wind would howl through the boards that made up the side of it. It came down very soon after I curled there."

Many curlers of her generation share similar experiences. Russ Howard played on an open-air rink fashioned by his father in the Georgian Bay backyard of his youth. Most, if not all, of the men who represent Saskatchewan can trace their first rocks thrown to little houses on the prairie with one or two sheets of ice.

In Tonkin, just to the east of Yorkton, McCusker played in a kid's league, and on a regular basis during the winter the whole student body of her rural school was bussed to the curling rink. "We all played in the junior league. The older kids played with the younger ones and we all learned to curl," she remembered. Natural ice was a given in the small clubs, and it made for some interesting times. "The old Pierce brothers who ran the rink were complained to bitterly about how slanted the ice was. So after Christmas they slanted it the other way for us so that we could learn the other turn," the former Olympic champion reminisced.

Saskatchewan was once dotted with one-sheet rinks, and I can recall a television feature on one of them—a place called the Skull Creek Curling Club. From the exterior, the club looked like a long, white tunnel of snow, stark and simple against the rural backdrop. The club had been built in 1962 by local people and operated by farmers and their families who volunteered to pebble the natural ice or make ham sandwiches in the minute kitchen. Every year since its opening, the club has staged a bonspiel lasting a full week and involving the entire community. "As I remember, everyone that was eight or older generally curled," one father who was skipping against his son pointed out. "Warm and friendly is a good way to describe it."

Warm may have been a feeling that came from within. The temperature inside the rink was surely sub-zero and the misty exhalations of the curlers drifted about the icebox as they shuffled up and down the length of the playing surface. The surface itself was painted white under the circular target areas at either end, but the natural ice in the middle was a steely and frigid-looking grey. "It's a little swingier on cold days," the volunteer ice maker offered. "If there's frost out there it gets a little heavier. But on good days it's as keen as artificial ice."

The fans appeared to be keen as well. There they were, huddled on a couple of rows of wooden benches that rose in the warmth of the viewing area. They wrote their comments on sheets of white paper and pressed them against the glass to get the message across to their favourite curlers, who were also likely to be their cousins. "A Little Heavy," one of the elders wrote. Then again, it's hard not to throw heavy when you're on natural ice. It wasn't until she went to the larger centre of Yorkton and played on an artificial sheet that Joan McCusker developed a subtle touch to her game.

"There's so much tradition out there but the smaller clubs of Saskatchewan are struggling to make a go of it," McCusker lamented. "To have enough money to put the ice in. That's a shame and they really have to look at the business of curling and how to sell it and how to make money to pay the bills, which never used to be an issue."

In Skull Creek, the people looked to be making a go of it. Nobody minded putting in a few hours to care for the place. Layers of bulky sweaters draped on top of long underwear neutralized the numbing cold. "It's just a small community rink in the middle of nowhere," one man said. "A gathering place for everyone in the winter time." The clubhouse of this farming settlement is an oasis where friendships have been fostered and ambition ignited.

The old one-sheet buildings so important to curlers like McCusker are a lasting physical reminder that curling's history is firmly anchored in what's left of rural Canada. Like so many others, curlers are moving to the cities where there are more opportunities on better, longer-lasting ice.

But that doesn't mean the country rinks have lost their importance. "How long will it remain?" the TV reporter asked, as he wrapped up his story on the Skull Creek Curling Club. "That depends on the will of the people and a little cold weather. Two things you can pretty well count on around here."

I had to get to a small rink. To see why it, and others like it, are so important to the culture of curling. Randy Ferbey, the Brier champion, had lived up to his word and put me in touch with a man named Kevin Robertson, who lives in a spot called Eagle Hill. Kevin was surprised when he took my phone call, dumbfounded that I would want to come and look at the little arena and visit a few members of the club where he was president. Still, in a shy monotone, he read me the directions with great care. Eagle Hill is not on the map and "you could get lost in a hurry," he cautioned. It lies an hour and fifteen minutes from Calgary—sort of on the way to Edmonton—and Kevin gave away a part of its charm as he said, "When the oiled road jogs over the bridge, you'll know you're close."

Early in the morning, the snow is whipping the highway and it shrouds the roads of Alberta's countryside in a threatening sheet of white. Off the big thoroughfare and onto Highway 27 heading west, I go by the Gopher Hole Museum just before the community of Olds. Pickup trucks are legion and they plough through the bad weather as a matter of course. I'm squinting now and frantically searching for the unmarked "oiled road" that Kevin mentioned.

There's another panicky phone call and Kevin, so calm on the other end, tells me that the road is exactly fourteen

miles west of the cutoff from Highway 2. Too late, I haven't
been watching the odometer and I'd have to do a conver-
sion from kilometres to miles anyway. Finally, miracu-
lously, I find it, County Road R 4–00, and I make the turn
heading north over the little red bridge, which spans a racing river, and onto the unpaved path ascending to Eagle
Hill. There is a church, a gate with a wagon wheel, and a
sign that says "Eagle Hill Simenthals." I'm in the right
place. The bulls are out in the yard and they take no notice
of the solitary car groping by. At the bottom of the hill is
the centre of town. The Co-op store. The rink squats
directly across the road.

"It's supposed to be on the map. They said it would take
five years to get it done." Doug Paton welcomes me into
the sanctuary of the Foothills Curling Club. "That was ten
years ago."

Paton rumbles with laughter. He's a sturdy man in working clothes—ball cap, drab green trousers and jacket, a
checkered flannel shirt. He works a herd of cattle called
Gelevieh. "Are there any others?" he asks jokingly. Paton is
seventy years old and proud to be an original member of
this club founded in 1947. The current structure dates back
to 1966 and is made of concrete blocks. Sawdust concrete
blocks, as Doug points out, meaning that wood shavings
have been mixed into the stone and allowed to set. "Good
insulating qualities," he says with a wink as the blizzard
howls off the porch of the rink.

Inside, Doug leads me through a little mud room where
you can drop your boots, hang a bulky coat. To the left and
down a couple of stairs there's a miniature compressor, and
the ice plant, for the moment, purrs like a content cat. The

The kitchen at Eagle Hill: Warmth after the game

floor down there is so clean you could eat off it. We emerge through the door and into the heart of the club where a father and his son are there to greet us.

Adam Robertson is seated on a permanent swivel stool, one of half a dozen that line up at an old-fashioned kitchen counter. Kevin's standing at the stove warming up a kettle for some instant coffee. If I didn't know different I'd assume we were at the luncheonette at Woolworth's. The menu, written in magic marker and hanging above the cooking area, offers twenty items. Homemade soup is a buck. There's a box of plastic kids' toys off to the side and the membership dues are advertised clearly on the wall. They range from student fees of $15 a year to the tariffs for an entire family, which can soar as high as $100 a season. "Farming hasn't been paying that good." Doug notices me perusing the price range. "That can hurt our membership."

In a hamlet with no population listed, they weather the winters in the safety of this little building. It's neat as a pin and obviously cared for with a tender vigilance. There are eight teams and a total complement of forty curlers. Kevin Roberston is the president and has held the position since January. For the thirty-six-year-old cattle and grain farmer who has been curling since the age of fourteen, it's a second kick at the office. "I was the only one stupid enough to take it," he says. I can tell he doesn't mean it as he carefully wipes the counter, removing a slight spill of milk. His dad, Adam, came to the club in 1948, the year after it was opened, and quickly understood its importance. "It's all tied together," he explains. "You have to wonder if we didn't have the curling club, would our community still be here? Would the store be here as well? Would the hall across the road be there?"

People live here and enjoy the pleasures of companionship. There's a notice on the corkboard asking for participants to enroll in something called the "Granny Spiel." Entries are governed closely. "Must be a grandmother. We will accept authentic ultrasounds," it states.

"Sometimes the curlers sitting on the bench are a lot better than the ones on the ice." Adam snickers as he points to the permanent stands in the viewing area. The stands are impressive; rising in three steps and spanning the width of the club they seem a bit out of proportion to the rest of the tiny building. They are fully padded and reminiscent of the bleachers at a softball diamond. Clean and inviting. Most of the time the people who park their seats over the length of them are discussing not just curling but local business as well. "Did you ever get a bunch of farmers that don't talk farming?" Adam asks in a knowing way.

"They come up to visit and watch the curling even if they don't curl. That's the way it's always been," Doug chips in.

Kevin is motioning to a narrow staircase that descends to another level. "We try to make sure everyone is comfortable here," he prefaces our arrival in what's known as "The Snake Pit." It's just a recreation room with a dartboard and a few wooden card tables and chairs, the ones you might see at any church hall or small community centre. What distinguishes this space is an elaborate mural painted by the locals across the wall at the end of the landing. Snakes are depicted curling with cigars or pipes dangling out of their mouths; some wear tams, some are clad in tartan. Kevin stands in the

The snake pit: High times in the foothills

middle of the room and both of us just avoid wedging our heads into the extremely low ceiling.

"Out on the ice you spend a lot of time standing next to the other guys," he explains. "Then you go downstairs and drink with them." The two older fellows snigger as they hold their hands in their pockets and I sense that they telepathically share countless tales of the nights spent in "The Pit." I'm honoured to have been invited into the inner sanctum of these people's lives, like the adult who gets a peek at the secret tree fort built by a society of adventurous kids.

"The merchant spiels used to get a little rowdy," Doug confesses. "You'd curl all day and the prizes were a flat of eggs, a few cans of fruit, or a bushel of grain put up by one of the local farmers." He laughs with the rest of them, and I can tell that the more important statistic has to do with the barrels of beer that were consumed once the curling was completed. "There's nothing too serious ever happens here," Kevin says. Doug's of the same opinion.

"It's a social event really," he confirms.

"And things have tamed down a lot," Adam adds, with a note of barely concealed regret.

The only comprehensive and recorded history of what is now known as the Foothills Curling Club exists in the form of a 1997 poem written by Alma I. Bisenthal to celebrate the fiftieth anniversary of the original building's opening. It tells of local farmer George Gibson donating logs from his land to be used as construction material. The rest of the community quickly organized to provide the labour and everyone was involved. "Not a slack one among them or so it's been said," Bisenthal writes.

The raising of the building was done by members of the local Co-operative and completed in good time. A land lease of ninety-nine years was donated by the general store, also owned by the Co-op, and the original lighting system for the two-sheet rink consisted of gas lamps. There was no artificial refrigeration apparatus, so the first ice at Eagle Hill was dependent on the forces of nature. A series of giant shutters on the sides of the building were regularly lifted to allow the wind to whip through on colder nights, firming up the playing surface as it blew. "One time they opened the flaps and an old fella rolled in," Adam Robertson recalls. "He was clutching a bottle of booze."

The first membership fee was five dollars a season. In 1948, in an effort to raise more money and secure a commitment to look after the rink, the directors of the club sought an increase. Female members would continue to pay five dollars but henceforth the male curlers would be levied double that amount—though those men who donated their labour free of charge could still pay the five dollars. Indoor plumbing facilities were not available at first. "The cold outdoor privies, were oh so sublime," Bisenthal teases. "No danger for any to spend overtime. There was one for the ladies—I tell you that's all—so where did the men go to answer the call?"

Ice didn't go in until Christmas when a man named Albin Johnson flooded the two sheets with a barrel of water that rested on a stone boat. At the back of the contraption and attached to a smaller tank was a pipe with holes pierced in it. As the liquid spilled into the reservoir it was dispersed as evenly as could be expected, the whole thing being hauled the length of the rink by a draught horse (sharp shod, of course). Later the farmers dug a well and with a gas engine pumped water into a trough installed in the rafters. The rink could then be flooded with a hose and the horse spared his or her duty.

Electricity didn't arrive until 1951 but interest in a game lit by gas lamps was high. Evening curling was conducted using a square draw of two sessions on each night, Monday through Saturday. Sunday was a mandatory day off. This system allowed a maximum number of twenty-four teams to curl two evenings a week during the long winter months. There were also occasional bonspiels to be played out on weekend afternoons. The entry fee was a meagre two dollars and the women took turns preparing lunches in the little kitchen.

Fees steadily increased for the men who curled in the community but the women's annual ticket remained at five dollars. It was thought that men who farmed were able to pay more. It was also acknowledged that most of the volunteer work as well as the day-to-day organizing of social activities was undertaken by women. Regardless of the division of labour, the Eagle Hill Club was open to both sexes on an equal basis from its inception. There appears to have been no differentiation between the rights of male and female curlers at this two-sheeter.

The businesses of the community were squarely behind the little rink. Building materials were donated when the arena needed a new roof, and the Eagle Hill Power Company charged a mere fifteen cents an hour to illuminate the place. In return for shingles and light, the donors had their names marked down in the club ledger and dues were forgiven the following year. It was curling on the barter system.

The first caretaker was hired after a number of tenders for the job had been taken. The winning bid belonged to a man who promised to light up the fire in the clubhouse wood stove before scheduled games and to keep track of the number of hours the lights were turned on. In addition, the caretaker claimed as his responsibility the pebbling and sweeping of the ice after each session and when the weather turned too mild, the barring of eager curlers from further play. (On this matter tensions could run high as many of the farmers were anxious to extend the season for as long as they could.) In return, the benevolent and patient caretaker would receive a monthly salary of fifty dollars, not to mention plenty of headaches for his trouble.

Expenses swelled as the rink matured through the 1950s and into the 1960s. There was fire insurance to pay, rocks to be sharpened and maintained, ventilators to be installed in the building, firewood to purchase, cut, and stack—the list went on and on. At one time, some members of the club considered a proposal to transform the rink into a rifle range during the off season. The plan was eventually abandoned. The majority of the congregation vowed not to let anything of the sort trespass upon their sacred curling sanctuary.

The biggest cost faced by the club was the purchase of two matched sets of rocks. From the time of the club's founding, the stones used had been a bizarre collection of odds and ends. Varied in size, shape, and weight, the rocks went a long way to explaining the inconsistent brand of curling that came to be identified with Eagle Hill and many of the smaller rinks throughout the prairies.

"Of course when we started curling they went to Calgary and bought one set of rocks." Doug Paton, one of the original members, tells the story. "They had what we called little teakettles and great big blockbusters and everything in between. Some were sharp and they would curl and some were dull and they would slide and the skip had to remember what everyone's rock was going to do. Everything was different. No two shots were the same."

Adam Robertson weighs into the conversation as the subject turns to the intricacies of rocks and ice in the old days. "You had to throw them a lot harder," he says of the oddball stones. "And when one of those big blockbusters hit . . . boy, would they move the others in a hurry." Adam smacks his hands together for effect and all three guys rumble with laughter. "That's when curling was curling," Doug insists. "Rocks have always been different to me. There's real fine granite that really slid nice. Then there were others, my brother Don had a set, second-rate rocks. They were a little coarser and they sure did pick up a lot more junk on the ice."

Adam and Doug both remember there being at least a ten-pound difference in the weight of the teakettles and the blockbusters. It made for a game of strategy, where the experience and guile of those who had been around the block a few times were a huge advantage. Appropriately enough for the curling farmers, the highest yield would go to the skip who considered the raw materials he was working with most carefully.

The Rocky Mountains can play havoc with winter's predictability. Eagle Hill, being barely an hour's drive from Calgary, is considered to be in the foothills. So it was that the natural ice in an enclosed facility became a hit and miss proposition. The annual chinooks warmed the air outside the club but created bumps on the ice within. The club needed to modernize, and even though the participation level in the community was still strong, the quirks of the very basic rink were becoming a bother. When they opened the flaps to let the cold air in, snow drifted onto the sheets and it was often too breezy to play comfortably. Still, the originals like Doug Paton regret the levelling of the playing field and the gradual passing of natural ice; most especially they miss the mysteries presented to avid sportsmen and women. "You were talking about the Brier and all the great shots they make. Well, the ice is so much better. I mean, our ice, you know, we had rocks that draw and sometimes you had to use negative ice. To me when they made the ice flat they wrecked the game. They took all the strategy and thinking out of it."

The door to the left of us flings open and winter's breath darts through the building. Then a squat man who is heroically wearing an unzipped windbreaker slams the door shut. Paying us no mind he flips on the lights and peers at the empty lanes of smartly groomed ice before him.

"He's our iceman. Our volunteer iceman," Kevin reveals. Turns out he's Don Paton, Doug's brother, another of the early members here in Eagle Hill. The boys warn me he doesn't take too kindly to those who question the quality of his playing surface or of any other playing surface, for that matter. Apparently Don's from the old school, the ice you get is what you get and you should feel lucky to have it. The curlers should just keep their opinions to themselves and play.

"If I don't hear any more complaints than I heard after the game last night then I'll be fine," Don chimes in without looking around. He's making reference to the match he watched on TV from the Brier. "One of the guys from Ontario was yapping. He'll just have to figure it out a little quicker today or tomorrow." The lights have taken a while to fizzle and flare to their full effect but the rink is now illuminated. The ice looks straight and true and cared for. "We say it's just the outside sheets that are bad here." He tips back his hat and offers his assessment in a deadpan way. Behind me the three other guys are snickering again. It takes me a second to clue in. Of course, in a two-sheet facility both would be on the "outside."

"It's the same story with a lot of the older rinks," Doug figures. "The centre ones were good but the frost on the outside of the building got onto the sheets and caused them to heave a little bit." Any variance in the ice is barely detectable as I remove my shoes and pad around the surface.

The frozen sheets: "Just the outside ones are frosty"

There are none of the chips and gouges that can be found in a small-town hockey arena. Everything has been smoothed and flattened as if by a carpenter with a level and plane working to exact specifications. Then again the people who use this ice try to complement the terrain by gliding over it, respecting its minor undulations as well as its flatness. Curling acts in concert with the ice, not against it. "It's not like hockey," Kevin Robertson estimates. "When you're out here you're not trying to rip some other guy's head off and banging around." The three wise men of Eagle Hill have followed us in procession and nod their heads in unison. Not one of them has a bad thing to say about this little haven of theirs.

By the mid-sixties conditions in the twenty-four-year-old building had deteriorated to the point where something needed to be done if curling was to survive another unpredictable winter. The community went to work en masse yet again to erect a much sturdier structure on the grounds of the Vale View School, just across from the Eagle Hill Memorial Community Hall. It was at the hall, a simple barn of a building opened in 1949, that the moccasin dances, cabarets, and banquets the curling club relied upon were staged. Fundraising went into overdrive in 1966, and the blocks were all hauled in by local labour. So was the sand that forms the current floor of the curling club. Still, there was no refrigeration plant, and once the roof was insulated and the base ready, two blocks were removed from the wall, one on each side, to allow air flow. Once the cold breezes were trapped and the ice had frozen stiff, curling began in earnest again. Things improved quickly at the new and solid house in Eagle Hill. Indoor plumbing facilities were added in the 1970s, and this time there were facilities for both sexes.

The people of Eagle Hill cling to an agricultural and rural livelihood and have persevered through their own ingenuity and a spirit of shared reliance. The history of the curling rink is likely a mirror of how the settlement itself has survived and flourished. Something as simple as the purchase of a secondhand ice-making plant from the nearby community of Pine Lake in the early 1980s was translated into hope for the little curling rink and in turn, optimism and a renewed sense of vigour on the part of the membership. "As artificial ice later made its debut," Bisenthal waxes, "A wee bit of heaven came shining right through." And on the subject of the advent of the long kitchen counter and the seven permanent stools, Bisenthal reserved praise for the efforts of the female curlers who made things that much more efficient. The club was undoubtedly assuming its place as the hub of winter activity. It may be modest in appearance but its women members would make sure it had all the amenities. "With a whole lot of work and the odd bit of bitchin'— The curling club ladies took over the kitchen. Down in the basement a bar was assembled—Where after 5 drinks you could feel all a trembled—'The Snake Pit' they dubbed it— 6 drinks made it crawl. Especially when eyeing the snake on the wall."

As I sit drinking coffee at the same kitchen counter with my new friends in Eagle Hill, I am struck by the stark contrast between the relative grandeur of the Pengrowth Saddledome in Calgary and this unremarkable building. Vastness compared to close quarters. An ultra-modern sports facility and the backyard rink. Still, one cannot survive

Ties that bind: The Robertsons and the Patons

without the other. At the Brier I had been surprised by the intimacy of the huge event. The acceptance of people from all regions of the country and the familiarity they demonstrated across the board was both amazing and encouraging. I admit to having never seen the like of it. Today, sitting with my mug of hot coffee and sharing a few moments with these three farmers, I know where it all begins.

Kevin Robertson had taken at face value my call from Calgary and an out-of-the-blue request to see the rink at Eagle Hill. He opened it up and invited the last of the original members still curling, Doug Paton, to tell a few stories of the place. His dad, Adam, was there too and the ice maker, Don Paton, had dropped by to eavesdrop on our conversation as much as anything else. They had brought along Alma Bisenthal's poem and a couple of pages of neatly written notes. They delivered them to me without question and with unassailable pride.

"You come out and meet your neighbours." Kevin tries to explain the reason for the rink's survival. "Otherwise you would never see them, I guess. There are probably people that you would never go to visit unless you came here to the curling rink to see them every once in a while."

In that respect it's like the Brier, only on a much smaller scale. And here the community of curling is even more important to this way of life. Something to cling to in the face of the big city's lure, a gathering place and a source of comfort for people who are separated by distance and a harsh climate.

"I think it holds the whole community together." Adam Robertson's assessment is very clear.

"Sure it does." Doug Paton echoes the sentiment. "It's not only that. It's what keeps the community going and it helps the store and the hall across the road. This rink is where it's at around here."

These days there aren't many one-sheet rinks still operating in Alberta. There may be a few more in Saskatchewan I'm told. But where they do exist across this country, community curling clubs still serve an admirable purpose. I remember the television coverage of the Brier the first time it was held at the Saddledome in 1997. The broadcasters marvelled at the ability of curling to fill the cavernous place. More than 18,000 seats—packed. As juxtaposition, they ran a short segment from a minuscule place called Seebe, Alberta—"The Little House on the Prairie," they dubbed it. Whereas the Brier's host city of Calgary had nearly a million people, Seebe boasted about eighty. The massive arena had been constructed in the shape of a giant saddle at a cost of tens of millions of dollars and with the promise of the Olympic Games to pay for its enormous expense. The rink in Seebe, one sheet of ice and a little lounge for viewing the action, had been built with materials from reclaimed construction shacks in 1949.

Every year in Seebe they stage a week-long bonspiel, just like they do at the Brier. There are sixteen teams and it takes a full week, Monday to Sunday, to play. The grandstands are always full for the bonspiel with people holding signs and doing the wave. "At Seebe we've put in a few bus seats," Terry Cummings, the volunteer manager and ice maker pointed out. "Here our capacity is about ten or twelve maybe." There's a sign that says, "Seebe Welcomes You," tattooed onto the ice just beyond the hog line.

The little houses in Seebe, Skull Creek, and Eagle Hill are all facing challenges that threaten their existence. There's the unpredictable weather that plays havoc with the havens of natural ice. "We've got ice plant problems here," Don Paton remarks. "The chiller went in February." Once again it was the volunteers of Eagle Hill who had to go to work, operating a lottery and casino in Red Deer to raise more funds to keep the machinery going. They brought home $17,000, devoured immediately by the repairs that were needed. I notice, though, that the ice plant does, at times, sound less like the purring of cat and more like the growling of an unsettled lion.

It's getting tougher to nourish the grassroots of the game. Joan McCusker had said as much as she took in the splendour of the Brier. "I know where I come from, my brothers are all farmers and they are curlers and they are not curling in the home club," she noted. "They are going to bigger centres to get more competition. The ice is better and the level of competition increases. The old club is still there but it isn't used as much. They didn't have the men's league this year. They're alive but they have to be careful."

Doug Paton remembers when, in the worst weather, the curlers would brave storms on horseback across the back forty to get to the rink at Eagle Hill. He recalls building this place and the one that preceded it, with his own hands and in the company of his relatives and lifelong friends. His youthful bulk and ruddy complexion belie his more than seventy years and he's determined to help keep this rink going.

The memories of how it started are remarkably fresh for men like Doug and Don Paton and Adam Robertson. I notice that Kevin, the next generation of Eagle Hill curlers, is doing most of the listening now. The older fellows tell tales of days when you didn't wear sliders but just sort of waddled out and released rocks before the tee-line. In "The Eagle Calls: A History of the Eagle Hill District," published by a group known as the Dorlas Ladies Aid, the first bonspiel champions are recognized. Jim French, Clint Bishop, Roy Harper, and Alex Buckley won "beautiful sweaters as first prize." That's about all that was written.

Doug claims a team from Eagle Hill got close to representing Alberta at the Brier in the early sixties. He can't put his finger on the exact date. That's not what counts, though, and he wonders aloud at the purpose of my questions about talented curlers who might have emerged from this rink to star on a wider stage. That's not the point, according to Doug Paton. "On many nights those bleachers are plumb full," he says triumphantly as he indicates the little grand-stands. "They come to watch and visit. There's neighbours there beside each other."

This is the odd but irresistible majesty of the little houses of curling. The boys of Eagle Hill can't make it any more plain. The bank mortgage is paid off and they own this club of their own making. "Just read this," Doug Paton says, as he points to the last paragraph of Alma I. Bisenthal's poem:

"It just goes to show that with honest endeavour,
What people can do when they all pull together:
Long life to our club, may it strongly endure,
And our social life, stand, both safe and secure—
For if we can manage expenses and fears,
We just might be around for 50 more years!"

Suzanne of the Island: 2001 World Junior Curling Champion
Suzanne Gaudet of Summerside, P.E.I.

CHAPTER EIGHT

YOUNG HEARTS

CURLING IS OFTEN CLASSED AS A GAME THAT BELONGS to the more mature among us. The skeptics suggest it inspires the young at heart—which, translated, means it is a sport best played by the elders of a community. With such sweeping sentiments, curling is dismissed as nothing more than the pastime of old folks. The perceived appeal of curling is further limited by the arbitrary, regional boundaries some would put around the game. The popular contention is that the best curlers invariably come from the heartland of the west, with any place east and south of Thunder Bay relegated to the hinterland. But such casual and ill-informed notions quickly melted away when I attended the World Junior Curling Championships of 2002. There, in Kelowna, B.C., I learned how easily curling can breach generational and geographical divides.

Kelowna is a settlement of relative youth when judged by Canadian standards. Incorporated in 1905 and in the middle of British Columbia's Okanagan region it is one of the fastest-growing urban areas in the country. The Kelowna surrounds are rich in agricultural produce and famous for their abundant yields of pears, apricots, and, most significantly, apples. Once a tobacco-growing hub that has since abandoned the crop to the more lucrative industry in southern Ontario, the Okanagan district boasts a moderate climate where long seasons for both skiing and golfing mean they co-exist.

According to the latest statistics, Kelowna's population is now in excess of 100,000 and a whopping 18.4 per cent of residents are beyond sixty-five years of age, a figure well above provincial and national averages. Kelowna has become a burgeoning retirement community, and with more than twenty golf courses in the immediate vicinity, the city has identified itself with the concept of leisure. There is, as a result, a less than frenetic beat to life in this place.

The Kelowna Curling Club, one of two in the city, is immense. It has twelve sheets of ice and is located in an industrial part of the town where its neighbours are the B.C. Fruit Packers plant, the

Twilight in the Okanagan: The Kelowna Curling Club

Sun-Rype Fruit factory, and the warehouse of Calona Vineyards. A huge sign moulded into the shape of a curling rock hovering over the parking lot reminds me of the entrances to amusement parks I have visited. The month of March has three days remaining and the weather is positively tropical. Convertibles pull into rapidly disappearing spaces with their tops down and radios blaring. I have to remind myself that I was at the snowbound Brier in Calgary barely ten days ago.

Inside the front door, which has been adorned with the flags of the eleven countries taking part here, things are abuzz. "Hi. How are ya doin'?" An official-looking fellow is hustling by but interrupts his progress to make sure I've got everything I need.

"Just on my way to see the last draw and would sure like to get to the grandstand before it starts," I reply.

"You bet. Just head upstairs and they'll get you fixed up with a program and all the rest of the goods." The bespectacled man is off and almost running to his next appointed task. Meantime, I'm heading up the stairs in the opposite direction, grateful for the assistance but wondering exactly who he was.

Flipping through the program, I discover biographies for all the curlers in attendance as well as the complete history of the World Junior Curling Championships—an event that has not, however surprisingly, been dominated by Canadians. The defending champions on the women's side of the competition are here and they do hail from Canada. Not from a reputed curling powerhouse, though. Suzanne Gaudet and her foursome have emerged from the smallest province to get to the top of the heap. They're from Prince

Edward Island, and I shake my head as another myth about curling evaporates. I also read that the men's champions from a year ago have moved into the senior ranks—that would be Brad Gushue's rink from St. John's, Newfoundland, making it an Atlantic sweep for the up-and-comers.

Jeff Timson is one of the media staff assigned to generate material for reporters covering this event. He's more than generous with the valuable moments he has available and helps me get settled in before the first rock is thrown at 6:30 p.m. Pacific time. "Who was that guy in the blue sweater and the glasses?" I ask him. "Looked like he was in charge or something." Jeff grins and shuffles the pages in the glossy magazine until he arrives at the right one. "That, my friend, is Rick Folk. The last man from Saskatchewan to win the Brier. A legend."

It turns out Folk is the co-chair of the event and has helped mobilize a volunteer corps of more than 300 locals in order to keep things running smoothly. He's revered as one of the most dignified curlers in the history of the game and won Canadian and world championships in 1980 skipping for Saskatchewan. He turned the same trick fourteen years

The master: Tournament co-chairman Rick Folk

later, representing his adopted province of British Columbia. Folk went to the Brier on four occasions and emerged from each as the all-star skip. He's regarded as a masterful shot maker, but perhaps in a more enduring way as a defender of the game's etiquette and tradition. The presence of this steward of curling at an event showcasing the sport's rising stars seems more than appropriate. I make a note to track him down and get his perspective on the game.

Downstairs, at ice level, the players are parading about in brightly coloured team jackets. They mingle with rivals from halfway around the world waiting for the procession that will take them to the ten active sheets for tonight's curling. It is like a carnival, a mini League of Nations where young curlers from Scotland, Japan, Sweden, Italy, Germany, Norway, and Switzerland, among others, assemble to share a burgeoning love for this game.

On the information booth, which now doubles as the results centre, someone has pinned up the blue flag of the City of Summerside for all to see. Suzanne Gaudet hails from Summerside, and next to the capital of Charlottetown, it is P.E.I.'s largest city—"up west," as an Islander might say.

"There's a decorating committee and everything." Basil Stewart, the mayor of Summerside, is suddenly at my shoulder. "You have to be careful but we figured they wouldn't mind us waving the flag a little."

Stewart is a heavyset man in a Team Canada jacket. He's been the mayor for as long as anyone in Summerside can remember and he's tireless in his promotion of the city as a place to live and do business. "We call ourselves the sports-hosting capital of eastern Canada," Stewart boasts. "That championship we staged in January was the most successful

Down to business: Scenes from the 2002 World Juniors

and had the largest crowds ever for Canadian junior curling. Having said that, we're here sort of beating the bushes for the world junior championships in 2004 or 2006."

As Stewart beams with satisfaction, I notice the motto sewn into his jacket beside the Canadian maple leaf. "Can't Hide That Summerside Pride." Indeed, Stewart has reason to be a bit lofty when describing the success of the Canadian junior championship hosted by his city not so long ago.

Attendance records were smashed as tens of thousands of enthusiastic fans from all over the tiny province showed up to cheer on the young curlers.

Not for the first time "His Worship" is at the head of a large contingent of Summerside fans here to witness the proceedings and provide much-needed support and fortitude. He wouldn't think of missing the opportunity to carry the colours and neither would the elders of the community who surround him. "I have known the skip's parents for a long time and I have known the families of the others as well," the mayor brags. "It was quite an experience when I went down to Ogden, Utah, last year and that's where the Summerside team, the Prince Edward Island team, won the title. That was a tremendous feeling to be there, sitting in the stands thinking that we were there from a tiny little city on the other end of the continent. We were representing Canada and completing a tremendous achievement. Here we are again tonight after going through the Canadians in January and now to the Worlds. It's just a tremendous feeling to be here as the mayor of that little city."

Seems like everyone else from the city is here as well. As they scurry to the ice, the Island girls get the biggest hand from the crowd in the bleachers. Seats are in hot demand, and some of the fans have been held up in their little nests of thick wool blankets and fluffy cushions since about four in the afternoon. This is not the Brier or the Olympic Trials and the arena is not commonly used for other sports like hockey. The Kelowna Curling Club is a traditional venue and the temporary stands erected along the sides of the building are where the heartiest of fans congregate. It's like being on the top shelf of a giant refrigerator.

The Canadian women are about to battle Sweden and their classy skip, the raven-haired Matilda Mattson. Mattson is a twenty-year-old bank clerk who is making her fifth trip to the world championships as leader of her team. She won it all in 2000. In the crowd is the father of the Swedish lead; he has their surname, Hammarstrom, embroidered across his yellow and blue sweater. Somewhat annoyingly, he's dangling the giant triple-crown flag of Sweden off the end of a fishing pole directly in front of the faces of the Canadian contingent. After the national anthem is sung by a young virtuoso, the rocks begin to fly and so does Hazel Webb—right out of her seat and in a flash, the mother of Canada's second, Carol Webb, is whispering harsh words into the Swedish fan's ear. Almost sheepishly he takes his assigned place, and the flag is quickly furled away as we all turn our attention to the match, which will determine first place heading into the playoffs.

"Summerside tends to go a little nuts over her." Mae Cameron leans back and explains the intensity of Suzanne Gaudet's fans. "It's very important for the self-esteem of the town. Everyone kind of identifies with her. She is the world champion, after all. It brings a name to Summerside as well, and it's kind of neat that the champion comes from such a small place."

Mae Cameron, a dead ringer for Anne of Green Gables with red hair and a goodly number of freckles, happens to be Suzanne's best friend, has been since elementary school. Cameron has come all the way to the tournament from Fredericton, where she's a science student at the University of New Brunswick. She's wearing Gaudet's white Team Canada windbreaker and is surrounded by the relatives of the other Canadian team members.

When appropriate, Mae honks an air horn, joining in the enthusiastic noisemaking that accompanies every successful shot. "Bio-mechanically she's got all the angles. It's a very difficult sport, you know. It's got everything, involving psychology too. It must be mentally tough to come out and do what she does time after time. It's very important to concentrate on the game. I don't curl myself but I imagine that it would be very difficult." Mae Cameron crinkles her nose and twirls back to the action in time to see Suzanne prove her right. The Canadian skip coolly draws to the four-foot and takes a single point in the first end to go ahead of Sweden. The celebratory racket in our section of the stands is almost deafening, and I can't for a minute understand how any competitor could concentrate in the midst of it.

In spite of the setback, Papa Hammarstrom is up and waving the flag again. This time he breaks into song, drawing on the courage provided by a few pre-game ales. The more reserved of the Swedes ignore him while the Canadian faithful have reluctantly adopted him as a nuisance to be tolerated for the time being. He's part of a more eclectic crowd than one would see at a national championship and, as might be expected, the Scottish fans on the other side of the rink are even more boisterous than the Swede. They assemble under a banner proclaiming the presence of "The Tartan Army" and their hero, skip Kenny Edwards, is putting up a fight against Leo Johnson of the United States.

I notice a youngish man ogling the Swedish side from the grandstand beside me. He whispers to his buddy every time one of Mattson's rink delivers a rock. Kevin Folk is the gawking twenty-something—part of the team from Kelowna that won this title in 2000 and the son of the revered Rick Folk.

Unfortunately for him, he's having little success distracting the Swedes, who are hanging tough against Suzanne Gaudet's foursome. Gaudet, who has been far from dominant, is just able to steal one point in the second to increase her margin.

The juniors are only so in terms of their age. The designation says nothing about the quality of curling currently on display. The composure of the players on the ice and the way they are able to block out the noise and activity that surrounds them is remarkable. Teenagers, pursuing the world championship in a sport marked by finesse and exacting standards, they seem to carry the load without hesitation or modesty. They look like pros.

"The big thing is she is absolutely fearless," Paul Power claims of Suzanne Gaudet. He's the coach of the Canadian women's team and while still a young man in his thirties he assumes the position of the wise adviser to this foursome from the Island. He's been with them for a couple of years and was on board when they won the world title last year. Power brings perspective and a high level of playing experience to the mix. He was part of the team led by Jim Sullivan, who won the world juniors in 1990 and represented New Brunswick in the final of the 1990 Brier. It was a closely fought match but in the end the young Atlantic team lost 5–4 to the titans from Ontario, the rink skipped by forty-two-year-old Ed Werenich. Still, New Brunswick had rarely come closer to winning the Canadian championship and Sullivan's men, Power included, had proven that experience wasn't everything in curling.

"She's not scared of anything." Power continues his assessment of the skip he tutors. "Even a lot of the good men's and women's teams that we see around the bonspiels look for an out when they have to play a certain kind of shot. They look to do things a less difficult way—not Suzanne. She just puts the broom down and away she goes. Whether there are two rocks in the rings or four rocks in the rings, she just puts her down and fires away."

Doubt cannot be a part of the equation for a curling skip. To be successful, you have to take chances and demonstrate confidence. The same principles apply regardless of age, and so it is that Suzanne Gaudet has captured the attention not just of those in the audience but of thousands at home on the Island.

Rebecca Jean MacPhee has a sister on the Canadian team. Robyn is eighteen years old and playing third for Suzanne Gaudet—she played second on last year's winning team. Rebecca watches intently from the green bleachers and evaluates each of the shots the Canadians throw. She is acutely aware of the strength of the entire foursome but most importantly, she's accurately deduced the potential of the skip. While still only twenty-eight years old, Rebecca has three times been the provincial champion in P.E.I. and carried the Island's colours to the Scott Tournament of Hearts in Vancouver, Calgary, and her native Charlottetown. She senses Gaudet will graduate from junior competition to become a force in women's curling.

"These girls are good. Anyone will tell you that," MacPhee acknowledges. "For the Island they have done a lot. Not only winning the Canadians and then going to the Worlds but they've helped to dictate curling in the Maritimes these last two years. Whether it's the ladies or the junior field, they are in the hunt. Certainly they are making their city and their province known."

Ages on the Gaudet team range from Suzanne at twenty to Kelly Higgins, the lead, who is just seventeen and still in high school. Higgins and her skip come from Summerside, and Robyn MacPhee is from Charlottetown. Carol Webb, the second, comes from near Saint John, New Brunswick, but attends the University of Prince Edward Island. Add to the collection the alternate player, Shelley Nichols, who is a proud Newfoundlander, and the squad embodies an entire region's youthful curling hopes.

"It puts us on the map," Rebecca Jean MacPhee says confidently. "The kids back home want to see them play, and it's really helping junior curling by bringing the youth into the sport. The Charlottetown and Summerside clubs are full of juniors. The team is doing fantastic and it couldn't be any better for any of us."

Things could be somewhat better for the resolute Suzanne Gaudet. While she remains singularly focused on the task at hand, the big shots are not going her way. Her rink is blanked by the Swedes in the third end. On the ice the Canadian sweepers are down to their shirtsleeves. In the bleachers, the folks from Prince Edward Island are huddling a little closer together now. Tension heightens when, in the fourth end, Mattson completes a perfect hit and stick to narrow Canada's lead to a single stone.

"It's definitely a scenario for maximum pressure," Tara Costello estimates. A consultant who works in the sport leisure program at the Atlantic Tourism and Hospitality Institute in Charlottetown, she's also the Canadian team adviser, psychologist, and chaperone. While she applauds the support shown by family and friends, Costello also understands the weight their expectations place on the young athletes' shoulders.

"It would be hard to paint a more pressure-filled situation," Costello explains. "But Suzanne is playing for herself in many ways and she has always been able to do that. While it's really nice that other people are going to feel good about it as well, you are the one out there. You are the one that has put all the hours of hard work into it. You therefore have to play for yourself and that's what we get them to focus on—their own reasons for wanting to do well."

As I observe Gaudet and her team struggling in the middle ends of the match with Sweden, Tara Costello's analysis seems startlingly accurate. The large group in the stands, just a few feet away, remains completely supportive of the reigning world champions. Still, the air begins to hang a little heavy with an oppressive desire for them to make every shot, claim every end. It's as if the reputation of the Island is riding on the top of each rock as it lumbers unwittingly to the target area of the house at the far end. The teenagers are forced to be resilient in the face of swinging emotions and the natural momentum of the game. At times it doesn't translate and they become kids again. When one of Kelly Higgins's stones fails to find the correct place on the ice, she is dejected and there is a fight to hide a few tears.

"What makes it more difficult when you have three other individuals on the team is that you are not just letting yourself down if you don't do well," Tara Costello points out. "They have to help each other deal with the misses and that's something we've been working on a lot. Something as simple as standing beside someone who has missed, a little punch in the arm, a little analysis to understand why you have missed. That part of the game is huge in terms of the psychological skill it takes to get re-focused. It's something that players will consistently have to work at. I'm not sure you ever get that one licked."

Gaudet and the rest of the team give Higgins the high five in spite of the errant first rock. Even the impatient crowd seems willing to forgive and forget an error—this time. There is a danger, Costello suggests, in young athletes trying to do too many things in this kind of setting. "There is a difference between an expectation and a goal," she says. "The words have a different connotation and what we want them to focus on is the goal. It's what you want. I think it's true that the girls like having their families here for the most part. It brings comfort. It also adds pressure. Everybody's watching. Everyone is here, wanting the girls to do well. If they focus on that it's worse."

I watch the band of Islanders rise from their seats and hold their collective breath until the Canadian stone discovers the right path and it seems clear that the Island youngsters, while trying to win for themselves, are also paving the way for the unselfish supporting cast to enjoy a small moment in the limelight.

Suzanne Gaudet's résumé is an impressive one. She began curling when she was eight, and in the last dozen years she has earned a sparkling record. Included on her side of the ledger are five provincial junior titles, two national championships (following a close second-place finish to Saskatchewan in the year 2000), and a silver medal playing third in Grande Prairie, Alberta, at the Canada Games of 1995. She speaks very few words on the ice and is not as demonstrative as some of the other elite curlers I have met. Gaudet is, however, intense. As she delivers her rocks, it's like she's locked into the target area. She'll emerge from the hack in a fairly upright position, compared with some others. Her eyes widen, become fiery. Suzanne throws with the left hand, which adds to her complexity. You are forced to watch her as much as you watch the rock. If you don't, you'll miss the subtlety that makes her so special.

Suzanne's dad is pacing behind the protective glass at the end of the rink. His daughter is getting into hot water in the fifth end. The Canadian skip has missed a takeout, racked up on one of the Swedish guards, and now has to call for a measurement to avoid a major turning point in the game. "I don't get nervous. I just watch the game," Gaudet claims. Nothing could be further from the truth. Noel Gaudet can't seem to stand still as he chatters away with fellow parent Bill MacPhee and Carl Delaney, the manager of the Silver Fox Curling and Yacht Club back in Summerside. Wearing one of those red Team Canada poor-boy hats made fashionable at the recent Olympic Games, Gaudet speaks with a slow sort of drawl almost as if he hails from the southern United States. Every once in a while though, a clipped plural will underscore his Acadian background. His first language is French but Noel's family name has become corrupted over the years and besides, his daughter likes it that way. "It should be pronounced 'Gaud-ette' because that's the way it's spelled." He shrugs. "But back home it's different and she will not change it. A lot of places you go they try to call her Suzanne 'Gaud-ette' and she wants Suzanne 'Goody'."

He's like most hockey dads I've met. Noel's intensely proud of his talented child and has obviously made adjustments to his family's life in order to ensure that an individual's ambition can be realized. He speaks of "we" as if

Suzanne's triumphs are a collective endeavour, to be attributed to the entire clan. "Last fall we played Colleen Jones at one of the ladies' spiels in Halifax and we almost won." His eyes widen. "We're just as good as anyone and all we've been doing in the last four years is playing in the ladies' super league anyway."

The patriarch is expressive when he gets onto the subject of his offspring's accomplishments, but his comments are not overtly boastful or smug. He quietly beams at the mark his daughter has made while mindful of the humble beginnings she has come from. Noel and his wife, Elaine Gaudet, operate a small convenience store in Summerside. They are the kind of general merchants that still thrive in smaller communities across the breadth of Canada. The operation is called S & E Grocery and Noel named it with his wife and only daughter in mind. They have regular and loyal customers; they also remain firmly planted in the seaside settlement and rarely, if ever, has the thought of leaving Atlantic Canada crossed their minds. They are Islanders first and foremost.

Noel winces only slightly as he peers through the glass to see that Suzanne has lost the measurement in the fifth end and has given up a steal of three points to Mattson of Sweden. The world champions are suddenly down 4–2.

There are three children in the Gaudet family and Suzanne is the baby, which makes her the object of special affection on the part of her parents. While Elaine defers to Noel on all subjects worthy of bragging, they both agree that their daughter took to the game quickly and enjoyed success almost from the time of her debut on ice. Suzanne's older brother Mike also curls and can look back on his own enviable record as a provincial champion representing the Island at the 1994 Brier in Red Deer, Alberta. Unintentionally, Mike was the one who got his sister into the game in the first place.

"Way back in 1990 he was supposed to babysit her because there's an eight-year gap, you see." Noel smiles. "We were working at the store, I guess, but Mike couldn't stay home because he had to go and practise curling. He took his eight-year-old sister down to the club and sat her on the ice so she could watch the game. She came home that night and said, 'Dad, I'd like to try that sport.' So we went down and registered her. I think it was twelve dollars for the season, and we signed her up at the Silver Fox."

Suzanne gave up figure skating and gymnastics and concentrated all her efforts on curling from that point forward. Through Elm Street Elementary School, Summerside Intermediate, Three Oaks Senior High School, and on to the University of Prince Edward Island, where she currently studies, the most accomplished of the curling Gaudets has always lived within a couple of blocks of her teammates. "It's all just a matter of dedication, hard work, and practice, practice, practice and she was willing to do that," says her dad. "I used to pick them all up in the van and take them to the curling club, watch them throw, and then take them back. That was six days a week. Now she goes on her own. She goes to the Charlottetown Curling Club and throws rocks every day. It's the only way you're going to make it."

There's a haunting but comforting tone to the conversation I'm having with Noel Gaudet. It's reminiscent of simpler times and what used to motivate young people to participate in sport. Here is where Gaudet diverges from his hockey counterparts. He is not talking about Suzanne getting to the next level, of signing with an agent, or making a fortune when she collects her first professional paycheque. Noel prefers to relate stories of his daughter's competitiveness, her passion for the game and a burning desire to be the best.

"Her best friend Mae Cameron is in the stands and they play ball in the summertime—oh yeah!" Noel exclaims. "When she goes there, she goes to play. There is no fooling around. They don't win everything but they go in with the intention of winning. She has no fear. Either that or she's not telling us anything about it. The better the team that's ahead of her the more she likes it. She has no fear of anyone. We are tremendously proud. She's a great kid," Gaudet finally admits. "You know, you never think that your own child will be a first-class world athlete. As far as I'm concerned, she's known all around the world. We played Sweden last year and we still keep in touch with them [the Swedish players]. They know Suzanne and how she curls. You read something in the paper and you say, 'Jeez, that's my daughter.' Just a little girl from a little town and here she is known right around the world. It's a nice feeling."

Spirits are sinking perceptibly for the Canadian women as the game wears on. Missed opportunities by Suzanne Gaudet and her mates lead to a succession of minor gains for the Swedes. Having relinquished the lead in the calamitous fifth end, the reigning champions fall farther behind and the match is growing beyond their powers of recovery. While the number of hoots and hollers from the partisan crowd diminishes somewhat, the roar of the rocks is relentless. Twenty teams in full flight, young men and women, all of them possessed by soaring hopes of a world championship.

On the far wall, hanging over the heads of Scotland's Tartan Army, is the commemorative banner that acknowledges one of this club's most savoured curling achievements. "Proud Home of the 1994 World Men's Curling Champions," it declares. Rick Folk, the man who led the way that year, is casually attired in a cardigan he might wear to curl in as he quietly checks on all the little details. As the co-chairman of the tournament, he leaves nothing to chance and revels in an atmosphere where athletes from around the world can submerge themselves in the game he loves.

"I've thoroughly enjoyed this because you can add something to events knowing that you have played in them. You can make things happen from a player's perspective," says Rick Folk. "It's neat to watch all these young players developing. Some might come back for five or ten more Canadian championships. Some might never come back so you want the event to be the best it possibly can be. You want to provide conditions that allow them to play their best and to have the finest teams move on. It helps their curling careers."

Rick Folk's career is as close to legendary as can be found in all of curling. But in addition to public triumphs, there were solitary days at the Nutana Curling Club on Saskatoon's Main Street. There Folk, the son of a furrier, honed his craft and paid his dues to a game where accepted, almost ritualistic practices endure. "The game itself drew me in," Rick says. "I have early memories of my dad taking me out to watch the city Brier playdowns in Saskatoon. I was really young, six, seven, or eight years old. I would watch and he would explain what was going on. He would tell me that I should copy some of the guys that

The elder Folks: Rick Folk's curling ancestors (his father, Alex Folk, is far right)

were out there. They were some of the best in the world, my father would say, and it kind of got me hooked."

Rick Folk treasures the long road he travelled to get to the top and the valuable lessons he learned along the way. "It's the way it's played and what it stands for," he concludes about curling itself. "I used to take a rubber boot with me to school. The other kids went out and played hockey. I'd walk through the alley to the Nutana Curling Club and don this rubber boot and still have one slippery shoe on which to slide. I'd bug the ice maker until he'd let me out there. That's the part of the game that I like. You kind of have to cut your teeth so it shows that you have a determination to stick to it."

Folk's victory at the 1980 Brier was a milestone for Saskatchewan. It put him in select company, which included the famous curling Richardson brothers, and solidified his popularity throughout the province. But even though Folk won the world championship that same season the title guaranteed nothing over the long haul. "I really believe that our Brier champion has to be the guy who starts right at his club and goes through the same things that everyone else does," he says. "The year after we won, on January 2, we started our club playdowns with sixty-five other teams and we never made it out. We were defending world champions and when our city playdowns came we were just watching."

Nothing is taken for granted, but prestige comes with curling stardom in parts of this country and Rick Folk knows that all too well. After the 1980 successes at the Brier and on the world stage, he was elected to the provincial legislature and served a term as the minister of Sport and Culture in the Progressive Conservative government of Grant Devine. Holding office meant closing his curling shop, trying to live another kind of life. But Folk couldn't shake the lure of competition and what it meant to be a champion from the prairie province. "There was something about that first time I put on the Saskatchewan sweater, the first year we even won the high school championship," Rick fondly remembers. "It ran tingles down my spine, there's no doubt about that. Every time after that when we won a provincial men's title and then put on our Saskatchewan sweaters at the Brier, that purple heart, it was hard to describe, it was an unbelievable feeling."

1968 high school champs of Saskatchewan (skip Rick Folk is far left)

Folk ran for re-election in 1986 and was defeated. Then in an effort to re-establish himself in the sport, he pulled up stakes and moved to Kelowna where he opened Folk's Golf and Curling, a modest shop on Pandosy Street in the heart of the community. I had stopped by the store on my way to the Kelowna Curling Club and noticed among the racks of sports attire, brooms, and shoes, a clock in the shape of a curling stone, "Rock-Tock" it said. A picture of Rick's 1980 world champions was tucked inside the front door, and plastered to the window was a flyer for an upcoming Saskatchewan reunion to be held in Vernon, B.C. It was obvious that Rick Folk's ties to home had not been severed.

In the 1989 Brier, while curling for British Columbia, Folk was involved in an incident that solidified his reputation as a fierce defender of the rules of the game. Late in a match with Manitoba, and directly in front of the rabid fans from that province, a Manitoba rock was clearly kicked, or burned. Members of the Manitoba team were willing to let it slide but Rick Folk and his team were not. Folk walked out in front of the disbelieving crowd and removed the stone from play. "I had to go out and do it," he stresses. "There were about ten thousand people there and we happened to be playing right beside the Manitoba section. To say the least, they didn't like it but it had to be done. All the way along, part of curling has been the act of self-policing and the notion that you should call it yourself. But if you don't then the other team has to do it. I feel strongly about that."

Folk went on to win another Brier as the skip of British Columbia in 1994. The banner that hangs on the wall here in Kelowna is a constant reminder of the so-called Super Team that assembled under the Saskatchewan native's leadership. The squad included elite curlers Pat Ryan, Bert Gretzinger, Gerry Richard, and the fifth player Ron Steinhauer. This was a team that could have won a lot of money had curling

Folk's curling corner in Saskatoon: The first store

Rick Folk's Brier and world champions, 1980

been a professional sport and had the prizes on the cash-spiel circuit been more lucrative. Rick Folk was a determined competitor who gave no quarter—he suffered each loss as if it were his first and only setback. "The way I grew up in curling was very intense," he admits. "It means a lot to me, win or lose a game, to be able to sit down and be comfortable afterwards that I gave it my best effort. My dad taught me that. Win or lose, feel good about the way you play."

Folk feels more relaxed now. He still curls but seems to relish the place he's carved out for himself as a role model for the next generation of great players. It's not an expression of vanity but of responsibility to a game reliant on its honourable past. He is not a swaggering man and few people pay Rick Folk much attention. He's just another onlooker, a respected sage watching the talent develop. Curling is a game, Rick Folk helps me understand, where the past has its place in the unlimited potential of the future.

Rick points out the game between Japan and Russia on Sheet D. He focuses on the exploits of a twelve-year-old named Kazuki Sishihata, representing the Minami Furano Curling Club. "It's fabulous; where else can you get a twelve-year-old out there against a twenty-one-year-old and holding his own? Who knows, in eight years' time we could be watching him as the skip of Japan dominating at the world level. We can say we saw that guy in Kelowna and he was good." This is the vision of Rick Folk. The game is growing and the seeds are taking early root.

Even at this level, curling is not all fun and games. The juniors engaged in this international competition are ambassadors for their countries and shoulder the often heavy weight of expectation. Things are deteriorating for the Suzanne Gaudet rink in the late ends and soon there will not be enough rocks left to catch up to Sweden. The loyal supporters who have not strayed from their positions beside the ice slump back in their seats. While Hammarstrom, the Swedish flag bearer, is up to his old tricks, the wind has clearly gone out of the Islanders' sails. It's 8–3 for Sweden after nine ends, and the Canadians, having given up hope of finishing in first place, make an early move to shake hands with their rivals. This is not the way the home team wanted to finish the elimination round of the bonspiel, but the champions are cornered, if only for the time being, into an act of concession. It seems strange that Gaudet and her group would not fight until the mathematical possibility of victory was erased. Perhaps in curling it's not the way. The

lesson here is that supremacy on the day is to be acknowledged and applauded. In this sport, humility is accepted
early in one's competitive life.

There are tears, particularly on the part of the youngest
of the Canadian players. Kelly Higgins is almost incon-
solable. After the handshakes, she rushes from the ice and
sobs with her back turned to the others. They give her room
and in time Noel Gaudet embraces the seventeen-year-old.
The calming effect is immediate.

"I think it's great to be where we are," Kelly Higgins says
once she has composed herself. "I feel very honoured to do
so well and especially to start at such a young age. I was only
thirteen when I went to my first national championship and

Mending broken hearts: Noel Gaudet and Kelly Higgins

that's pretty young. I am very, very happy that we have done so well."

She reflects on the support she's received from the student body of her high school back home, where along the corridors they've posted signs bearing her likeness in recognition of what she and her teammates have brought to the community of Summerside. "I think it means so much," she says. "They are supposed to be making a statue of us and they're putting it downtown to honour us." Kelly's eyes widen behind her spectacles and she looks very much like a kid. It's as if her status as a world champion and her estimation of herself are strangely opposed. She's obviously still learning the ropes and at times, it's all a little overwhelming.

"It feels great when you do it right," Kelly figures. "You just look at Suzanne and she says, 'Nice shot!' It's the best feeling in the world. When you don't make the shot you don't have a good feeling. You feel kind of lonely and like you let your team down. I love it when we are all happy, playing well and everything is good. We are unbeatable when we are all happy and laughing."

Tonight is not one of those times for the rink from Summerside. Kelly Higgins has come to grips with that. With a brave face, the lead for the world champions reflects on the wise leadership to be found in the ranks of her squad and the reason why the skip holds the position of prominence she does. "Suzanne makes the great shots and she knows the strategy," Higgins says of Gaudet. "It's like she thrives on the pressure. It doesn't bother her at all."

In the aftermath of the game, Suzanne Gaudet makes her way toward the small scrum of reporters that inevitably await a Canadian skip at events like this. They are present,

Grace under fire: Suzanne Gaudet answers all questions

win or lose, and seem endlessly curious about errant rocks and missed opportunities. The stoic Gaudet shrugs her shoulders at the suggestion that the loss to Sweden might be considered an upset. "They've been around for years and they're a great team," she counters one reporter's query. "Other countries are getting better and better every year. But Canadians are still the greatest."

Even at age twenty, she doesn't give much away. She's practical and tempers the expectations she carries with a no-nonsense approach to every big match. "I feel like the favourite every time I step on the ice as the world champion," she states unequivocally. "I think as a team we are supposed to feel like that. I also think that we have a better-than-average chance to win every time we play. I hope that's what people who watch us think too."

It's not quite bravado but Suzanne Gaudet oozes confidence. "We have worked hard to do this," Gaudet says. "We've worked as hard as anyone from anywhere else would have worked, say, from Ontario or Alberta. We are very happy and honoured by what we've done."

Some observers have called Gaudet one of the most promising talents, male or female, in the world of curling. She's put together a tremendous string of successes in her short career. Her remaining ambitions include winning the Scott Tournament of Hearts and an Olympic gold medal. She even harbours hopes that someday she might modestly cash in on her enormous talent. "Later on I'd love to win more money," she admits brightly. "Hockey players and football players make millions and curling is growing tremendously in terms of the number of fans. It only makes sense. The priority right now is just to be able to do well and play well and win. I'd still just like to be able to win because that feels best of all."

In a sea of curlers from all over the world, the youthful skip from Canada is seen as the prime prospect. Unlike a young hockey star, though, there will be no lucrative contract to help secure her dreams. She will go out into the wider field of competition armed with few tools other than a soft touch, a keen sense of strategy, and an ability to handle enormous expectations. Once she gets to that bigger stage, she will be on her own and all that will count is the maturity she has gained while paying her dues.

"We love the support. Having our family and friends here makes us feel great," Suzanne Gaudet acknowledges. "But I'm not scared to play anybody. I'm a competitive person and I want to do well. There is no room to be scared. I just don't think you can be."

As I watch her walk away from the reporters and toward the throng of curlers who are simultaneously her friends and rivals, I wonder what Suzanne is thinking. Is it about the loss she's just suffered or the sudden-death game she'll have to play against the United States tomorrow? Perhaps thoughts of continuing to grow in the game are most important to her now. "I wouldn't trade this for anything," she says to me. "No way!" After pausing to accept condolences from two-time world champion Rick Folk, Suzanne disappears into the crowd and I feel sure she is plotting her next move en route to yet another victory.

Making my way out of the Kelowna Curling Club late that evening, I duck into an open door just beside the main entranceway. In the centre of the kitchen, I spot Bill MacPhee and Noel Gaudet, both clad in aprons, getting set to dump numerous bags of shellfish into a vat of boiling water. "It's Canada Night tonight," says Bill. Noel's eyes gleam and he rubs his hands together. "A hundred pounds of P.E.I. mussels and a bunch of salmon from the west coast!" he confirms, with great satisfaction. "We're having a little party!"

The elders are putting on a meal for the young folk and for now the stress of competition simmers on the back burner. This is the way things are done in curling—these time-honoured traditions. I'm told it's been like this since anyone can remember.

*The elders plan a feast: Noel Gaudet and Bill MacPhee in the
kitchen on Canada Night*

Prince Edward Island's largest curling rink: The six-sheet Silver Fox Curling Club in Summerside

CHAPTER NINE

THE ISLAND WAY

I FIRST WENT TO PRINCE EDWARD ISLAND IN THE
mid-1980s to work on a supper-hour news and current
affairs show *Compass*. Very soon after my arrival, I was able to
secure the position of sports reporter, a designation of some
import on the Island. I quickly learned that most of P.E.I.'s
110,000 or so residents could not have cared less about the
National Football League or Major League Baseball. Instead
they craved news of action much closer to home. They lived
and died with the fortunes of hockey's Charlottetown Abbies
and Tignish Aces. They anxiously waited on the results from
the Charlottetown Driving Park, the dirt oval where harness
horses like Angel's Shadow and Rev Your Engine trotted and
paced, racing toward an elusive track record, which in my day
stood at a miraculous one minute, fifty-eight and four-tenths
of a second. From Souris in the east to Miminegash in the
west, these were the kinds of stories that mattered.

During my time on *Compass*, I learned to delight in the
understated majesty of the standardbred horses and the "Old

Home Week," a gathering that concluded with the presentation of the revered Gold Cup and Saucer. Every year, ten thousand Islanders made the pilgrimage to witness the late-summer race steeped in tradition. I also celebrated the heated intensity of Island junior hockey where the games were played in matchbox houses and the cigarette smoke hovered in a thick, blue cloud over the ice. I even came to grips with the insanity of stock car racing over the crimson clay loop in a place called Oyster Bed Bridge.

I did, however, receive more calls to cover curling than anything else. "The Canadian Postal Championships are going on up here in O'Leary, boy," someone would point out. "How about doing a special on that? There are rinks here from all over the country including Upper Canada!" Several such requests came to my attention. I wasn't getting enough curling on the air and the locals gently warned that I had better get my act together. Admittedly, I did spend some time in curling rinks following the likes of Peter Gallant, who challenged for the Canadian Mixed title in the mid-eighties, and Kim Dolan, the provincial women's champion whose family owned the Old Dublin Pub, a favourite watering hole in the capital city. Still, I stubbornly resisted most of the pleas from curling fans. Perhaps because I had "come from away," I just couldn't understand how close the game was to their hearts.

There is something special about being a Prince Edward Islander, and unless your kin actually comes from the tiny landmass floating in the Gulf of St. Lawrence, it's difficult to claim the intangible status of citizenship. "I feel like an Islander," I told a man named Roddy Pratt, after I had been on the Island for a couple of months. Pratt was the father of one of our camera operators, a curler from a small place in the eastern part of the Island called St. Peters, and, at the time, the Minister of Fisheries. "Boy, if you were born on the ferry boat ten feet off the shore at Borden and your mother was herself third generation from Summerside," he bellowed, "you would still never be an Islander!"

On a regular basis, though, I did reach many Islanders in the intimacy of their living rooms, and after a while, I was able earn the status of a respected immigrant. Eventually, I was made an honorary Islander, complete with an Order in Council bearing the impressive official seal of the Chief Justice of the Province of Prince Edward Island, himself a long-standing member of the Charlottetown Curling Club. When I left the Island for Montreal and the chance to work on *Hockey Night in Canada*, I felt like I was leaving home. But, in retrospect, I cannot deny that I didn't get enough curling on the air. If the truth is told, I opted for what I knew best, which was hockey. I can't help but think that had I spent more time in the seven curling clubs—from Alberton up west, to Montague in the east—I might have learned a lot more about what it means to be a real Islander.

The curling rinks of the Island are found at the major intersections of the key settlements, and you can visit them all in a few hours, just as you can drive the length of the Island in a leisurely afternoon, completing the trip in not much more time than it would take to travel from Toronto to Ottawa. In spite of its size, the province has a complexity all its own. There are pockets of affluence and hardship, counties where those of Scottish descent dominate the population and contrasting French-speaking villages where Acadian culture flourishes. Some places are dependent on the sea for their survival, others on the land. The Island has its jealousies and its rivalries and seems at times to be a miniature reflection of the country itself, and the curling rinks here are a testament to that notion.

The largest is in Summerside, Prince Edward Island's second city. The Silver Fox Curling and Yacht Club boasts six sheets of ice and is one of only four in the entire Maritime region that can make that claim. The Silver Fox is now more than twenty years old and when I speak to the manager of the place, Carl Delaney, he has a good handle on the burgeoning membership. "Five hundred and fourteen," he says without a moment's hesitation. "When I got there eleven years ago we had about 273. We haven't increased the size of the ice plant and now we have 514. Things like having the world champions in your rink add to the interest of curling."

Delaney is of course referring to the impact Suzanne Gaudet and her team have had since winning the world junior title in 2001. Young people are flocking to the game, and there are now 120 kids in the membership of the Silver Fox. Four afternoons during the week, ice time at the facility is devoted to teenagers and those even younger. At the other end of the demographic pole, the more senior members of the club are also very active. "It's a big thing," Delaney points out. "The retired people get out. Senior curling starts at age fifty and we now have 120 people in that group. It's mushroomed."

Curling in the city of 14,000 goes back to 1926 when the first club was organized. They played the game on frozen outdoor ponds until the purchase of the old Crystal skating rink moved proceedings indoors. The old barn lasted until 1948 when, in the spring of that year, the community approved and then broke ground on a new building that would house three sheets of artificial ice and cost the princely sum of $55,000. From its very beginnings, curling has reached every level of Summerside's society. Early in the going, the ladies curling league became a lynchpin of the association, while the R.C.A.F. station at nearby St. Eleanors sent a contingent thirty strong. The Summerside rink, along with its counterpart in Charlottetown, became the first clubs in the Atlantic region to introduce high school curling for boys.

Now the Silver Fox is attached to a yacht club and is, according to Carl Delaney, the only non-profit community complex of its kind in the world. Here, you can curl as much as you like throughout the year for the grand sum of $293 and moor your thirty-foot sailboat for $800 a season. That berth includes access to cable television and a high-speed Internet connection. At the threshold of Summerside's harbour, the Silver Fox has become one of the busiest places in town, serving as a social centre in the non-curling months.

This season, which is rapidly coming to a close, has been an active one at the club. The Silver Fox hosted the Canadian Postal Curling Championship and the Canadian Police Championship. Though modest affairs by the standards of Canada's larger urban centres, both bonspiels enjoyed full representation from the ten provinces as well as the territories.

For the coming years, the Silver Fox has its energies focused on a chance to host the World Junior Curling Championships. The proposition, once considered impossible for a community this size, is a reflection of the city's ambition as expressed through the curling club. "As you know, we held the 2002 Canadian junior championships in Summerside, and we broke all the records for attendance. We took in over twenty thousand people and we beat cities like Calgary and Moncton. All the big cities in the country and we got more people. We couldn't have written the script any better," Delaney says with confidence. It's a small place but the people in this seaside setting believe curling can be a major proposition. In Summerside the game has found a near perfect ability to draw.

Although I lived in Charlottetown and ventured to Summerside on several occasions, I had never truly been "up west," as the residents of the Island refer to the territory beyond the major centres and in the direction of the North Cape. Up west there are villages bearing exotic handles like Tignish, Anglo Tignish, Seacow Pond, Christopher Cross, and Skinner's Pond, the hamlet where Stompin' Tom Connors spent much of his childhood. Then there is Alberton, the major centre of West Prince County. I admit that I've never before been this far from Charlottetown and still been on Island soil. It's a mere 143 kilometres by car and I once thought of it as a world away.

The Western Community Curling Club is the smallest of the Island's rinks. Due to a recent addition it now has three sheets of ice. For the longest time, though, it had been a magical two-sheet barn reminiscent of the facilities found on the prairie. Driving through the little town, I make a stop at the Irving gas station to get directions to the rink. "Well, she's right there, mister," says the friendly attendant. "Looks like you finally made her up here after all these years, eh? It's that big yellow building right there." He points to a

brightly painted clap-
board house. A small sim-
ple sign in the middle of
the front façade reads
"Curling Club" in bold
letters and is framed by
familiar crossed brooms.

Inside Pete Larter is
working with the local
school kids who curl at
the rink in the after-
noons. Retired after thirty-
five years of service with
the Island Telephone
Company, Larter volun-
teers his time at the club.
"Started curling when I
retired from Island Tel,"
he offers. "Now I can't get
enough of it. By the way,

*The Western Community Curling Club on the
main drag in Alberton, PEI.*

about forty years ago the club got into money problems and
they went to the town of Alberton for financial help. The
town bailed them out but they had written into the agreement that as long as there was a curling rink here, the school
kids could play for nothing."

It's a strikingly informal setting and the three sheets of
frozen pebble are buzzing with youngsters sliding over their
length. John Sentner is in his first year as the club president. His grandmother Isobel Clarke was an original share-
holder when the building was erected in the early 1960s.
"We have a tremendous turnover in terms of membership,"

Sentner says, with a slight sigh. "They'll stay for four or five years, leave the game and then they'll come back after a time away. We seem to be stuck at about seventy-five to eighty adult members."

It's not a bad total when you consider the town of Alberton is barely 1,200 people. But Sentner tries to cast the club's net out to the wider community with a population of about sixteen thousand. "We would like to get a hundred adult members," Sentner claims. What makes him happiest are adults who come through the doors having never curled before. This year the Western Community Curling Club had fifteen such customers, which is considered a major victory. The number of kids curling has been consistently strong—there are sixty-five in the youth group—proof of curling's popularity with teenagers in this part of the country.

Curling in Alberton dates back to the period just before World War Two. Former New Brunswicker W.P. Keenan interested a group of eight men in the purchase of eight sets of stones. They played on the local skating rink in the afternoons and over the course of a decade the membership grew to forty curlers. Competition was held on a single sheet of natural ice housed in the original arena until 1953. Then, according to local historians, "a new rink with two sheets of ice and commodious social quarters was built." Despite the suggestion of grandeur, the club was an intimate and close-knit association of curlers, and the building was in keeping with the spirit of the sportsmen and women who inhabited it.

Still, the modest rink, the largest building in Alberton, dominates the main drag of town. With the third playing lane now in operation and the installation of a new artificial ice plant, the length of the curling season has been extended, starting in the second-last week of October and wrapping up at the end of March. "A lot of farmers and fishermen are members of the club and they don't want to be tied up with curling come spring," John Sentner points out. "It's a very seasonal sport and that's perfect for the kind of economy that operates around here."

There is proud tradition at the club, and this past year they sent the provincial representatives to the Dominion Legion Championships. Their hallmark tournament remains strong. "No question the biggest event that we have every year is the fisherman's bonspiel," John Sentner says. "It's called the Blue Book Bonspiel. When it first began here only the captains of fishing boats could take part. In order to enter you had to show your blue book. Each captain had his licence bound in such a book. Now, in recent years they've opened up the bonspiel to other rinks and the result has been an annual entry of twenty-five to thirty teams in mid-February."

This universality is the key to the longevity of the curling rink in Alberton. To have remained a closed society offering privileges only to the select few would surely have spelled the end of it.

"Our bonspiels are always open to the public. Doesn't matter if you're a member of the club or not," Sentner concludes. "We figure if we can get them through the door for one weekend then we have a pretty good chance that they will join us." All he needs are fifteen more members to reach his goal of an even one hundred—that and the resilience of those who might have once considered straying. It sounds a lot to me like the ebb and flow of the

The Maple Leaf Curling Club in O'Leary: A shed by the bleachers of the ball field

population in Atlantic Canada. Like the region itself, curling may be a place you have to leave to fully appreciate it upon your inevitable return.

O'Leary is barely fifteen minutes down the road from Alberton, to the south and east—inland on the Island. Here the soil is as brick red as I have ever seen it and the potato trucks, laden with seed, crisscross the highway. This is spud country to be sure, and a sign on the road just before you pull up at the Maple Leaf Curling Club heralds the upcoming O'Leary Potato Packers Yukon Gold Fun Spiel. This tournament will bring the curtain down on the club's twenty-fifth anniversary season and they're expecting more than forty teams from all over the Island in early April. In spite of the local flavour of its title, the most successful annual gathering in this small corner of the world is sponsored by the provincial police.

From the outside, this rink is as unremarkable as most—board and batten with a peaked roof and a small awning over an anonymous white door. It's what's behind the fascia that is so reflective of the surrounding settlement. There are four sheets of ice, enclosed by a galvanized corrugated dome, which looks a lot like the elongated potato sheds found throughout Prince Edward Island. It's a building nestled beside the local ball diamond in the middle of a farmer's field, it's a structure that melds naturally with the landscape.

"The curling club provides exercise and fellowship," Debbie DeLong says. She's the president of the board of directors that oversees the operation of the building and everything that goes on within its metallic walls. "You pull your hair out wondering where the money is coming from sometimes," she laments. "There was a time ten or fifteen years ago when the club got into financial difficulty and some people paid a good chunk to save it. We made them lifetime members. They're probably just breaking even now in terms of what they've paid and how much they've curled."

Indeed, the Maple Leaf Curling Club has a dozen aging patrons who once anted up as much as $1,500 to curl for life. In the process they helped save a community institution and have seen it cling to life through some rough times. "Back then you had nothing else to do but go to the curling club," Debbie recalls. "Now there's so much to do for everyone with hockey and everything else. A couple, for instance, they both need jobs to make ends meet. There's just not enough time for curling."

The club's not what it once was. Membership's down to a group of about 150 but they have made adjustments to accommodate the maturing population of their town. "We've just undergone a renovation and become wheelchair accessible," DeLong points out. "We're assuming the rink will become more like a community hall."

The most revered member of the Maple Leaf Club and an almost mythical figure in these parts is a country doctor by the name of George Dewar. Debbie informs me that Dr. Dewar, at the age of eighty-seven, still curls four days a week. Once a member of the legislative assembly and a companion of the Order of Canada, he credits clean living and moderation with his longevity. "Dr. Dewar says curling is one of the best things that you can do for your health," Debbie preaches. "We had a testimonial dinner for him at the club and it was our best fundraiser ever. We had about 125 people because that's all we could hold. We took in $2,500 and cleared about $2,000 of that."

Debbie DeLong is an apt representative of her club's eclectic membership. She does a little bit of this and a little bit of that and works in a local bakery to supplement her income. She's been living in O'Leary for only a dozen years, having made her way to the Island from Saint John, New Brunswick. "I didn't curl back there, I bowled," Debbie says. "When I came to O'Leary there wasn't a bowling alley nearby but there was a curling rink so I came back to the game. I had once curled in the intramural league at Mount Allison University in Sackville."

Now she's hooked again and has made pilgrimages to the

The serenity of the Crapaud Curling Club on the Trans Canada Highway

world championships when they were held at Harbour Station in Saint John a few years ago and also to the most recent Brier in Halifax. "I just love sports," she enthuses. "Robert Campbell, the Islander who finished last, almost beat Randy Ferbey the last day. Just about anything can happen, you know." I reckon the continued existence of the Maple Leaf Curling Club proves she's right.

Halfway between the two large centres of Summerside and Charlottetown and just off the undulating Trans Canada Highway, is the Crapaud Community Curling Club. You can't miss it, the parking lot's huge and the building is stark white against the emerald green of the lawn surrounding it. A stylized maple leaf and the number 1967 are carved into the cornerstone of the foundation marking the curling rink's creation in Canada's centennial year. It serves a population of just under a thousand people, if you count the development over the next hill, and is as active as any on the Island.

The club in Crapaud (a French word meaning toad) is known for extending the curling season in these parts. In the warmer weather, Russ Howard, the former Brier champion, has come over from New Brunswick to play in the odd bonspiel, and rising superstar Suzanne Gaudet has used the ice for practice sessions. "The Summer Spud is our claim to fame," says the manager, Carolyn Lowther. "Inevitably we have it on the hottest weekend of the year. It'll be 34 degrees out and almost everyone is on the ice running around in their shorts."

The Summer Spud bonspiel was launched more than thirty years ago by one of the more successful farmers in the area, a man by the name of Alan Robinson. They flood the rink in the middle of August and invite between forty and fifty teams from the Maritimes, Ontario, and the eastern seaboard of the United States. It started out as a gathering of Robinson's business acquaintances and has developed into a tradition for off-season curling. Participants golf for a day and then curl for three. The funds raised have, on occasion, been in excess of ten thousand dollars and have helped finance the club's activities in the regular season.

"Sometimes it's the only ice on the Island," Paul Noonan confirms. He's one of the nine members on the board of directors. The first mate on a ferry boat that runs between the south shore of New Brunswick and the tiny Island of Grand Manan, Noonan lives in Borden, which is about twenty minutes from Crapaud. This curling rink has become a seafarer's tie to the land. "We provide a place for people to come to," he says. "Sometimes they just come to play cribbage. Heck, I probably know more people in Crapaud than I do in Borden."

Noonan doesn't get a cent for his efforts to keep the club's membership of about 130 busy and happy in the immaculate rink. Its interior walls of richly panelled wood literally gleam. The four lanes of ice will glisten deep into April each year. "We call that final bonspiel the Crapaud Meltdown," Paul says, eager to impress. "It gets our name out there but you know we've always had a name for having good ice."

House-proud, that's the aura that surrounds the community curling club in Crapaud. It sits by itself but assumes a huge place in the lives of the people who frequent it. It's a concert hall; Wayne Rostad of *On the Road Again* fame loves playing at this venue. It's also become a drop-in centre for young people who want to gather and play pool in the middle of the summer. "We use it for community school. We've used it for meetings on the watershed. We use it for everything," Carolyn Lowther says.

Lowther is barely thirty and brings absolutely no curling qualifications to her job as the manager, one that she's held for just about two years. Until she came back to the Island from the other side of the country, she had played a total of four matches in her life and admits to taking the club for granted in many ways. Having graduated with a diploma in business administration from the Island's community college, she went to the opposite coast, to Vancouver Island to work for a time on the Social Planning and Research Council of British Columbia. Carolyn had taken part in environmental assessment and community developmental projects before she gave in to the tug to come home. On her return, she applied to be the first full-time manager of the Crapaud Curling Club.

"I was coming back to the Island and this job came open," she says. "I thought it was an ideal way to come home and reconnect myself with my community." As a young woman who considers herself a curling outsider, Lowther had to adapt in a hurry. "Someone would phone to ask the score in a bonspiel and I had no clue what to say," she recalls. As manager she has "55,000 functions to perform." She must take regular shifts tending bar, scheduling ice times, and overseeing a rash of little kids' birthday parties (taking youngsters curling has become a popular thing to do). Lowther tackles each task with vim and vigour, all the while reminded of the important position she now holds in the day-to-day life of Crapaud and its surroundings.

"In the last two years we've seen a marked improvement." Paul Noonan praises the young manager. "Carolyn has done an outstanding job and there were a lot of hours that she has put into this place that she didn't get paid for. The result has been that this is as nice as any club on the Island."

"One day I found myself pebbling the ice, which I had never done before," Carolyn tells me. "An older gentleman watched me very carefully and when I was done he came over and actually congratulated me. 'You know, young lady, I've been curling for thirty-five or forty years and I've never seen a woman pebble the ice. You did a very good job.' I felt as if I had made it."

Paul Noonan is pleased to report that because of good times in Crapaud the board of directors will be able to raise the hourly wage they pay to part-time bartenders at the club and Carolyn's salary has been modestly hiked. For her part, Lowther has taken a job at Canada Customs but hopes to retain her duties at the curling club on a part-time basis. "I've learned so much but sometimes you have to go where the money is," she says. "Not that money is everything but it's nice to have a little in your pocket."

Carolyn's family goes back many generations on the Island and her involvement with the club connects her to that history. "The club's been a central place for as long as I can remember," she admits. "Someone once told me if you want to learn what the community is really like, then go spend some time at the curling rink. I've done that and now when people call during a bonspiel, at least I can tell them what the score is."

Heading to the east and just before you cross the North River into the outskirts of Charlottetown, you travel through Cornwall. It is often considered to be a suburb of the capital, but the locals resist that classification. It wasn't until the early eighties that the residents here banded together to get a recreational facility of their own. The curling club in this smallish town has come to represent a form of modest independence from the influence of the big city. The four-sheet rink

The Cornwall Curling Club: Independence for Charlottetown's suburb

attached to the Cornwall Civic Centre, financed through a
federal grant, a loan from the village, and funds raised by club
members themselves, is something of Cornwall's own making—a place where local heroes will be made.

Heidi MacLean's been the duty manager at the Cornwall
Curling Club for the last four years and performs most of the
administrative functions for the full-time manager, Gordie
Lank. "He's a Conservative, you know," she whispers in reference to the former MLA who is now her boss. Politics has
always been an obsession on the Island, perhaps the most
hotly contested of all sports. Tories and Grits still dominate
the vast majority of discussions at gas stations and water cool-
ers, and the drama of provincial elections, as I distinctly recall,
is met with greater anticipation than overtime hockey games
or a photo finish down at the Charlottetown Driving Park.

I had originally hoped to touch base with the manager,
Lank, or the club's president, Derek MacEwan. "Why
would you need to talk to them?" Heidi asks the question in
a singsong sort of way. "I know just as much if not more
about what goes on around here."

The Cornwall club wasn't even imagined until 1979 when
the then village commission committed itself to develop
recreational facilities for the growing population. The curling
rink was to perform a modest function—it would be an
arena for those interested in a social game and there would
be emphasis on cultivating new and junior curlers.

In its first years the club suffered from a lack of ice-making
experience. The wooden planks on the walls and ceiling
failed to absorb as much humidity as was intended and there
was a struggle to find the exhaust contraptions that would
ensure the surface hardened. Cracks appeared and the surface

was uneven, even though an old ice-burner from O'Leary had been purchased to free the Cornwall club from its dependence on ice makers from Crapaud and Montague.

In spite of these difficulties, the club, sustained on an entirely volunteer basis, grew. But in the early nineties participation dropped severely. There was too much work to do and people had too little time to pursue their everyday lives, curl, and care for the rink. With ownership came too heavy a burden of responsibility.

The board of directors staged a major recruitment drive and hired paid staff to look after the duties of managing the place, making the ice, and perhaps most importantly, running the bar. With the pressure of the day-to-day operation of the club lifted from their shoulders, members were able to enjoy playing the game. Today, Cornwall has a registration of 110 junior and 280 adult curlers, making it the third largest fellowship of its kind in the province.

"It seems to be an up-and-coming thing these days," Heidi MacLean is proud to report. The club's duty manager lists off a series of bonspiels that begins in mid-October with the Transition Spiel where members golf for half a day then put away their clubs to hit the ice. Included on the calendar are the P.E.I. Firefighters Championships, the Cavendish Agro Farmer's Spiel, and the Countryview Golf Closing Spiel on the last weekend of March. Before the ice is taken out, the "L'il Rockers" have their skating party, and in May there will be the annual meeting of the club's membership and an awards night. Reviewing the week-by-week schedule at the Cornwall Curling Club is like taking a peek at the date book of an entire town. There are special occasions marked—sleigh rides, "the silly Olympics," car rallies,

Busy times at Cornwall's community-run rink

golf tourneys, dances, parties, and regular trivia contests. It is very clear that the curling club has become the way for a large number of people here to organize their social lives and remain in their own surroundings. This is not just a curling club—it is the clubhouse of the community. It's been worth the time and effort everyone's put into it.

Cornwall has also produced Island champions in its short history, including Nancy Coffin, Mark Kinney, Tyler Mackenzie, and Meghan Hughes. The junior ranks at this club have yielded some of the best curlers in the province, perhaps a dividend of the annual free curling school that operates on the last weekend of October. It's not a competitive history to rival Summerside's or Charlottetown's, but then again the rink at Cornwall wasn't made for that purpose only. It's nice to have representatives who can carry the name of your town further afield. Here, though, it's much more important to have a place where families can go to be together.

"You can rent the whole arena for $110 for two hours," Heidi points out. When I hear that, I envision inviting thirty-one of my favourite friends and conducting a private bonspiel. It couldn't be done where I come from, not for hockey, curling, or anything else. There was a time when the people of Cornwall had to go somewhere else and use somebody else's ice if they wanted to play among themselves.

"It's our place." Heidi MacLean sounds not only like the administrative secretary of the icehouse but its protective mother. "It's a place we can call our own."

In Montague there exists the eastern outpost of curling in Prince Edward Island. It is a house of four sheets that has descended from a one-lane ice building once attached to an ancient skating rink. The Montague Curling Club was first organized in 1927 and, for a time, dominated the competitive ranks of the sport in this province. In 1936, teams from here made a clean sweep of the Island's most revered prizes, winning the MacArthur Trophy, the Gaboury Trophy, and the British Consols Trophy.

Montague's club had an original membership of twenty-four interested citizens and grew steadily through succeeding decades as it moved into a two-sheet facility in 1949 and welcomed the arrival of artificial ice in 1955. The new club, with its clapboard and peaked roof, looks like the other smaller rinks on the Island and was completed in 1979. There are a total of 222 adults, juniors, and seniors on the roster at Montague.

The eastern part of Prince Edward Island has seen tough times in the recent past. The ship-building industry at Georgetown has all but disappeared and now that more people are driving across the Confederation Bridge from New Brunswick to Borden in the western part of the province, the ferry at Wood Islands has become nothing more than novelty. It's tougher to get traffic into the area east of Charlottetown, although golfers are starting to invade the region's growing number of championship courses.

Still, there is a wide and varied group that curls in Montague—agricultural families, fishing families, business and retired people as well as young people from the area. There is a banquet hall that can handle up to a hundred people, and Burke Dyck, the club's manager and a retired R.C.M.P. officer, keeps the room busy by hosting dances, the annual Rotary Club dinner, and the rotating constituency meetings of the local political parties. There's a fashion show that raises funds every year and they cram as many tournaments as they can into a season.

This past year Montague hosted the Lady Scott's at which Suzanne Gaudet won the provincial crown on the way to a brilliant showing in her first Canadian women's championship. The P.E.I. Masters and the annual "Milk Can," the end-of-season gathering named to reflect the dairy industry of the region and attracting thirty-six to forty rinks, were also held here. "We have as many bonspiels as we can," Burke Dyke explains. "It's one way of doing well at the bar, and it helps satisfy the constant need to raise money."

He vows to keep up the fight. If the Montague club ever folded it would mean that curlers would have to get to Charlottetown or Cornwall to engage in their favourite winter passion. For the resilient people of this area that would never do. It would be too much like giving in to the growing urbanization of the province as a whole. Some things are worth preserving.

"I'm pretty competitive," claims Burke Dyck. "I can tell you every member here by name. As long as there's a spot for me to be the manager of this club I'll take it. When they hired me they didn't talk about the length of employment and so far it hasn't been discussed. I'm here to do the best I can."

Outwardly, the most permanent looking of the Island's curling clubs is the one on Euston Street in downtown Charlottetown. The square brick block occupies a place of prominence on the capital city's physical and historical landscape. The curling club was formed in 1887 with a membership of ten men. Now there are 511 members, and what was once a bastion of the clubby elite in a very old Canadian community has evolved into a gathering place for youth and senior citizens, men and women alike.

"Traditionally, this is by far the most competitive club on the Island," Kaye MacFadyen is telling me. She's the fifty-eight-year-old manager of the five-sheet rink and is just finishing up her second season at the helm. "I'm on the three-year plan," she chuckles. "Every day is just a challenge. The ice plant will break down or whatever. The building is in disrepair and I've only blown my stack twice since I've taken the job."

Kaye flips on the lights and the ice sparkles to life. She has opened the door to the club for me not knowing who I am or exactly what it is I'm after. Still, she quickly gets the picture and begins rummaging through her little office, awash with schedules and bills to be paid—trophies are stacked up in the far corner. "There's no formal history of

CHARLOTTETOWN
CENTENNIAL BONSPIEL

MARCH 21st to 26th - 1955

THE CHARLOTTETOWN CURLING CLUB

*Programme from the
centennial bonspiel at the
Charlottetown Club, 1955.*

the place," she mutters to herself. "But a couple of University of Prince Edward Island students once did an essay on the administration of the club."

She hands me a seventeen-page paper authored by April Hicken and Angela Sutherland titled "The Charlottetown Curling Club." A brief sketch reveals that from its beginnings the association of curlers in this town has been dominated by a board of directors with power akin to any elected assembly. At its genesis, this board had as its patron the Lieutenant Governor of the province, and included a minister of religion. The board oversaw the growth of curling in Charlottetown through the first indoor gatherings at the Excelsior rink until it burned down in 1910. There followed fairly unsuccessful attempts to curl on the frozen ice of the harbour and local ponds before a new facility was built on the waterfront just before World War One. Then in 1945 the five-sheet natural-ice palace on Euston Street opened its doors.

In the first sixty years of the club's existence the city's male establishment ruled supreme and membership was not extended to women. It wasn't until 1950 that women were admitted though the board of directors made the conditions of their acceptance very strict. The men would be given priority on the ice, and during bonspiels women would be required to work in the kitchen. Amazingly, it wasn't until 1978, nearly three decades after women began curling in

Charlottetown Centennial Curling Bonspiel
March 21 - 26, 1955
PRIZE LIST

General Motors Products of Canada Limited .... 4 beautiful, 3-piece international silver service, Heritage pattern, and 4 embossed and engraved 20 inch matching coffee trays.

Macdonald Tobacco Company Limited, Montreal. 4 Sheffield plate, heavily embossed and engraved 24 inch coffee trays.

T. Eaton Company (Maritimes) Limited .... 2 Trapper Point blankets; 2 engraved 28 inch coffee trays.

Charlottetown Wholesale Grocers .... 4 chrome plated curlers Desk Lamps, matched plastic shades, matching stone designs.

Maritime Central Airways Limited .... 4 beautiful tri-floor lamps

R. T. Holman Limited .... 4 sets engraved marble book ends decorated with gilt curling stones and crossed brooms. 4 sets, 6 each, ebony tumblers, decorated with sterling silver curling figure, stone and brooms.

W. G. Barbour Limited .... 2 Nat Gordon tartan skirts (pleated) with vests and centennial crests.

Simpson-Sears Limited, Halifax .... 4 engraved old English reproduced copper base trays.

Prowse Bros. Limited .... 4 men's Stetson Hats, any size and shade.

County Construction Company Limited .... 4 large desk brass ash trays with curling figure in center.

Island Construction Company Limited .... 4 attractive large table lamps

A. Pickard & Company Limited .... 4 beautiful table lamps

Robinson Supplies .... 4 travelling electric irons

Moore & McLeod Limited .... 4 men's Vyella tartan shirts with centennial crests

Imperial Oil Company Limited .... 4 large lazy susans

British American Oil Company Limited .... 4 engraved silver butter dishes, curling stone design and 4 attractive men's cuff links.

Henderson & Cudmore Limited .... 4 men's tartan shirts with Centennial crests

Sunter's Ladies' Wear .... 1 lady's Nat Gordon tartan skirt (pleated) with vest and Centennial Crest.

Nat Gordon Inc., 423 Mayor St., Montreal 2 .... 1 lady's tartan skirt with vest and Centennial Crest.

W. W. Wellner Limited .... 4, 1847 Rogers 14 inch silver trays suitably engraved.

Morrison & MacRae, Summerside .... 4 beautiful engraved onyx desk sets with large curling stone emblem |and fitted with modern fountain pens.

Lord Calvert .... 4 forever sharp Sheffield Carving Sets.

V-O .... 8 modern Ronson cigarette lighters.

Ch'town Branch, Canadian Tire Corp. .... 2 Ottawa Valley, 100% Virgin Wool Blankets.

Oland & Son, Halifax .... 4 engraved pewter steins with Centennial Badge brazed on sides.

M. F. Schurman Co. Ltd., Summerside and 4 General Electric Food Mixers, full powered, Charlottetown .... does every mixing job from heavy batters to fluffy meringue.

Bill Dunham, St. Stephen, N.B. .... 4 engraved miniature rose bowls.

Charlottetown, that they were given the vote at board meetings. In a rink that had hosted the Canadian Men's Curling Championship, the Canadian Mixed Curling Championship and the Canadian Ladies Curling Championship, victories for the female membership were won with patience.

Kaye MacFadyen was at one time a provincial fire arms officer and has spent much of her working life in the Island's civil service. Now she runs a curling club, the most historic and arguably the most significant in Prince Edward Island. MacFadyen was one of the first females to sit on the board of directors of the club when she began curling here in the 1980s. Almost in passing she once mentioned to her predecessor, John Likely, himself an Island men's champion who had competed at the Brier, that if he ever left she'd like the job.

Kaye won't deny the challenges she has faced guiding the club through the first years of the new century. "We're always trying to raise money," she says. "That's what the arguments are inevitably about. It's about the facility and how to raise money to fix it. When you deal with a board of directors, you find that people have very different agendas."

Still, Kaye is getting the job done in fine fashion and the place is thriving. There are forty kids at each session of the L'il Rockers, where the smaller twenty-pound stones come into play. The P.E.I. Barspiel is becoming a tradition with thirty taverns from around the Island invading the club to stage a much anticipated year-end celebration. There are commercial leagues, competitive leagues, mixed leagues, leagues of every description and the club is frantic seven days a week over the course of the entire season.

On the way out of the Charlottetown Curling Club, I notice a sign above the driveway. The coat of arms of Prince Edward

Island is flanked by curling brooms and special greetings for a newly married couple. "Congratulations Candace and Robert," it says. This place is at the centre to be sure. It's not what it once was—a fraternal organization, that is. It's open to everyone, and that includes the woman who presides over the board of directors and steers its course. Just like this Island's revered junior champion, Kaye MacFadyen has managed to win a lot of hearts and more than her fair share of allegiance.

At the centre of the community: Wedding greetings for Charlottetown's curlers

By my calculation there are 2,063 registered curlers in a province of not much more than a hundred thousand citizens, proof that curling is blossoming on the Island. The sport has broken through economic barriers, gender discrimination, and regional isolation. The seven rinks on the Island survive because they have embraced one of curling's most fundamental principles: it is a game open to anyone who is willing to play along. I see now that when I lived in this province, a place that guards with such vigilance the distinctiveness of its identity, I might have come closer to a feeling of belonging had I paid more attention to something that matters so much to the Islanders themselves.

The Pied Piper: Guy Hemmings of Quebec at the 1999 Brier in Edmonton

CHAPTER TEN

OUR SECRET HANDSHAKE

THE SPECTACLE OF SPORT HAS A LOT TO DO WITH STAR power. It is the heroic and tragic figures of a game who are essential to securing the lasting loyalty of real and potential fans and to connecting spectators to the story unfolding before them. In curling, as in anything else, there is a need for a charismatic, large-than-life figure capable of lifting the drama off the ice and into the stands.

Guy Hemmings may just be that figure. I can clearly recall two consecutive Briers in the late 1990s that commanded my attention where previous competitions had slipped beyond my notice. At the centre of the championships in Winnipeg in 1998 and at Edmonton's Skyreach Centre a year later was a greenhouse owner from St. Aimé, Quebec. Guy Hemmings was a tomato grower who skipped a rink at the Tracy and Outrement curling clubs in his spare time. He was, when I first saw him, unshaven, and a brilliant cowlick adorned his abundant head of hair. Hemmings spoke a fractured hybrid of English and French that wasn't always decipherable but translated surprisingly well on tele-vision and in the arena. Deep in the heart of curling coun-try, the ultimate outsider was making a splash and quickly becoming the darling of the western crowd.

Down 2–0 after two ends to Ontario's young hotshot Wayne Middaugh in the 1998 Brier final, it was clear Hemmings had also won over veteran play-by-play man Don Wittman. "The fans in the Winnipeg Arena love it. There's a pro-Quebec crowd here in the Manitoba capital, and Guy Hemmings has endeared himself to this gather-ing," Wittman crooned.

Hundreds of banners punctuated the stands. "QUEBEC RULES—GUY ROCKS," "GO GUYBEC GO," even, "HEMMINGS HAIR SALON." The underdog from la Belle Province had them eating out of his hands. "Do you get the feeling that Hemmings has lost both his hairbrush and his razor?" Wittman's question was in keeping with the mood Hemmings's presence had inspired. He was the story and everyone knew it.

"I read that the last time he combed his hair was before his first communion," Sandra Schmirler said from her commentary position. "He didn't even comb it when he got married."

Hemmings came out of the hack in his brilliant, double-blue shirt emblazoned with fleur-de-lis. He pulled the string coming up just short on a draw, thus allowing the big red machine from Ontario to steal a point and a 3–0 lead. Hemmings shook his head, plastered an impish grin back on his face, and rushed to the sideboards to sign autographs. This fellow obviously knew where his bread was buttered.

A thousand instances of Hemmings's charm were sprinkled throughout that Brier final in Winnipeg. His foursome, made up of three French-speaking players and a single anglophone, Dale Ness, the lead, were able to communicate brilliantly, swinging the conversation back and forth between the two languages. "*On reviens*," Hemmings said to Pierre Charette, the vice-skip, in the sixth end, while considering a shot that might cut into a 4–0 Ontario lead. "Juste off nose," he continued for the benefit of Ness, whose expert sweeping would be required to get the rock to exactly the right place.

Hemmings came roaring out of the irons, barking his instructions. The crowd held its collective breath and watched an immaculately conceived double takeout of the Ontario stones stacked ominously in the house. It was what's known as a circus shot, and in the end Quebec had three rocks closest to the button. Suddenly the match stood at 4–3, Ontario's lead reduced to one. The fans were on their feet cheering. "*Guy, Guy, Guy,*" rang through the arena like it once had at the Montreal Forum for hockey legend Guy Lafleur. There was Hemmings bowing to the four corners of the stands like a carnival magician who had just completed a sleight of hand.

In the eighth end, with the Quebeckers down 6–3, a blackout enveloped the stadium. When the generators kicked in and the broadcaster regained power, pictures revealed Guy Hemmings sneaking down to the scoreboard, jokingly putting extra numbers on his side of the ledger. The fans clapped and urged him on—even Middaugh got into the act. The clown prince was making it the most memorable Brier in ages and everyone in the building and watching across Canada was pulling for him in one way or another. "Has the game started yet?" he was overheard saying while posing for a few snapshots rink side as he waited for the lights to go back on. "Tell me when we're curling again."

Ontario won the 1998 Brier by a score of 7–4. But it was a Quebecker who won the allegiance of countless fans across Canada. Flashing his boyish grin, Hemmings waved to the crowd, acknowledging the chant of his name and a prolonged standing ovation. They loved him and it didn't matter where he was from or what language he spoke. He curled with character and in the process became an instant celebrity.

"It's a game, up four or down four—we're still playing curling. It's not a job," Hemmings said in the television interview. His English was far from perfect, but the sentiment was right on the mark. "You gotta enjoy it. And we do enjoy it. The fans are cheering for us and it's tough not to enjoy it."

Hemmings was in the Brier final a year later in Edmonton. Deeper into the Canadian west and the Quebecker's aura had grown exponentially. This time he faced a former world champion, Jeff Stoughton of the Charleswood Club in Winnipeg. Hemmings and his teammates, Dale Ness, Guy Thibaudeau, and Pierre Charette, were underdogs once again. There were some, however, who believed that Montrealers might just become the first Quebec rink to win a Brier since Jim Ursel completed the task in 1977. A victory this time would be even sweeter though. Ursel had been a transplanted Manitoban when he won. Hemmings was well aware that he was the French-Canadian flag bearer for a developing cultural diversity within the game.

Throughout the week's competition, Hemmings culti-
vated support, going out of his way to get the Alberta crowd
on his side. "This is what has endeared Guy Hemmings and
the entire team to the fans of Skyreach," Vic Rauter, the
voice of the championship match, noted. "He's been out
and visiting schools, and despite the fact it's the final he's
still doing what he does best and that's being a friend to anyone who wants an autograph or a picture."

In the early going against Stoughton, Hemmings fared
well. In the sixth end, Hemmings attempted to hit an
opposing stone and run it back onto another, leaving his
own to count. The camera stayed with Hemmings as he
released the granite and slid out beyond the hog line. It was
a narrow miss. The run back removed Quebec's red stone
while Manitoba's yellow stayed to count. After the dust had
cleared, Jeff Stoughton and his rink had a steal of one and a
6–4 lead. Hemmings shook his broom and wailed to the
crowd as his stone was erased. Then he bowed his head and
crawled off the ice on all fours. The mass of supporters
groaned in sympathy. Even in failure, Guy Hemmings was
their hero. Escorted by a man in a big, black cowboy hat,
Hemmings shuffled to the sideboards to dutifully pose and
scrawl his name on T-shirts and pictures. Guy Hemmings's
smile was back, even as another Brier seemed to elude his
reach. A placard just above the spot where he gathered with
his disciples said it all. "GUY! MISTER PERSONALITY!"

He fought back to get one in the seventh end, but that
was as close as Guy Hemmings and Quebec would get to
Manitoba that day. Trailing 9–5 in the tenth and final frame,
Hemmings, in grand curling style, gave up the good fight
and conceded the match. The requisite hugs among the

competitors seemed more genuine this time. One could almost believe that the classy Stoughton had secretly been hoping for Hemmings to sneak out the comeback and win.

The provincial flags of Quebec waved throughout the stands of the huge hockey rink, the home of the NHL's Edmonton Oilers. An enormous scrum of reporters swallowed up Guy Hemmings. Patiently, delightedly, he answered all their queries. "Victor, he's what curling needed," Ray Turnbull, the former champion turned analyst, proclaimed.

"Right you are, Ray," chimed in Rauter. "In the world of curling Guy Hemmings is a true rock star."

After a respectable showing at the Ottawa Brier of 2001 the popular skip put curling aside. He travelled to Niort, France, where he and his wife, Josée, had opportunities in the computer business. The game had lost, for the time being, its most popular and identifiable star and with him a lot of the momentum his presence had built. Curling was determined to get him back.

In the fall of 2001, the Canadian Curling Association made Hemmings an offer he could not refuse. Hemmings signed a three-year contract to act as an ambassador and promoter of the sport across Canada. "The Guy Hemmings Rockin' the House Tour" would take the most popular player in the country to eight cities a season. From Halifax to Kelowna, Hemmings would conduct clinics, visit hospitals, make speeches, and sign autographs. With the sheer power of his personality, the French Canadian would reach beyond the usual patrons of the game, so extending its borders.

"Little did I think when the doors of the Outremont curling centre swung open one frigid Saturday morning in

January that I was embarking on an adventure that would soon take over a good part of my life," the promotional material quotes Hemmings. "That visit to the curling club, which seemed insignificant on the face of it, would subsequently result in career choices being made in later years, affect my family and social life and forever alter my views on the rest of Canada."

The contract's worth was not made public, but it allowed Hemmings to return home with his family of four to curl full-time. In addition to travelling the country he continued to play in cashspiels and in the provincial playdowns with his eye still on the Brier. There was a TV commercial for a broom company, and TSN recruited him to do colour commentary on their curling telecasts. Hemmings was the poster boy for curling—its hope for coast-to-coast, multicultural appeal. About these ideals, the Canadian Curling Association and Guy Hemmings had no qualms at all.

"The sport took me to all corners of my country where I discovered people of all ages in major Canadian cities and far removed places had the same passion, the same life choices, and the same ambitions as I did," Hemmings explained in signing on. "These were people who could get over linguistic or cultural barriers just to share some time on the ice or even become good friends, regardless of age differences, social status, or language. That, in my opinion, is the richness of curling which makes it Canada's true national sport."

The last stop on this, the first year of his tour, is in the far west. Kelowna has warmed to Guy Hemmings and the turnout at the curling club is amazing. More than a hundred youngsters, most with no curling experience at all, await the

The ins and outs of

icon's arrival. The people who are to help with this clinic are stars in their own right: Pat Ryan is a three-time world champion, Bert Gretzinger competed at the Canadian Olympic trials as did Bob Ursel, the son of Quebec's Brier winner. On this occasion they will play a supporting role as the new darling of the game takes centre stage.

Hemmings arrives in jeans, a bomber jacket, and the bed head that has become his trademark. He's lugging around a vat of Tim Horton's coffee and chatters away with an enormously muscled bald man, André Proulx, his handler. If the truth be told, Proulx is an Ottawa firefighter who met Hemmings while driving competitors around the nation's

the in- and out-turn

capital at the 2001 Brier. They became fast friends and Proulx jumped at the invitation to accompany Hemmings on his pilgrimage through curling's heartland. "The province he's known least in is his own," remarks the engaging Proulx.

On the ice, the crowd gathers around him, and Hemmings immediately assumes his character. He's the minstrel of this motley crew—boys and girls, big and small; some have dreadlocks and are new immigrants to Canada. Within moments they're playing the game. "Anybody know why Guy Hemmings would do this job and nobody else?" The sage beckons. "I hope it's because I'm better looking." He's got them right where he wants them.

Throughout the session the air is filled with laughter and the clatter of brooms whacking the ice—a thousand pratfalls. Many of the kids are without sliders so Hemmings has instructed the volunteers to wrap clear plastic packing tape around their sneakers. He wants them to feel what it's like to zoom from the hack toward the other end of the ice. One little beginner gets it right on the first try, moving with a newfound grace and complete control. "Not bad," croaks Hemmings. "But you know he's a left-hander so there is no hope!" The prize student, embarrassed, bows his head while the group chuckles at his good form and even better fortune at having been singled out by the leader.

Hemmings divides his time carefully and devotes attention to each of the kids. He puts his arm around some to provide comfort, whispers words of encouragement in the

The first steps: A youngster gets set to rock the house in Kelowna

ears of others as they steady themselves to try this new and strange thing. He is the master of having fun, and the group appears to lose itself in the experience. He speaks so quickly with an accent many of them have little experience with, but in no time they all get the picture and the synergy that develops is fantastic. Soon Hemmings has those who cut corners on their delivery and others who miss the broom paying a price. "Drop down, eh," Hemmings demands with a phony harshness. "Gimme fifteen pushups!"

In the moments after his show Guy Hemmings returns to his now tepid coffee and drinks lustily. "They might not get it right away or join the next year," he says of the potential new recruits. "But a couple of years from now someone will talk to them about curling and they'll remember that and maybe try it again. In the long run it will be very positive."

Hemmings is unfailingly positive and is able to infect others, regardless of their backgrounds, with his enthusiasm. "Coming from Quebec in this sport has been very interesting," he admits. "When you are a francophone living in Quebec you are thinking about western Canada in an interesting way—not the nicest of ways. But I remember coming out here and one of my best memories in curling was playing that Brier in Edmonton. There were kids in the stands with their faces painted blue and white, the colours of Quebec."

He has been able to tear down some walls and, along the way, helped to widen the game's appeal. But Guy Hemmings refuses to take credit for revolutionizing curling. He believes in the universality of the pebbled ice. "That's one of the great things about this game. You travel to Yukon

or P.E.I. You get into a curling club and there is no barrier
to language. There is no salary barrier. Everyone is playing
the same game, their game, at different levels, and they are
working as hard as they can at it. They have a drink after, a
beer or a pop. We'll get together and shake hands before the
game and shake hands after the game. It's really a social
sport where everyone appears to be equal."

Hemmings loves to talk and he is a great storyteller.
Listening to him, it's easy to believe that somehow he stumbled into his role as the game's icon. He is a kind of "every
man" blessed with special powers of attraction and like a mag-
net he draws everyone and everything around him a little bit
closer. "It's a fun game." Hemmings shrugs and grins. "I have
been curling for sixteen years myself, and I have yet to run into
someone who comes back after trying it and claims it was
more boring than they thought. I'm trying to coach these people who enjoy watching curling to give it a try," he explains.
"To trade a bag of chips for a couple of hours with a broom."

The overriding message Guy Hemmings will continue to
deliver with each rock he throws, even in the most intense
of competitive situations, is that curling is a blast. "I like to
see myself as a kid living in an adult's body. I'm a fourteen-
year-old in a man's frame," Hemmings laughs. "I enjoy playing any kind of game, and curling is a game I am able to
play at the highest level. If I am not enjoying myself at the
Brier, I'm losing my time. I put lots of effort, time, and
money to get to that level. Once you get there, if you're not
enjoying yourself then you're wasting your time."

The new face of curling loves the camaraderie above all
else. Hemmings is empowered by his affinity for the people
who populate the game. They are, he has discovered, his

people. "Curlers across the country are similar in nature," Hemmings claims. "When you are inside the curling club you feel like you are home. You feel like people know you. It is a family thing. Not only the family in terms of playing with your dad and your kids. You go to different places and you feel like you know them too."

In everything he says, Guy Hemmings reveals his love for the game. He's found the thing that binds him to his

Guy Hemmings and André Proulx

neighbours, to his friends, and to the thousands who have come to know his name across the country. He relates it to the team he plays with—to Dale Ness, Guy Thibaudeau, and Pierre Charette. "In curling you have to play with a teammate," Hemmings explains. "You can't be a bad person or you'll have to work really, really hard to find people to play with. You might have to find three other bad people and in this sport that's not easy to do."

My time with Guy Hemmings is nearly over and his road show is wrapping up for the season. Soon he'll be going back to his greenhouse in Quebec and tending to his tomatoes. There too his patience is coupled with tremendous energy as he nurtures his seeds through to the harvest. "You can't forget the grassroots of curling," he says, waving his broom toward the ice beyond the glass in Kelowna. "If I could help the sport, that would be wonderful. The sport has been really good for me. I'm not talking money-wise, I'm talking personally. As an individual I have improved a lot by playing this game. If I can help kids to discover the same path that I discovered sixteen years ago then I will be proud of myself." André Proulx, the big bald genie, comes to whisk Hemmings away and I feel like I've just met Peter Pan on a whirlwind visit to Neverland.

The Los Angeles Kings needed something when I ran into them in Calgary that day. The team had gone through much of the season crippled by injury. Star players were lost, many of them with concussions, and some wondered if their careers would be able to withstand the recovery period. The Kings, generally a talented bunch, were forced to rely on skaters called up from the minor leagues while the others

Behind the bench: Andy Murray of Manitoba in Los Angeles

convalesced. It was only January, but their chances of making the playoffs were already waning. And so it was that the Kings got together and spent a day at the curling rink.

"It was team building to take them out," said the coach, Andy Murray. The fifty-one-year-old team mentor hails from Souris, Manitoba, about thirty miles to the southwest of Brandon. He has curling in his blood, and at a time when his hockey team needed to rally, he drew on the strengths of Canada's other ice-bound game. "You talk about the social dynamics of curling and how you have to work together and communicate. We wanted a chance to be together, to laugh and smile and we haven't had much of an opportunity to do that the whole season what with all of the injuries."

That night before the Kings' game against the Calgary Flames, the players I talked with were eager to tell me of their misadventures at the Calgary Winter Club. It was as if the time away from hockey's battles had provided a salve for their aching wounds, both real and imagined. "We are having real difficulty," agreed Mathieu Schneider, the club's highest-scoring defenceman. He leaned over the boards during the warmup looking a little worse for wear and knowing that if the Kings were going to make a run for the post-season, it would have to start almost immediately. Schneider is an American and had played pro in big cities like New York, Toronto, and Montreal before getting to Hollywood. "A day off yesterday and a little curling." He sounded like a regular. "It was a team event and it brought us together. Hopefully it will help."

Jared Aulin, a twenty-year-old forward who hails from Calgary, had been pictured in the local newspaper that morning holding a curling broom and standing in the con-centric circles of the Winter Club. Surrounding him was a minefield of yellow and red rocks. He was beaming in the middle of the confusion, though not quite dressed for the part in a pastel Hugo Boss shirt and gleaming white train-ing shoes. "For many of us it was our first time curling." Aulin grinned as he completed his pre-game workout and headed for the dressing room at the Saddledome. "But it was fun and I'm pretty sure it was worth it."

It was not the first time that Andy Murray had tried this tactic. Two years ago before a period of tremendous success for the Kings, a wave they rode into the playoffs and to an eventual elimination of the powerful Red Wings, Murray had gathered the troops, put them on a bus, and taken them to the curling rink for the first time. Many of the players had balked at the idea. The most successful left-winger in

hockey, Luc Robitaille, who has since left the team for
Detroit, was among the naysayers. "We heard we were going
and we thought we didn't want any of that shit," Robitaille
recalled. "We got there and we started playing and we all
thought, 'This is awesome!'"

Robitaille developed an appreciation for curling though
he struggled with its execution. "Hilarious," said Andy
Murray, in estimating Robitaille's prospects from hack to
hog line.

"I was pretty good!" Luc Robitaille looks shocked on
hearing his old coach's evaluation. "The only thing was, I
had no style. Every time I threw a rock I'd flip over on my
side. I didn't find it difficult. I found the aiming part quite
tough, though. I watch the curling on TV now and that's at
a different level. What we did was fun."

Andy Murray shook his head as he reflected on the afternoon he'd shared with his players away from one rink and in
another. A meticulous man, a strategist known for his attention to every one of hockey's details, Murray seemed most
interested in the intangibles as he explained the purpose of
his field trip. "If you're in Canada in the winter and you're
not playing hockey, then you should be curling," he
preached. "The other reason that I picked it was because if
you're going to pick a sport to do as a distraction and you're
the coach, you have to pick something you're good at. I
knew that these other guys weren't very good and I know
that I'm not great but I figured I might be the best."

Murray has been a professional hockey coach much of his
adult life and has been onside for Canada at the Olympic
Games and the world championships. The most vivid
memories he has of growing into his craft involve not one

but two sports that shared the arena in his small hometown. "In rural Canada all the curling rinks were connected to the hockey rinks," he recalled. "You had the high school or the youth curling, and then you would go to your hockey practice. If you were lucky enough, you could stand around and see the men's team and if they had someone missing from their night draw. You'd be able to jump in and fill his spot and therefore you'd spend the whole night at the rink and you wouldn't have to do any school work."

The relationship between the two games was standard fare for Manitobans like Andy Murray, growing up in places like Wawanesa and Elgin. Some rinks even had a walkway connecting the curling and hockey facilities. He remembers hearing the rumble of the rocks amid the slap shots and blasts from the referee's whistle during a hard-fought hockey game. Pausing at the bench between shifts, young Andy wondered what was going on with his dad Ewart's foursome as they faced the others in the local elite league.

At certain times, like the annual bonspiel, the curlers displaced the hockey players, and four sheets of pebbled ice were fashioned over the arena's frozen surface. Murray learned a lot. "I love the strategy and figuring out the angles," he told me. "It's all about how you can make things happen. Maybe that's why I like coaching so much because you're always trying to stay one step ahead of your opponent. I think curling as much as anything I did when I was younger helped me coach. It was because I was a skip and as a skip you had to do those things to survive."

Andy Murray is not convinced that the results of his curling outing with a professional hockey team will reap immediate or concrete rewards. He does know that it has had a

King of curling: Andy Murray returns to the pebbled ice in Calgary

relaxing effect on a team preoccupied with its recent bad luck. They had fun at the Calgary Winter Club, and the resulting buzz in the locker room was a tangible thing. "We as coaches have always had a good communication level with our players, it's something we've worked on even during the tough times," he stated. "We're not looking at it as impetus for the rest of our season, and I had planned to do it whether we were ten games over five hundred or two games under five hundred. It's team building, the ability to laugh and smile and do something different."

They were millionaires almost to a man, flopping around the ice trying a sport they knew little about. Two of the brightest stars in the game of hockey, Jason Allison and Ziggy Palffy, the former from Toronto, the latter a native of Skalica, Czechoslovakia, were suddenly humbled when confronted with the intricacies of curling. "They had all watched it before and I had told them beforehand it was difficult," Murray laughed. "The funniest part was watching those two guys argue over how to score the thing. They had no idea where the numbers were supposed to go."

In the end, Andy Murray was the best of the curlers that day—even among his proud hockey players. "They'd say, 'Look at this guy. He can't shoot a puck anymore or skate but he sure can curl,'" the coach said, with more than a little satisfaction. It brought back memories of his own youth and the wonder he'd once experienced when asked to share the ice with those he respected most.

"I had never curled before," he started the story. "I was just there at the rink one night and they asked me to come and play. My grandfather, whose name was also Andy, told me to put both feet in the hack and take the rock and push it. I got hooked on it right away. To be with my grandfather was the big thing. I remember the guys on his rink to this day and how they helped me. The big old sweaters they used to wear and the gigantic fedoras. To be out with these guys as a nine-year-old, well it was unbelievable that they would even ask you. To me the importance of curling was the chance to be out with the older people."

He cautioned me against reading too much into what, on the surface, was a playful distraction for a struggling professional hockey team. "It was really something unique," he would admit. Other teams, including Washington, Buffalo, and Vancouver, had tried it, always on a swing through the prairie west. Some of the coaches had thought of it as a way to reconnect with something truly Canadian—get grounded and be reminded of the grassroots of the country where most players hailed from.

"There was one other thing that happened yesterday," Andy Murray offered before his last pre-game meeting with the Kings. "I said to them that we were going curling, and the guys immediately asked me if we were making a big trade. The last time we curled here two years ago was in the afternoon. We traded Rob Blake that night. Mathieu Schneider was laughing and asked me if we were making another. He remembered it because of that."

Rob Blake, one of the best defencemen in the NHL, had indeed been traded to Colorado following the last Los Angeles Kings curling trip. Mathieu Schneider, the star player who reminded Andy Murray of that fact, would be dealt to the Detroit Red Wings in a matter of weeks, something he would never have expected as he tried to master the out-turn that day on a curling rink in Calgary.

The view from Outlook is a whole lot brighter than it was in 1981 when Bob Stephenson first returned to his hometown in rural Saskatchewan. He had been away playing pro hockey in Birmingham, Alabama, with the World Hockey Association Bulls and for a short time after that as a member of the Hartford Whalers and the Toronto Maple Leafs. Stephenson's road to the pro game began in Nova Scotia where he was a star at St. Francis Xavier University in Antigonish. He's covered a lot of ground in his career and now he's the mayor of a community of 2,300. Fifty miles south of Saskatoon, a couple of hours from Regina, Outlook is perched smack dab in the middle of curling country.

"It's an integral part of town," Stephenson says, bragging about the new four-sheet rink that's finishing up its second season of operation. "Actually, we make our last payment on it this year. Because of all the in-kind labour, we built the thing for about a million dollars."

Stephenson is speaking from his office in the Irrigation Centre Motel, which he and his wife, Sandy, a music teacher and native Alabaman, have taken to running because Bob's father was having a little trouble keeping the place up. The motel has become the family meeting place and a focal point for the town, though nothing can rival the curling rink in that regard.

"Our old one was built by the collective," he explains. "Everyone in the town, all the curlers that is, threw in a number of dollars and everyone got a share in the club which really meant nothing. It was turning out to be a disaster, warm weather, cold weather, the ice heaved up and down like the waves on the ocean." To build a new rink would require a substantial investment, and the population base of Outlook was stretched thin by the financial demands of the endeavour. "You know, in rural Saskatchewan where you've got a decline in population, you get a little antsy as to whether you should go out on a limb and build a new one," the mayor says. "But the town bit off its share and they raised funds like the devil. In western Canada all of these projects are based on volunteer labour so there were guys who put in hundreds and hundreds of hours, if not thousands if you really counted them. We saved a lot of money that way."

The result has been the rejuvenation of curling in the town. The club has been an economic boon and a feather in the former hockey player's hat. The popular mayor took a chance on Canada's quiet obsession with curling and it's ended up paying dividends. "It's unreal how many people come to see the curling," Stephenson enthuses. "It's great for us because it keeps our kitchen running almost full-time, which helps support the rink's economy and in turn the community's. That's why we built it."

There are now 130 active members and a strong seniors group curling in Outlook. The club, Bob tells me, has played host to the provincial junior championship and become a sort of curling hub for the surrounding area. "It's just a facility you've got to have if you want to survive here," Stephenson believes. "If you want to draw people into your community and give them opportunities, particularly in winter sport, it's a must. I don't know what you'd do here in the winter [otherwise]. Snowmobile maybe, but sometimes the snow doesn't come either. Curling is always there."

Bob Stephenson marvels at the power of the game he knew so well as a child growing up in Outlook. Curling brings together people from all walks of life. He points to the early experience of his wife, whom he met while he was skating as a Bull and she was working at the University of Birmingham. Packing up her life in the early eighties to move to rural Saskatchewan was a monumental challenge.

"Big time! It was a culture shock for her. You're telling me!" exclaims the mayor. "I think my sisters thought we'd last about a year. They didn't say anything for the first ten years or so of our marriage and then they told her, 'Oh God, we never thought you'd make it.'"

Sandy Stephenson has more than made it in Outlook, and curling was one of her first ways to connect. For the adventurous spirit, throwing a rock and making it stick in the house was symbolic of her willingness to build bridges with strangers in a strange place. "She liked to give everything a go," Bob figures. "It was her way to get into the community. That's the thing with the curling rink. It's a point of contact. Heck, we even took the Alabaman in the mixed spiel a few years back and, much to everyone's surprise, we won the thing!"

Sandy doesn't curl much anymore. She's taken on a large number of piano students and her own kids play hockey. All the after-school activity means that curling suffers, something that Bob laments. He's only now finding time to get into the full swing of the men's league again. Still, he relishes the chance to find new converts and show them what really matters to the people of Outlook. It's like he's campaigning for curling itself.

"I know the young kids are taken down to the club by people in the town. They get the public school kids and get them indoctrinated. There are a lot of kids getting back into it," he proclaims. "And you know, we've got a South African doctor here so we had to indoctrinate him into the game." The word indoctrinate, far from sounding sinister, takes on a welcoming connotation when spoken by the mayor of Outlook as he glorifies a sport akin to religion in this part of the world. "We golfed a lot and I told him we'll have to try curling. Now he's hooked on it. He just loves it. He's one of those guys who gets into sports and doesn't just do it for a little recreation. He's actually studious and likes to know the game."

I imagine, through the telephone line, that Bob Stephenson is about to beg off our conversation and take to the streets recruiting even more people to his beloved curling house. Its

continued existence may be the greatest accomplishment of
his time as mayor and the reason he remains optimistic about
Outlook's future.

Before ringing off I ask how much longer the former pro
hockey player, irrigation system salesman, and motel pro-
prietor can continue to fulfil his duties as a popular politi-
cian. "Elections are coming up so who the heck knows, eh?
I'll tell you one thing," he says, before bidding farewell. "It's
hard to find a free night to curl!"

Ken Lynch is sounding very much like he misses Canada.
He moved to Florida half a dozen years ago to pursue his
career as a mechanical designer. Showing his origins, he's
talking about the Tampa Bay Lightning of the National
Hockey League and their prospects in the upcoming Stanley
Cup playoffs. And he's talking about curling.

"It was a hot one here today." I can envision him mop-
ping his brow in the living room of his home in Ellenton,
Florida, where the breezes from the Gulf of Mexico blow
warm mid-March. "Curling was the only thing I missed
when I moved out of Canada."

Lynch is on the board of directors of the Florida Curling
Club and is one of the association's founding members. The
game is a recent phenomenon down here and something
very foreign to the native population. The "snowbirds," as
the migrants from the northern United States and Canada
are referred to in these parts, have seen to it that curling can
grow even where conditions are hardly favourable for a
wintertime passion.

The major mover and shaker behind the Florida Curling
Club is Rich Rosa from Connecticut. Rosa saw the game for

the first time on a giant outdoor TV monitor while attending the Salt Lake City Olympics. "They had the curling on," Ken explains. "Rich and about two hundred other Americans stood out on the street and looked at it. They had no clue what they were watching."

As the story goes, Rosa was so enthralled that when he returned to his Florida residence he established a web site and called a meeting for people interested in finding out more about curling. Ken Lynch found himself surfing through the site of the United States Curling Association when he saw the link for the Florida Curling Club and decided to attend the get-together. About thirty-five people showed up, half from Canada, half from places in the northern United States like Michigan, Wisconsin, and Minnesota.

The next step, once interest was piqued, was to find a place to play. The flock discovered that the nearest ice rink was a place called the J.P. Igloo in Sarasota, managed by a former resident of Waterloo, Ontario, named Kerry Leitch. Leitch coaches figure skating and runs the facility, which boasts two ice pads and a roller hockey rink. When he heard that the curlers had no place to throw their rocks, he offered up one of the ice surfaces, told them they could paint circles on it and do whatever they pleased.

"We were able to get five curling sheets out of the one rink," Lynch says. It took us a few hours to get the painting done and then we discovered that we had no rocks and there were none even close."

Not to be deterred, they contacted the United States Curling Association and found out that if they conducted a clinic for all interested parties in Florida, the U.S.C.A. would help them find the tools to make it happen. So it was that seventy-five Floridians signed up for the opportunity to curl, and a truckload of stones, brooms, and hacks was dispatched from the closest curling club, which, strangely enough, was located in Gatlinburgh, Tennessee. The arrival of the supplies was greeted with the same enthusiasm given a giant care package delivered to homesick kids at summer camp. "It took us three months of searching before we could purchase our own rocks after that," Ken chuckles. "We located them at a club in North Carolina. To be kind, they were an older set of stones."

The early gatherings of the Florida Curling Club were a far cry from Ken Lynch's decades of curling in the Ottawa Valley and later Elmira, Ontario, not far from Kitchener. Now they have five sets of "older rocks" and six solid teams who compete in an open division. "Generally it's pay as you play," Ken sighs, sounding like a scratch golfer doomed to play a par three course for the rest of his days. Still, he and his wife, Carol, both avid curlers, are eternally thankful for the Florida Curling Club.

"A curler is a curler wherever you go," he admits. "If you know you are a curler then you can sit there and talk to anybody. I've been to the Brier and just started up a conversation with Eddie Werenich. At the Scott Tournament of Hearts I could talk to any one of the very best women in the world. It's just that kind of camaraderie that you don't get in many other sports."

Every once in a while, Ken Lynch gets frustrated at the low level of curling he is currently subjected to, though even that seems set to change. Still in its infancy, the club is growing rapidly. There are now ninety paid members, and about a third of them curl on a regular basis. The rest pay $50 a year to curl whenever they escape their permanent homes in the north and fly south for all or part of the winter.

"I hope it will grow even more," Lynch says. "Now that we've got it here with a modicum of an organization, the marketing is the next step. What we're battling here is that there is so much [else] to do. In Canada, where I come from, one of the only things to do was to go to the curling club. Here you can go golfing or fishing anytime you want. We have to target people from the north. Develop a 'snowbirds' league or the large retirement groups that come down to Florida."

Although recent curling coverage by the major U.S. television networks has sparked a wider interest in the game, Lynch worries the neophytes are not getting the whole picture. "So far they've made inroads but at the Olympics and the world championships they only showed skip's rocks," Lynch laments. "When we talk to people here, they are surprised to learn that everybody gets to throw a rock. Most think you are either the sweeper or the thrower. You have to go right to the basics and show the rotation so that everyone can see that all four people are involved in every aspect of the game."

The weather's good and there's curling in Florida. Yet there is a note of regret in my conversation with Lynch. He tells me that he made a pilgrimage to his old haunt of Elmira not long ago. He wanted to visit home but more importantly, he wanted to be a spectator at the Scott Tournament of Hearts being staged in nearby Kitchener-Waterloo. Ken wore his Florida Curling Club T-shirt. He wanted to show everyone he is still part of the gang, that he hasn't lost touch with what is really important.

"Everybody in this game is receptive," he says with reverence. "When I was at the Hearts they all noticed my shirt. People wanted to know all about it. They stopped and talked even though they didn't know me from a hole in the ground."

Lynch spent his time in southwestern Ontario among friendly curlers, just like the old days, and the resulting warmth rivalled the still unfamiliar temperatures of the "Sunshine State." "I actually met the guy who packed our rocks and shipped them down from North Carolina." He still marvels at the coincidence. "People who love curling will talk for hours about ice. No matter where they come from."

Seeing curling at its most competitive reminded Lynch that the game celebrates a kind of gentleness. Respect outdistances the win-at-all-cost attitude that dominates other sports. For Ken Lynch, it is comforting to know that so little has changed. "It always appears to embody a friendly rivalry," he suggests. "People are always complimentary to their opponents. There never seems to be any reason to hurt anybody."

They're getting ready for the end of the curling season in Florida. In defiance of the warm climate, people like Ken Lynch are making a go of it because without curling they feel empty, like a snowbird with a broken wing. Without curling in his life the rhythm of his days is interrupted—one more reminder in a land devoid of seasons that he has left the challenges of his country behind.

"We seem to have this common thing between us," says Lynch. "If you are a curler you just know what it takes. It's not that it's uniquely Canadian. It's just that it seems to be uniquely curling."

Talking with Canadians as diverse as Ken Lynch, Bob Stephenson, Andy Murray, and Guy Hemmings, I have come to appreciate curling as a special secret we can all share and would readily agree that Canada and curling do somehow go hand in hand.

Return to form: Author gets a hand from Olympian Mike Harris at the Kitchener-Waterloo Granite Club

CHAPTER ELEVEN

BACK TO THE HACK

NEVER HAVE I FELT MORE LIKE AN OUTSIDER IN A curling nation than on that day as I hurtled west along Highway 401, bound for my inevitable return to the ice. I had fretted over what to wear and worried about whether I could maintain my balance. It seemed certain that I was about to make an ass of myself in front of an Olympic silver medallist. Mike Harris was waiting at the other end of the line, at the Kitchener-Waterloo Granite Club, where he was conducting a clinic for young curlers. He had volunteered to watch me throw my first rock in a quarter of a century and would, no doubt, welcome me with open arms.

The Granite Club was celebrating its seventy-fifth anniversary season and acting as the co-host for the Scott Tournament of Hearts. Although the games were being held at the nearby auditorium, a much larger facility with a greater seating capacity, the modest rink in the heart of old Kitchener was floating on the excitement. There were half a dozen yellow school buses parked outside when I arrived,

75th Anniversary: The Kitchener-Waterloo Granite Club

just like the good old days at the Avonlea Curling Club on Railside Road. The last of winter's snow was stacked beside the entranceway.

Beyond the foyer, where a collection of sepia-toned photographs was arranged, I could hear Harris's familiar voice emanating from the lounge upstairs. "It's important to communicate something," he was teaching. Walking obtrusively through the door, I was astonished to see hundreds of young people on benches and sitting cross-legged on the floor. They were riveted by Mike Harris as he worked a pointer over projected images of concentric circles. He was lecturing on "a system of zones." "It's what separates the best teams from the ones that don't get the job done at the end of the day," he stressed. The finest high school curlers in the region were hanging on his every word, making notes on the split timing of how long it takes to get from the hack to the hog line. "It's less about feel and more about the technical," Harris continued. The curlers nodded in agreement. "The education of the ice makers has made conditions more consistent, and rather than focusing on the skips we now focus on the sweepers."

I took my place on the cold tiles in front of his podium, feeling more fearful with each passing moment. I was not ready for curling to become technical. I was counting on it being like riding a bicycle, you know, something you just always know how to do. Harris winked at me, acknowledging my arrival and then he introduced me to the assemblage. "Scott Russell of *Hockey Night in Canada* is paying us a visit," the Olympian announced. "He's writing a book on curling and wants to come out and throw a few rocks." Now the pressure was really on. Glancing down at my all-terrain cross-trainers, I could sense disaster looming.

Once dispatched to the ice, the young people proceeded with great purpose and an aura of expertise. I followed sheepishly and was greeted at the threshold of the playing surface by a man named Gary Crossley. He offered his hand and said that we had first met at the Canada Games in Kamloops, B.C., a decade ago. It turned out he was now teaching at Cameron Heights High School in Kitchener and acting as the staff adviser for the curling team. "I'm really a track coach," Crossley said with a shrug. "But our kids have fallen in love with curling."

After a brief conversation, which I gratefully used to stall for time, Crossley looked down at my feet and shook his head. "You'll certainly need something for those," he insisted. Gary polled his friends and came up with an extra slider, which he foisted upon me, no questions asked. I could barely fit the thing over the tread of my immense shoe but I somehow managed to make it work. "Otherwise you'll come to a grinding halt on that first throw," he said. "Maybe go ass over tea kettle!"

Equipped with my slider and armed with a brush (not the broom of my earlier curling career), I stepped gingerly onto the pebbled ice. I pushed weakly with my back foot while keeping the slider-clad front one rigidly still. I felt as if I might topple at any moment. All around me youngsters were zooming up and down. Some were pasted to the ice on the trail of giant, rumbling rocks. Others escorted the stones effortlessly, heeding the calls to sweep from their skips. Harris slid by. "Balance is everything," he said, leaving me in his wake. "You have to get on the ice and learn to get your feet under you. Especially when you're sweeping." He was gone in an instant to watch a nine-year-old deliver a hunk of granite with the most delicate touch I had yet witnessed.

"Those kids are from the Fergus Curling Club." Bob McConnell beamed. The group of pre-teens was here representing the oldest curling club, dating back to 1834, in the province of Ontario. "We've got 250 members," McConnell continued. "I'm talking about old guys like me." Clearly, in Fergus at least, the so-called generation gap of curling was a thing of the past.

I took comfort in the diverse group that surrounded me, hopeful that I could lose myself within it. Teenagers wearing "hoodies" and looking more like rappers than curlers swarmed the place. Young men and women, in equal numbers, took their turns in the hack. Their teachers were also

there throwing rocks, and any differentiation in age and status was strangely lost. I thought fleetingly of my old basketball coach, Mr. Heffernan, and wondered if he was still at it,
if he was still captured by this surprising game.

A youngish teacher was suddenly at my arm handing me
a camera and asking if I would mind taking a picture of him
and his students. Jeff Collard and his group were from the
Koinonia Christian Academy in Bloomingdale, about ten
minutes outside of Kitchener. The entire student body is
made up of twenty-nine souls. "Curling has become a great
way for us to be involved," Collard explained. "We don't
have the numbers to do tackle football or anything like that
but curling we can do. We've done it fairly well, and we've
even won a few games in the high school league."

Mike Harris and the clan from Fergus, Ontario

The youngest curler from the oldest club: A nine-year-old from Fergus settles into the hack

I admitted to Collard that, after all these years, I was a little hesitant about getting back on the ice myself, though I felt it necessary if my observations about curling were to have any credibility at all. "When I was thinking of what sporting activity we could do I thought of curling," he countered with confidence. "That's the first time I'd ever done it. It didn't take me long to get some of the basics down so that I could play. It's inclusive. That's the great part about it."

Relieved to be in good and sympathetic company, I made my way down to the far end of the sheet, to the awaiting iron of the hack and my unavoidable appointment with Mike Harris. The sliding seemed to be progressing reasonably well but the prospect of actually throwing the rock still terrified me. Better just to get it over with, I thought. "You can look dumb but you won't look dumb for very long," Mike Harris said with a wry smile. "Everyone gets so self-conscious on the ice, and it's the adults who are a lot more worried about failure. A kid will get out here and slide four times. He'll fall on three occasions but the one shot he makes is the only one he remembers. The adult remembers falling three times." I wondered immediately what it was I would later recall about this afternoon, besides my sweating palms and the now harrowing realization that the rock seemed very much larger than it had been in my curling days gone by.

"It's not about power," the Olympian cautioned as I crouched in the takeoff position, a subtle warning not to lift the rock but instead to grip it, using the momentum of my body to propel the thing forward. "People try to do too much, they kick out too hard, and they fall or they flip over," Harris explained, with a grin.

If this all seems too much prelude to a simple act, consider the pressure I was under. There I was, having not touched a stone like this in a quarter of a century, a complete amateur trying to impress one of the best curlers in the world and the man who had narrowly lost an Olympic gold medal. I suddenly felt very small in the presence of the giant rock. An eternity away, a kid from the Christian Academy was holding the broom on target and signalling the out-turn. Fat chance, I thought, I'll consider it a major victory if I get this thing beyond the hog line.

"Stay within yourself." Harris resorted to a last-minute cliché. Then he settled me down and took a few seconds to explain himself. "It's like any sport, and because I'm a pro golfer I always go back to that one. Any player in curling can experience what it's like to make a really great shot. It's like hitting that perfect drive. It's feeling like Tiger Woods feels. You and I can't hit it 350 yards every time and experience that part of it. But you can have the satisfaction of doing it just once."

Just once, I thought. If I could get away without making a complete hash of this solitary delivery my mission would be complete and I could rest easy. The moment of truth had arrived and I made a move. Right hand on the rock, right foot in the hack, I eased out of the ready position and rose just slightly. Harris was beside me and already on the slide—he would accompany the rock to its eventual destination.

I was on the runway now and feeling improbably well balanced and in complete control. The brush was there at my left to prop me up but I wasn't leaning on it. My fingers were touching the big stone only lightly now and it felt joyous to be along for the ride. As if by instinct, my left foot curled at the toes; the slider-clad heel arched off the glistening surface and tucked directly underneath my torso, becoming the centre of my form and my essential point of contact with the ice. The trick was to look up, to take my focus away from the red handle embedded in the granite and glance at the kid holding the broom at the other end. Just for a moment I did just that, and based on my calculations I made a slight adjustment to our collective course. Our sliding progress was beginning to die. I was still some distance from the hog line but the point of no return was upon me. It was time to let go.

Here, I remembered from all those years ago, one of curling's most basic principles. The trick to accuracy, I

Back to the hack and back in business: Author and Mike Harris in Kitchener

recalled, was not to push the rock at the last second but to let it slip from your grasp. This gentle motion allowed the handle to turn ever so slightly, thus beginning the curling motion of the stone—the source of the sport's subtlety and allure. There it was, the rock was on its own now. I had done everything in my power to pave its way. Even Mike Harris lifted his broom and just watched it lumber to the other end.

You can't know the relief of making the first stone count. With my body glued to the pebble, flat on my stomach, I was transfixed. So too were the others on this lane of the Kitchener-Waterloo Granite Club's ice. My rock made it all the way. It slipped past the far hog line with ease and slowed to a halt just biting the blue paint of the twelve-foot ring. It was in front and at the centre of the playing field, exactly where a good lead stone ought to be. I had done my job and thrown the great shot that Harris had spoken of, though there was no time to admire it. The next kid was roaring out behind me and his takeout erased my artistry in an instant.

"It's all about perspective," Mike Harris said, by way of congratulations. "As long as you take it for what it is. You can walk into any curling club you know. I haven't heard of any club that is turning away members. Walk through the front door. Someone will help you and you'll be in a league the next week if you want to be."

No borders—just common ground, I thought—a beautiful sentiment offered by an Olympian to a hacker trying to get a handle on this game. Curling was not beyond anyone, not even me. Still, I was eager for Harris's evaluation of my delivery.

"You were smooth. As smooth as silk," he crooned. "Twenty-five years, you say? I would have guessed fifteen tops."

Not long after I curled with Mike Harris, I contacted Mr. Heffernan, my old basketball coach. Something about the trek through curling's heartland drew me back to my first contact with the game. Throwing those few rocks on an afternoon in Kitchener had conjured up a welcome and familiar feeling. I realized that through all my memories about curling, I could think of nothing negative. There were no enemies among the people I had left behind those many years ago. I felt only a deep nostalgia for the warm times I had experienced in the company of my curling friends. They say you can never go back, but I wondered if it wasn't worth at least making an effort.

"I appreciate so much the gesture of Mister," the coach responded in his e-mail. "Let's now communicate on the same level. It's 'Heff' or Grant—no more Mister!"

He said he would come by to visit me in a week and informed me that there had been two recent reunions of the Victoria Park Secondary School gang. I had missed them both because of work commitments or other excuses equally convenient. Heff wrote that my curling buddies, Ken Pearce, Bruce MacInnis, and "Ace" had all attended. "I remember so many great moments from those teaching days," he concluded. Now it was my turn to make a promise. I'd get in touch with every one of the schoolboys and see if curling still had a place in their lives.

Ken Pearce answered the phone and was eager to talk. A business and securities lawyer with one of the largest firms in Toronto, he's a busy man. He married his high school sweetheart, a girl named Brenda Ritchie, with whom he had curled in the mixed bonspiels. "She probably had a record of 129 and 1 as curler," the former champion joked. "She always had the good fortune to play with a great team." He effortlessly recounted stories from those days, like the time Brenda fell in front of one of his perfect draws and the second, good old Bruce MacInnis, had the presence of mind to sweep her right out of the way, so allowing the rock to nestle close to the button. His rivalry with Rollie Hamar remained fresh in his mind as did the sadness of having to cut Ace from the rink in his championship year. Pearce recalled the blue leisure suits that his foursome wore to all the functions at the national championships. "Our suits were just like something Herb Tarlick would wear on that show *WKRP in Cincinnati*," he sighed. "We looked like clowns but then again, so did everybody else."

After Ken left high school, he continued to curl with his father in the elite league at Avonlea. He became a "super sub" for rinks skipped by Brier winners like Ed Werenich and Paul Savage. "I was not a sweeper," he admitted. "I was a shot maker."

That's exactly what I remembered about Ken Pearce, his precision and the Zen-like calmness he unfailingly demonstrated while under fire. Far more talented than the rest of us, he was able to rise above his rivals on every occasion. Ken was the one guy I imagined would always be a curler. On the ice he was a leader, on the ice he claimed excellence.

"I miss it," Pearce reflected. He has not curled for a number of years. His career places heavy demands on him, and besides that his kids are deeply involved in hockey. So while he has spent some time behind the bench coaching, there is just no time left for curling.

Before signing off, he suggested it was time he got back to the game and thanked me for reminding him of it. He shared one more memory of him and Brenda as newlyweds living in the small community of Cookstown. There they joined the local curling club. "We manned the bar and made drinks and we met our neighbours," he said. "That's what I loved. I loved the people and the etiquette and the fact that it was so much fun."

"I still curl," Bruce MacInnis boasted. "When I tell that to business associates who work in the United States, they look at me like I have two heads. They think it's like shuffleboard." My old teammate was in a jocular mood and happy to be remembered after twenty-five years. He scolded me ever so slightly for not attending the reunions but seemed to understand when I told him I was at some hockey game or other in Vancouver or Edmonton or wherever. He was still the spark plug that I remembered. A powerful, stocky sort whose Rink Rat would echo throughout the club whenever he was sweeping. "Brushes were for wimpy European types," Bruce said huffily when considering the extinction of the old-style brooms. "If you were serious, you had to have a Rink Rat and the louder it was, the better. It frustrates me that people who have never tried curling think it looks easy."

Bruce has a family now. He works as a chartered accountant for a firm that's pioneering in fingerprint technology. He curls in the recreational league at the Donalda, one of the fancier clubs in Toronto, but he yearns for the days when there was "lots of drinking and carousing." "My first drink was in the men's locker room," he chuckled. "Even as a kid I grew up with it. Tuesday afternoons I went to the nursery at the club; my mum would take me so that she could curl. Friday nights I went to the men's league to see my dad play."

Unlike Ken Pearce, Bruce MacInnis was a sweeper, a workhorse who welcomed every opportunity for head-to-head battle. "It turns very quickly," he reflected. "The hardest transition to make in the game of curling is to become social after being competitive. Shots that you used to make in your sleep, you now miss."

Bruce came back to curling after a short crack at playing old-timer hockey. "I had to lose some weight and curling wasn't the way to do it," he claimed. But in the end, his experiences as a young man, experiences he would not have traded for anything, drew him back to curling. MacInnis credited the sport with "being an outlet for kids back then," something he regrets his own kids are missing. "My kids would think that curling is nerdy," Bruce grumbled. "Unless you do it and appreciate it, you can't understand. "

When Ace opened the door to his home in our old neighbourhood, my jaw dropped to the flagstone walkway. There he stood, six-foot-five, at least an inch taller than me. This was the same Brian Nicholls who had been too small for the bantam basketball team. The enthusiastic little guy relegated to the curling club who talked me into tagging along all those years ago. Things had changed.

"I loved the fact that anybody could play." He ushered me into his house and presented me with a picture of our old foursome. Our hair was ridiculously long, but we looked happy. Curling was one of the only after-school activities that Ace was involved in. "You made the basketball team, I didn't," he pointed out. "I made the track team, though. I wasn't a bad runner." Curling was what he cherished most. "You didn't need a lot of skill in order to contribute. You could out-think your opponent even if you couldn't outshoot him," my old friend observed. "Because I always liked math, I could really look at the angles and see how things could unfold," he said. "It's a game where many things can happen because of a single shot."

Even back in high school we all thought Ace, who was the smartest among us, would have something to do with computers when he grew up. Nowadays Brian develops software for the giant IBM. Of course, he still curls in his spare time. At work he has launched an annual bonspiel called The Silver Broom, named after the now defunct world tournament once sponsored by Air Canada. He furnished the tournament's simple but coveted prizes—brooms spray-painted in his basement. These treasures, he reminded me, were not unlike the trinkets made of thimbles and buttons that we used to compete for in our schoolboy days.

"On any given day anyone can win." Ace repeated one of curling's truisms. "The first year that Ed Werenich won the Worlds I played lead for the team that Werenich initially beat along the road out of the Avonlea club. It was a team skipped by a fellow named Vic Suzuki and I think we ended up losing by two or three. That was pretty good considering the super team that Werenich had. It's something that I can tell my grandkids. The world champion had to go through me and he didn't just blow us off the map!"

Ace had made good and I felt so proud of him standing in his foyer that night. "It could be mean at times, very competitive," he recalled of his time at the curling club. "The more important thing was to get along with people. It was the best way to form a team. I think for me it was a wonderful way to learn some leadership qualities by being a skip for a while." As always, Ace had figured all the angles perfectly.

Heff arrived at my house at the appointed time. He was as bowlegged as ever and he came bearing a shopping bag full of Victoria Park yearbooks and a couple of old shots from his lacrosse days that I had asked for. His full head of hair, once dark and flecked with grey, was now a deep shade of auburn. "Kids kept me young, Scott, and now I dye my hair," Heff volunteered, as he fixed me with that intense stare. "So I cheat a bit. I still coach some hockey here and there and you can't look like an old man coaching kids. You won't have the same credibility. I know the little old ladies like the grey-haired men but you can't do it if you're coaching."

It was oddly exhilarating to have him in my home. Heff was feared and respected when he was our coach— to call him a friend would have been a stretch. But here he was, talking to me like an equal. "I love the associations I had," he said. "At Victoria Park we had the best of times."

Grant Heffernan spent the better part of the morning regaling me with stories about his first days in the classroom and his lacrosse wars with the old Peterboro Lakers. "It was viciousness," he admitted. "Brutality and survival of the fittest to a great extent. Skill was often a secondary thing."

Curling, on the other hand, was not a game of his youth. In fact, he didn't try it until he was entering his middle years. Even then he only curled to placate his wife, Janey, who was accomplished at the sport. "I started because of her. It was no great passion for this unknown game. It was curl or you're in deep trouble," he confessed. "I got into it by accident in many ways. We went to a bonspiel in Lakefield. She was to curl and I was to be the observer. The other team was short one player and I figured I could play this game so I ended up curling against her and we won."

Heff still exudes a competitive spirit, and at a spry sixty-one years of age he looks like he could paste you into the boards of any hockey arena or run you right over while brandishing a twirling lacrosse stick. Not surprisingly then, what appealed to Heff about curling were its challenges. "It's very competitive so the gentlemanly aspect of curling never entered my mind. You shook hands. I could never get used to that. You'd say, good curling. I hoped the other guys never made a damn shot. That was my competitive nature," he explained. "It's a game and the focus is to win the game. What's great about it is that it takes incredible skill. You have to be far more skilled in curling than you do in most other sports like hockey because of the fine muscle touch. You are taking a forty-pound rock and trying to throw it three feet farther than you did the shot before. That's muscle touch."

There were important lessons, perhaps hidden beneath the surface of the pebbled ice that attracted my old coach to

319

what he refers to as an unknown game. "I found out in coaching and playing curling that teams that won had the skill and the discipline," he said. "You give the other team life if you don't execute your shots. You must have discipline in order to be successful. All of the good curlers had the good leadership skills."

Grant Heffernan is retired from teaching now. He still coaches a little lacrosse and hockey, but the sport he holds on to in the most active way is curling. He's thrown rocks with the best of them, including Brier winners Paul Savage and Alfie Phillips Junior. As if on cue, sitting in my kitchen, he looked at his watch and was suddenly up and on his way to the Bayview Curling Club, where he was scheduled to start play in the annual Energizer Bonspiel for senior curlers. "Trouble is I got half a knee replaced last summer." He gestured to his left leg. "It's not bad now and I've almost got the balance thing figured out on the delivery. But for October and November it was brutal because I couldn't tuck it back underneath." Heff gladly fought through the pain in the name of something that had become a passion. "Some people might argue that I've played the three great Canadian games at a high level," Heff grinned as he said it. "My best friends are curlers and I remain faithful to that."

"I don't think they have a curling club at Victoria Park anymore. It's really gone down," he said with regret as he made his way to the door. "The biggest thing about curling is what it offers to people. You don't have to be six-foot-four like you do in basketball. You don't have to have the great specific skill to handle a lacrosse stick or to pass and shoot a hockey puck. Curling offers the possibility that anyone can play."

When Heff uttered those words I thought of them all—my schoolboy chums and the legion of curlers I had met along the way. Here was a member of the Lacrosse Hall of Fame, one of collegiate hockey's legends, not to mention my favourite teacher, pointing me to the simple truth of the game and the magic I had discovered going back to the hack. Curling is an open house and anyone can enter.

Along curling's road: The exit to Baysville, Ontario

CHAPTER TWELVE

EXTRA ENDS

THE THING IS, IF YOU START TO PAY ATTENTION TO IT, there is the distinct possibility you'll get hooked on curling. I became a fan without really noticing. It was a natural progression as my flirtation with the game evolved into a romance over the course of a journey.

Bruce Cassidy was just completing his first year as the head coach of the Washington Capitals when I ran into him in the early morning at Edmonton's Skyreach Centre. His team was in the last stages of a rare sweep through the NHL's six Canadian cities, a string of consecutive road games north of the border that few American-based hockey clubs are ever subjected to, or have the pleasure of, depending on your perspective.

"Probably it's a way to reconnect with Canada," Cassidy figured. "I was born and raised in Ottawa and I've got a lot of Canadian in me. I just love coming home."

Cassidy preferred not to talk about the fortunes of the team but instead about the anticipation of returning to his nation's capital and taking a run at curling for the first time in his life. "My parents curled when I was younger, and I spent a lot of time in curling rinks but I was only four or five at the time so I've never actually done the sport," he admitted. "I've always watched it on TV, though, and I really got a kick out of it so I guess I'd just like to try it."

Curling for Bruce Cassidy had always been there—he had just never tried it. But now something told him that he should. "I've got to get caught up with it. I mean I even got addicted to watching the women at the Olympics. I was happy for Canada. Didn't they win both gold medals?" Upon hearing my answer that Canada won neither, Cassidy further betrayed his affection for something he considered close to the heart.

"Why didn't they win the gold? What's going on? Curling is one sport we should dominate, isn't it?"

So much has happened to the curling characters I had encountered along the way. Unlike all the other sports I have covered, here there are no stories of retirement or of the game passing anyone by. Curling has a way of staying with a person, weaving its way through a changing life. There are times when curlers come of age and graduate to the next level, as has been the case with Suzanne Gaudet of Summerside, Prince Edward Island. She had failed to defend her world junior title at the event in Kelowna. Still, at the age of twenty-two, Gaudet, the former champ, teamed with a group from Charlottetown to win her province's senior crown. In the winter of 2003 the Islanders, under Gaudet's leadership, were the most successful squad through round-robin play at the Scott Tournament of Hearts in Kitchener-Waterloo, Ontario. Their record was

Moving on: Suzanne Gaudet's rink gives thanks

ten wins and a single loss. The only defeat came at the hands of the reigning champion, Colleen Jones.

Commanding a side that included the three-time provincial champion skip, Rebecca Jean MacPhee, her younger sister Robyn, and a thirty-nine-year-old gift shop owner with four kids named Susan McInnis, Gaudet quietly established herself as the one to watch in the immediate future. She faltered in the playoffs and came home to Prince Edward Island without a national title, but her prize was more impressive. She had solidified the devotion of the faithful from Canada's smallest province.

Mike Harris, true to his word, got back to the competitive side of the game while maintaining his place in the broadcast booth. The former Olympic silver medallist lost in a playoff match pursuing the right to represent Ontario at the 2003 Brier in Halifax. Still, he was back to being at or near the top of his game. "You try to feel like you belong at this level," Harris had told me. It was clear that he had accomplished his goal, both on the ice and above it as one of the game's most astute analysts.

Returning to the ice must have been gut-wrenching for three-time world champion and Olympic gold medallist Joan McCusker of Saskatchewan. She carried with her the memory of her beloved skip, the late Sandra Schmirler. With Jan Betker, a mother of three and the former third, as the new strategist, the team was reborn and represented Regina's Caledonia Curling Club at the 2003 national championship. McCusker, who listed her professions as curling analyst and motivational speaker, curled in the familiar second position. Along with one of the originals, lead Marcia Gudereit, and newcomer Sherry Linton as the vice, the prairie four made it to the semifinal before bowing to Cathy Cunningham of Newfoundland.

It was, in so many ways, a victory for McCusker and for all of curling. The game continued to tug at the souls of these Saskatchewan-born women. It is the legacy of Sandra Schmirler.

Russ Howard went back to another Brier. He's become the senior statesman in the men's game, having called the shots at an even dozen national championships. His roar is undiminished as he commands the hesitant rocks to their proper positions. The fans continue to thrill to the sounds of Howard's urgings, and it goes without saying that his absence in the arena would mean the loss of some of the game's mystique.

The same is true of Guy Hemmings. Now the most recognizable presence in the sport because of his cross-country travels, Hemmings has returned to the front lines. He struggled to a losing record at the most recent Brier in Halifax but he attracted a huge following nonetheless. Undaunted, the greenhouse owner and Pied Piper of curling continues to play for hearts.

Rising star John Morris still goes to university. He lost to Alberta's Randy Ferbey in the Brier final of 2002 and his status as the heir apparent in this sport is far from guaranteed. Curling is not that predictable. This past season, as he tried to get back to the Brier, Morris lost to eventual Ontario champion Bryan Cochrane, an elementary school principal whose team has played together for a decade. The young Morris remains a student of kinesiology and of the capricious nature of curling.

The hottest team for quite some time belonged to Randy Ferbey of Alberta. After winning a second consecutive Brier at Calgary's Saddledome, the foursome went on an unprecedented run. They captured the ensuing world championship in Bismark, North Dakota, making up for their failure the year before in Lausanne, Switzerland. They then approached the 2002–03 season with a vengeance.

Dominant might be a good way to describe how Ferbey and his teammates, David Nedohin, Scott Pfeifer, and Marcel Rocque, have performed in competition. They captured events called the Continental Cup, the Canada Cup, and the Skins game on the way to winning more than $230,000 in prize money. A third straight Brier title followed in Halifax, putting Ferbey in the record books as the only five-time winner of the event.

The culmination of a dream season occurred when the Albertans captured a second consecutive world championship, this time before a partisan crowd in Winnipeg. As Switzerland's Ralph Stockli watched helplessly, a group of "ordinary guys" delivered the knockout punch. As Randy Ferbey had predicted when I met him the first time in Calgary, little had changed. Marcel Rocque was still paying for someone to be a substitute teacher for his class while he was absent. They would all be back at their regular jobs come Monday morning.

I distinctly recall, in the spring of 2003, hanging on the outcome of the final game of hockey's regular season to find out where I would begin my observance of the Stanley Cup playoffs. Vancouver was hosting Los Angeles, and my colleagues and I watched with great anticipation from a sports pub in Edmonton. Of the several monitors in the bar, all but one was tuned to the critical match between the Kings and Canucks. On the other, the one where my gaze frequently drifted and eventually came to rest, Colleen Jones and Team Canada were curling against Denmark in an early confrontation at the world championships.

"Two more for the good guys," I'd exclaim while jumping from my seat and pumping my fist in the air. The rest of the crew looked at me like I had two heads and then reverted to the scoreless tilt being broadcast from the Pacific Coast.

Curling had become somewhat of an obsession by this time and the fortunes of the self-proclaimed grinder from Halifax carried a special attraction. I knew Jones, I had spent time with her and had come to appreciate the bigness of her life and that the fact that nothing came easily to her and her collection of underdogs. There was something at stake every time she played. On the other screens things seemed less urgent.

Since our encounter, Colleen Jones had failed to fulfil her Olympic dream but had won two more Scott Tournament of Hearts titles. As the skip of five Canadian championship teams, Jones stood alone as the most decorated leader in the annals of domestic curling. She steadfastly refused to be mentioned in the same breath as Sandra Schmirler. There was still work to be done.

The hockey playoffs began but on that first weekend I was riveted in my Vancouver hotel room to the women's world championship curling final. Colleen Jones, then forty-three years of age, had won every one of her ten games on the way to meeting twenty-nine-year-old Debbie McCormick, a Home Depot associate from Madison, Wisconsin. Jones, the perennial long shot, was clearly the favourite now even though she had finished a disappointing fourth at the last World's in North Dakota.

Colleen had done it her way again. Never winning by much, relying on a conservative and calculating approach to the game, she wore other teams down just as she had throughout her amazing twenty-nine-year career. This time, I thought, she'd get the job done and be rewarded with the respect she so richly deserved.

It didn't turn out like that. McCormick's team played with fire and emotion, they took some risks, and the Canadian champion couldn't seem to get the upper hand. She came up short yet again, having been forced to steal in the tenth end to tie the score and hopefully push the game to overtime. McCormick made her last hit perfectly and claimed the first ever women's world championship for the United States by a score of 5–3. "It's huge, we just made history," McCormick enthused over the airwaves. "We've worked all year to get to this moment."

Though it made her no more qualified in the end, the Canadian skip had worked a lifetime to win in front of a crowd like the one assembled at the Winnipeg Arena. This was the very heartland of curling. Her voice cracked with emotion as she graciously accepted defeat. "We just wanted to get here and then to hear our anthem played" was all Colleen Jones could muster. Then she listened to the playing of the "Star-Spangled Banner." I learned later that Debbie McCormick, the American victor, had been born in Saskatoon.

For past three summers, I have travelled to Lake of Bays to relax for a while in Ontario's cottage country. On the way to the place I stay there is a turnoff from the highway marked by a simple sign that points right and says, "Curling Club." Every year I make the detour, take the fork in the road and find a basic little building shrouded by evergreens. In the warmth of the season, the tiny curling rink just off the busy thoroughfare is always closed and I have never actually been inside. Then again, I don't really have to. Having visited curling rinks of various shapes and sizes across the country I have a pretty good idea of what it's like in there. It's a place where people will live their lives, will build friendships and share laughter as they unravel the mysteries of a game that makes so much sense.

Baysville's open house

PHOTO CREDITS

André Proulx: 15, 280, 281, 285
Brian Nicholls: 16
Bruce Rainnie: 68, 76
Catherine Gregory: 331
CBC Sports Archives: 145
Derek MacEwen: 261, 264
Grant Heffernan: 20
Herbie Pile: 11, 216
Jack Cusano/*Calgary Sun*: 291
Jeff Collard: 302, 311
Jim Henderson/*Sweep* magazine: 3, 9, 96, 112, 114, 115, 138,
    148, 149, 154, 170, 175, 176, 180, 266
Los Angeles Kings/Juan Ocampo/Bernstein Associates: 281
Michael Burns, Sr.: 10
Royal Canadian Curling Club Archives: VIII, 13, 38, 42, 44,
    47, 54, 55, 57, 59

ACKNOWLEDGMENTS

There are so many people to thank. Most of their names appear in the stories within these pages. I am forever grateful for everyone's help and understanding as I sought to discover Canada and the mystical hold curling has upon legions of its citizens.

Maya Mavjee of Doubleday Canada had faith in this undertaking and took the risk of bringing me onside.

The senior editor is Martha Kanya-Forstner. She combines a myriad of qualities in a single person, including the strength to stand by a worthwhile idea, the patience to see it through, and an awesome gift for making words assume their rightful places. I thank her for all this and value her friendship more than I can properly express.

Scott Sellers has an enthusiasm that knows no bounds and a wondrous belief in me to go along with it. Wendy Thomas brought her precision and attention to detail to the project. Scott Richardson and the production team at Doubleday gave the book and its jacket everything I had envisioned and so much more.

I would like to recognize my trusted colleague and friend Chris Cuthbert, who understands this sort of endeavour. So do people like Nancy Lee, Mike Brannagan, Joel Darling and Chris Irwin at CBC—they encouraged me and made generous allowances as I traveled the road of curling. Trevor Pilling, Joe Recupero, Peter Ogilivie, Perry Lefko, David Moir and Bob Weeks fortified my research efforts with no questions asked. Jim Henderson has so much pride in the pictures he takes and was willing to share them. I am in their collective debt.

Phyllis Ellis provided inspiration and wisdom. Jeff Timson opened many doors. André Proulx was unselfish as he allowed the image of Guy Hemmings to come to life and Lloyd Lawless gave me a pipeline to the Island. Bill McAnally, the manager of the Royal Canadian Curling Club, was always welcoming. Eileen Pile painstakingly searched through the archives of her late husband, photographer Herbie Pile. Together with Dave Brown and Bruce Rainnie these folks connected me to my past and present as it relates to this wonderful Canadian game.

My constant friend Tim Currie is always worthy of special mention. He knows how much the late John Latimer meant to my life and my love of stories. The utmost affection is reserved for the late Joan Mead. She was born in the United States but came to treasure all things Canadian—curling above all else.

My mother Elizabeth and father Scott got me to give curling a try and I'll never forget their enthusiasm for the game. My sister Carrie seems forever interested in my progress even though she has a busy life of her own. These are great people to have in your corner. So too are

Catherine, Alex and Charlotte who know little of curling. They do, however, understand me and for some reason constantly give of themselves so that I can undertake such fanciful journeys. I owe them so much.

It's significant that my trek in search of the soul of this sport should culminate in a place where it's held so dear. I walked into a shop that sells curling equipment in Saskatoon not so long ago. This is the city where the last man from Saskatchewan to win the Brier got his start. It's also where the next Brier will be staged, no doubt with great fanfare. Adding to its mystique is the fact that both World Junior Championship rinks emerged from right here in Saskatoon.

Naturally, the door was open to me at "Folk's Curling Corner" on that bright, spring day. Sheldon Koch, Gerry Cooney and I talked about a winter's game and I felt so very close to home.

Scott Russell,
Saskatoon, Saskatchewan
May 2003

SCOTT RUSSELL is an award-winning sports journalist who has covered nine Stanley Cups, the Olympics, the Commonwealth Games and the Canada Games. Author of *Ice Time: A Canadian Hockey Journey* and co-author of the bestselling *The Rink: Stories from Hockey's Home Towns*, he lives with his family in Toronto.